MOBILE PEER TO PEER (P2P)

WILEY SERIES IN COMMUNICATIONS NETWORKING & DISTRIBUTED SYSTEMS

Series Editors: David Hutchison, *Lancaster University, Lancaster, UK*
Serge Fdida, *Université Pierre et Marie Curie, Paris, France*
Joe Sventek, *University of Glasgow, Glasgow, UK*

The 'Wiley Series in Communications Networking & Distributed Systems' is a series of expert-level, technically detailed books covering cutting-edge research, and brand new developments as well as tutorial-style treatments in networking, middleware and software technologies for communications and distributed systems. The books will provide timely and reliable information about the state-of-the-art to researchers, advanced students and development engineers in the Telecommunications and the Computing sectors.

Other titles in the series:

Wright: *Voice over Packet Networks* 0-471-49516-6 (February 2001)
Jepsen: *Java for Telecommunications* 0-471-49826-2 (July 2001)
Sutton: *Secure Communications* 0-471-49904-8 (December 2001)
Stajano: *Security for Ubiquitous Computing* 0-470-84493-0 (February 2002)
Martin-Flatin: *Web-Based Management of IP Networks and Systems* 0-471-48702-3 (September 2002)
Berman, Fox, Hey: *Grid Computing. Making the Global Infrastructure a Reality* 0-470-85319-0 (March 2003)
Turner, Magill, Marples: *Service Provision. Technologies for Next Generation Communications* 0-470-85066-3 (April 2004)
Welzl: *Network Congestion Control: Managing Internet Traffic* 0-470-02528-X (July 2005)
Raz, Juhola, Serrat-Fernandez, Galis: *Fast and Efficient Context-Aware Services* 0-470-01668-X (April 2006)
Heckmann: *The Competitive Internet Service Provider* 0-470-01293-5 (April 2006)
Dressler: *Self-Organization in Sensor and Actor Networks* 0-470-02820-3 (November 2007)
Berndt: *Towards 4G Technologies: Services with Initiative* 0-470-01031-2 (March 2008)
Jacquenet, Bourdon, Boucadair: *Service Automation and Dynamic Provisioning Techniques in IP/MPLS Environments* 0-470-01829-1 (March 2008)
Minei/Lucek: *MPLS-Enabled Applications: Emerging Developments and New Technologies, Second Edition* 0-470-98644-1 (April 2008)
Gurtov: *Host Identity Protocol (HIP): Towards the Secure Mobile Internet* 0-470-99790-7 (June 2008)
Boucadair: *Inter-Asterisk Exchange (IAX): Deployment Scenarios in SIP-enabled Networks* 0-470-77072-4 (January 2009)

MOBILE PEER TO PEER (P2P)

A TUTORIAL GUIDE

Frank H. P. Fitzek, University of Aalborg, Denmark

Hassan Charaf, Budapest University of Technology, Hungary

A John Wiley and Sons, Ltd., Publication

Library of Congress Cataloging-in-Publication Data:

Mobile peer to peer : a tutorial guide / [edited by] Frank H.P. Fitzek, Hassan Charaf.
   p. cm.
  Includes index.
  ISBN 978-0-470-69992-8 (cloth)
  1. Mobile communication systems. 2. Peer-to-peer architecture (Computer networks) I. Fitzek, Frank H. P. II. Charaf, Hassan.
  TK5105.525.M62 2009
  004.6′−dc22

2009007112

A catalogue record for this book is available from the British Library.

ISBN   978-0-470-69992-8 (H/B)

Typeset in 10/12 Times by Laserwords Private Limited, Chennai, India.
Printed in Great Britain by TJ International Ltd, Padstow, Cornwall.

Contents

Foreword

Numerous parallel disruptions are taking place in the software industry. These include the introduction of truly web-enabled mobile devices, large-scale use of peer-to-peer networking, and the new practice of social software engineering. In the emerging era of web-based, peer-to-peer mobile social software, applications live on the web as services that can be accessed with a mobile device. These services consist of data, code, and other resources that can be located anywhere in the world. The services and applications require no installation or manual upgrades. This makes the deployment of applications and services exceptionally rapid and simple. Ideally, applications also support user collaboration and social interaction, i.e. allow multiple users to interact and share the same applications and data over the Internet or in an ad hoc fashion, depending on their preferred form of communication.

This book has the ambitious goal of making sense of all the different techniques and technologies that fall under the peer-to-peer umbrella. To achieve this, it addresses the different bits and pieces that form the necessary technology basis for mobile peer-to-peer networks, as well as providing concrete examples of how to compose applications that benefit mobile peer-to-peer capabilities.

The book is authored by numerous researchers representing the different dimensions of the field. The chapters cover technology introductions and programming-level considerations, as well as introductory applications that have been implemented using the different technologies. The different dimensions that the authors address are well balanced, and when put together form a coherent story.

Based on my own experiences in all of the fields of technology covered in the book, I feel that this book is a welcome compilation of the different dimensions of the emerging use of mobile peer-to-peer networks. I am confident that it will encourage both researchers and practitioners to examine fresh approaches to application development, as well as being a source of useful information for a new generation of students.

Tommi Mikkonen

Professor, Mobile and Distributed Software
Department of Software Systems
Tampere University of Technology
Tampere, Finland

Preface

Mobile communication has been dominated by centralized architectures over decades. Direct communication among mobile devices was not the focus of researchers and not required by industry for many years. However, as mobile devices are nowadays fully programmable, this book aims to demonstrate the main motivation behind mobile devices clustering and making use of the developments in Mobile Peer to Peer (P2P). Mobile P2P describes the communication between mobile devices. The communication is realized by direct communication links such as Bluetooth or WiFi or via the network operator. It is important to note that the main services are carried out on the mobile device and no longer in the network.

This book presents insights into how to program such communication systems, referred to as mobile peer to peer (P2P), on mobile devices powered by Symbian OS (and one example is addressing JAVA as well). Mobile peer-to-peer communication systems are now receiving much more attention in research and industry than ever before. The direct communication among mobile devices is breaking ground for new services such as social mobile networking or cooperative wireless networking. Leaving behind the centralized world with strict point-to-point communication architectures, mobile communication devices are enriching our daily life. Such a pervasive communication world opens the door for new communication architectures.

About the book

The main motivation for this book project is to share the knowledge we have gained within our research groups in Aalborg and Budapest to build mobile applications leaving the old-fashioned cellular world behind. The book should help students or interested readers to gain the basic knowledge to build mobile peer-to-peer networks. Furthermore, it can serve as a textbook for courses in mobile communication, as the sources for all examples have been made available on the web (see below).

The book is divided into three main parts. The first part gives an introduction to mobile communication in general and some insights into mobile peer to peer (P2P). It is assumed that the reader is already familiar with the great achievements in the general area of mobile communication, which are normally given in the first 10 pages of such books, and therefore no overwhelming market sales information is given here.

The second part explains the basic programming environment and the basic wireless communication technologies such as Bluetooth, WiFi (IEEE802.11), and cellular communication examples. The programming language is mainly Symbian C++, as the Symbian platform is giving us by far the largest flexibility. One example is using JAVA as the underlying programming language.

The third part provides detailed examples of mobile peer-to-peer communication, including social mobile networking, cooperative wireless networking, network coding, and mobile gaming.

All programming examples can be downloaded from

http://mobiledevices.kom.aau.dk/mp2p

as source code and as executables, distributed in SIS files, that have been tested with a Nokia N95 8GB. The source code is made for the programming environment that is described in Chapter 3.

Note that, throughout this book, we will use the term 'mobile devices' instead of mobile phone, smartphone, or mobile/wireless terminal. The reason for this is that connections will no longer terminate at the device, as they have done with centralized communication systems. Furthermore, we would like to underline that we are not looking only at speech services. The term 'mobile' implicitly means 'wireless' in this context.

Frank H.P. Fitzek
Hassan Charaf

Acknowledgements

The editors and authors would like to thank Nokia for providing technical support as well as mobile phones for the testing. Special thanks to Harri Pennanen, Nina Tammelin, and Per Moeller from Nokia.

This work was partially financed by the X3MP project granted by the Danish Ministry of Science, Technology, and Innovation.

Furthermore, we would like to thank our colleagues from Aalborg University for support, namely Børge Lindberg, Ben Krøyer, Peter Boie Jensen, Bo Nygaard Bai, Henrik Benner, Finn Hybjerg Hansen, and Svend Erik Volsgaard.

We would also like to thank the Wiley team for their professional support in this book project. Special thanks to Jo Stichbury for her discussions and helpful reviews.

List of Contributors

Frank H.P. Fitzek
Aalborg University
Niels Jernes Vej 12,
9220 Aalborg,
Denmark
ff@es.aau.dk

Hassan Charaf
Budapest University of Technology
and Economics
Budapest, H-1111
Goldmann György tér
3. HUNGARY
hassan.charaf@aut.bme.hu

Lara Srivastava
Aalborg University
Niels Jernes Vej 12,
9220 Aalborg,
Denmark
ls@es.aau.dk AND
laraomnibus@yahoo.ca

Morten V. Pedersen
Aalborg University
Niels Jernes Vej 12,
9220 Aalborg,
Denmark
mvpe@es.aau.dk

Károly Farkas
University of West Hungary
Bajcsy-Zs. u. 9.,
H-9400
Sopron,
Hungary
farkas@inf.nyme.hu

Gergely Csúcs
Budapest University of Technology
and Economics
Goldmann György
tér 3, H-1111
Budapest,
Hungary
gergely.csucs@aut.bme.hu

Péter Ekler
Budapest University of Technology
and Economics,
Department of Automation
and Applied Informatics
Hungary,
H-1111 Budapest,
Magyar
Tudósok körútja
2. II/I.L.208.
peter.ekler@aut.bme.hu

Gábor Zavarkó
Budapest University of Technology
and Economics
Hungary,
H-1111 Budapest,
Goldmann György
tér 3.
IV/433.
zgabi@goliat.eik.bme.hu

Bertalan Forstner
Budapest University of Technology
and Economics,
Department of Automation
and Applied Informatics
Hungary,
H-1111 Budapest,
Magyar
Tudósok körútja
2. I/I.B.153.
forstner.bertalan@aut.bme.hu

Imre Kelényi
Budapest University of Technology
and Economics
Budapest,
H-1111 Goldmann György tér
3. HUNGARY
imre.kelenyi@aut.bme.hu

Janus Heide
Aalborg University
Niels Jernes Vej 12,
9220 Aalborg,
Denmark
speije@es.aau.dk

Leonardo Militano
Università Mediterranea di Reggio
Calabria - DIMET Department
Via Graziella - Feo di Vito - 89124
Reggio Calabria (RC), Italy
leonardo.militano@unirc.it

Part One

Introduction and Motivation

1

Mobile Peer-to-Peer Networks: An Introduction to the Tutorial Guide

Frank H. P. Fitzek
Aalborg University, ff@es.aau.dk

Hassan Charaf
Budapest University of Technology and Economics, Hassan@aut.bme.hu

1.1 Introduction and Motivation

The main aim of this chapter is to provide the reader with a good introduction to mobile peer-to-peer networks and to demonstrate the motivation behind mobile peer-to-peer network development – the basic purpose of this book. Mobile peer-to-peer networks rely on direct communication among mobile devices of any kind. Even though today's mobile communication architectures are mainly centralized and therefore based on preinstalled infrastructure, this book advocates mobile peer to peer (P2P), breaking ground for new business models and appealing services. To realize these novel communication architectures, a tutorial guide for different wireless technologies is presented in this book. Roughly speaking, this book deals with the potential to build mobile networks without or with the help of cellular networks, taking advantage of the short-range technologies Bluetooth and WiFi (IEEE 802.11) to communicate among mobile devices.

Peer-to-peer networks have raised a great deal of attention in the last decade. These peer-to-peer networks started in the wired domain. First implementations targeted file-sharing services and distributed computing. The main idea was to use distributed storage and computational capacity instead of one centralized server. Such an approach was less vulnerable to denial of service attacks and made the networks more robust. As most peer-to-peer networks started with music file sharing, they were often regarded as

Mobile Peer to Peer (P2P)   Edited by Frank H. P. Fitzek and Hassan Charaf
© 2009 John Wiley & Sons, Ltd

pirate networks. The new architecture was a huge threat to the music industry, and to this day several network and service operators are still frightened by the term 'peer to peer'.

On the other hand, peer-to-peer networks have shown their potential and advantages over centralized approaches. Inspired by the fixed domain, peer-to-peer networks are now penetrating the wireless and mobile domain. The goal of this chapter is also to show the potential of mobile peer-to-peer networks as an extension to existing infrastructure approaches. Therefore, network and service operators should see the mobile peer-to-peer networks not as a threat but as huge potential to make their existing networks and services more appealing, more robust, and less resource intensive. In other words, the peer-to-peer networks define the infrastructure for different types of protocol, applications, and services.

To the best of our knowledge, the first mobile peer-to-peer service was a dating client. The main idea was that people with the same interest in meeting other people could specify their interests and needs by using a mobile application, which was realized on a Symbian platform. Using Bluetooth, the mobile application looked out for *matching* partners having mainly the same interests and needs. This example gives a first idea of how mobile peer-to-peer application might look. However, as explained later in this chapter, new ideas of *social mobile networking* and *cooperative networking* are being implemented in the field.

In the following, the evolution of mobile and fixed communication systems is explained to provide a common understanding for the reader.

Today's dominant mobile communication architectures can be summarized as central-ized, which means that mobile devices, as soon as they are switched on, will search for any base station and/or access point, as they will assume that this is the main service access point. Once they are connected, they will search for content that is mostly stored in a centralized manner. The base stations cover a larger area by spanning multiple cells over it, one base station covering one or multiple cells by sectorized antenna patterns. But where does this centralized architecture have its origin? There are two main fac-tors. When the first mobile devices were created for voice services, they could already communicate between each other (just like walkie-talkies), but there was also the need to communicate with people connected through fixed networks, which had already been established decades before. So bridges from the mobile world to the wired world were needed – the origin of the base stations. The second factor is that wireless communication is mainly based on radio propagation, which limits the range of mobile-to-mobile com-munication with respect to power constraints. Therefore, the fixed networks with their bridging capabilities allowed two mobile devices to be connected over long distances, the fixed networks acting like virtual tunnels (see Figure 1.5).

This centralized architecture has been used extensively for second- and third-generation mobile communication systems, referred to as 2G and 3G. Mobile devices focus on base stations only, as these are the main source of any information. The 2G mobile services were mainly voice services and text messaging. With 3G networks, data communication has been boosted. While 2G networks allowed data communication at small data rates, 3G communication systems target data rates to support broadband Internet access. However, the centralized approach also has its drawbacks.

Following Moore's law, the computational power will double every two years, and the increased computational power will be transferred to new services for the mobile device, making it more attractive to the customer. These services include digital cameras, music

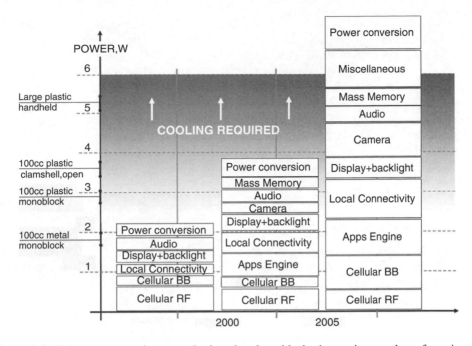

Figure 1.1 Power consumption over the last decade, with the increasing number of services on mobile devices. Reproduced by Permission of © 2009 Nokia. All rights reserved

players, games, and, of course, wireless technology. The latter is becoming dramatically more complex for the upcoming fourth generation (4G). On the other hand, we have the battery of the mobile device, which has to support the more complex services. Figure 1.1 shows the power consumption over the last decade. An increasing number of services and hardware will require more power from the battery. Unfortunately, battery capacity is not keeping pace with the development of computational power. Battery capacity has been almost doubled over the last decade. Thus, mobile users will find that their operational time, also referred to as standby time, may decrease in the future. This trend was already noticeable on transition from 2G to 3G, where 3G mobile devices had half the operational time of 2G devices.

Another paradigm shift is where services are generated for the user. So far, mobile devices have been used for voice communication between people who know each other, or for data connection to the Internet. With the high-capability mobile devices (we call them smart devices or smartphones) on the market, mobile devices are not only consuming content, they are also capable of producing mobile content and to store it on their large memory. Thus, in the future, the services we are looking for might not be stored in the backbone or overlay networks. They might be right next to us on a mobile device in a range of some metres.

After understanding the origin of centralized mobile networks, we will now explain some of the advantages of moving to a peer-to-peer architecture. As explained throughout the book, mobile peer-to-peer networks have the potential to overcome the aforementioned problems. As shown in Figure 1.2, 'mobile peer to peer (P2P)' encompasses different

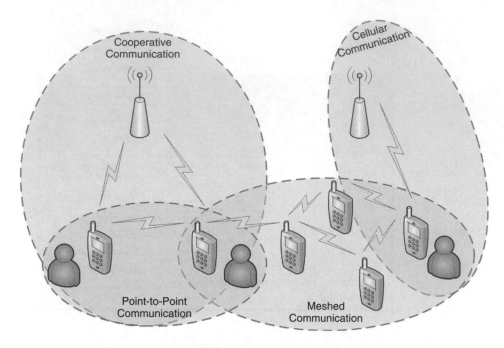

Figure 1.2 Overall architecture

architectures such as point to point, meshed networks, and cooperative networks. Network operators are often scared away by the term 'peer to peer'. This is mainly motivated by their existing business models and the fear of losing ground to peer-to-peer technology. However, network operators should regard peer-to-peer technology as a great opportunity to establish new services and break new ground to make money. Interestingly, in Africa, where fixed networks are either not established or only insufficiently so, wireless networking is growing dramatically. In dense areas, the centralized approach is used again, but, in less dense areas, new architecture forms, such as meshed networks, are considered for deployment.

1.2 Wireless Technologies

There are many types of wireless technology deployed on mobile handsets. Here we provide a short description of the wireless technologies used within this book. Enough information about the basic concepts should be provided for the reader to understand the following chapters.

In Figure 1.3 the supported data rates versus communication range are given for different wireless technologies. The figure shows 2G technologies such as GSM CSD/GPRS and 3G technologies such as HSDPA. Also, future technologies, referred to as 3.5G, are named, such as worldwide interoperability for microwave access (WiMAX) and long-term evolution (LTE). Furthermore, wireless local area network (WLAN) or WiFi technologies are presented, namely different versions of IEEE802.11 and Bluetooth. In the following subsections, these technologies are outlined briefly.

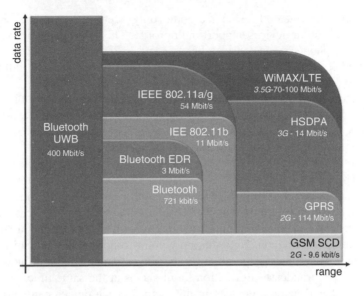

Figure 1.3   Wireless technologies and the supported data rate and range

1.2.1   Short-range Technologies

Here, the basic concepts of Bluetooth and WiFi (IEEE802.11) are laid out. We will mainly look into these technologies because they can be found on many mobile devices already. While Bluetooth is by far the most widely used on mobile devices today, IEEE802.11 is breaking some ground on the more advanced mobile devices, referred to as smartphones. We will not look into ZigBee, as there are only a small number of devices supporting it, and neither will we look into IRDA, as it requires line of sight.

1.2.1.1   Bluetooth

Bluetooth is a radio technology that operates in the 2.4 GHz band. It is often referred to as short range communication, as the range of communication is relatively small compared with cellular systems. The communication range is determined by the power class of the Bluetooth module. There exist three different Bluetooth classes, namely class 1, class 2, and class 3. Class 1 devices can have communication ranges of 100 m and even more, while class 2 and class 3 devices are limited to 10 m or less than 1 m respectively. Most mobile devices are class 2, while Bluetooth access points are class 1. Bluetooth systems are composed of a radio/baseband part and a software stack.

Originally, Bluetooth was intended as a cable replacement. The first applications of Bluetooth were described as connecting PCs and laptops to printers. Bluetooth has since shown a much wider range of applications. It eases the process of connecting cordless peripherals such as headsets or GPS modules.

Bluetooth offers different communication profiles to define which service can be supported at a given time. Voice profiles are used for headsets connected to a mobile phone, while the LAN profile is used for data communication between two peers for IP traffic.

In the early time of Bluetooth, a device could only support one of the profiles, while nowadays most if not all devices support multiprofile. This is needed, for example, in the case of a mobile phone connected to a headset and a PDA at the same time. Choosing the phone number on the PDA, setting up the call over the phone, and talking over the headset is only possible with multiprofile Bluetooth chipsets.

Bluetooth chipsets were advertized initially as a technology with a bill of materials (BOM) cost of $US 5. Unfortunately, today the chipsets cost around $US 30 if bought in small numbers. Even with a larger number, the $US 5 threshold cannot be achieved.

Bluetooth communication takes places between one master device and at least one but a maximum of seven active slave devices. All slave devices are connected to the master device only. The numbers listed here refer to active devices. As the master is able to park a device, the master could theoretically be connected to more devices, but the number of active ongoing communication partners is restricted to seven active devices. As a result of this architecture, slaves cannot communicate directly with each other and are dependent on the master to relay information. Note that only point-to-point communication is possible, and no broadcast or multicast is possible for the slaves. Some Bluetooth implementations allow the master to broadcast information to all slaves at the same time.

To discover other Bluetooth devices in the vicinity, each device can start service discovery. The service discovery will search for other devices and classify them into mobile phones, PCs, headsets, etc. Once these devices are found, they can be paired – a procedure by which devices are approved as communication partners. In the case of a large number of Bluetooth devices, the discovery process can take quite a long time. With more than 10 devices around, it can take minutes to discover all neighbouring devices.

One Bluetooth device has the ability to support three synchronous or eight asynchronous communication channels. The synchronous channels are used for voice services mostly, while the asynchronous channels are for data communication. As we use mostly data connections in this book, we will describe these in a little bit more detail.

Because Bluetooth operates in the 2.4 GHz bandwidth, it employs frequency hopping to make the entire communication less error prone in the presence of other technologies using this open ISM (industrial, scientific, and medical) band. Medium access is organized in a time division multiple access (TDMA) fashion, where the channel is split into 0.625 ms slots. Whenever one device is sending information to another device, the receipt of this information needs to be acknowledged in the next slot. In the case of unbalanced data transfer, such as the transmission of a photo from one device to another, one device is sending the data and the other one is just sending acknowledgements. The acknowledgements also occupy a full slot, which is not very efficient. To increase the efficiency, three or five slots can be bundled by one device and are acknowledged only by one slot. Furthermore, Bluetooth has the option to protect the data by forward error correction (FEC) information. Those with FEC are referred to as DM packets, and those without are referred to as DH packets. Each of these packet types can use one, three, or five slots, ending up with six different packet types, namely DM1, DH1, DM3, DH3, DM5, and DH5. Whether to use DM or DH packets depends on the signal quality. DH packets offer more capacity than DM packets, but it may be that these packets will be retransmitted more often as they are lost and therefore not acknowledged. DM packets have been used in cases where the wireless medium was highly error prone. Recent findings show that DH packets are more or less as robust as DM packets. This is due to novel achievements with hardware, more precisely with transmitter/receiver sensitivity. On this basis, new Bluetooth technologies such as ULE and UWB will not use DM packets at all.

Standard Bluetooth can achieve data rates of 721 kbit/s. Using the enhanced data rate (EDR), data rates of up to 3 Mbit/s are available, as shown in Figure 1.3.

Programming examples for Bluetooth are explained in Chapter 4 and used in some of the following cases.

1.2.1.2　IEEE 802.11

IEEE802.11 describes a whole product family. The 802.11 family is based on one medium access protocol and different physical-layer implementations. Initially, 802.11 had three forms of realization at the physical layer, namely direct sequence spreading (DS), frequency hopping (FH), and infrared (IR). As IR was limited to line of sight and FH at that point in time was more complex to realize than DS, all chipsets used DS. FH and DS were not intended to realize medium access but to improve multipath interference. The first DS realizations offered data rates of up to 1 or 2 Mbit/s working in the 2.4 GHz frequency band. Shortly after that, 802.11b was introduced, offering data rates of up to 11 Mbit/s. Three fully orthogonal channels can be used to avoid interference with neighbours. As the 2.4 GHz frequency band started to become crowded, IEEE802.11a was introduced, working in the 5 GHz band. More orthogonal channels are now available (depending on the region, up to 12 channels for indoor use), and data rates of up to 54 Mbit/s are supported. Besides the change in frequency band from 2.4 to 5 GHz, 802.11a uses OFDM for higher spectral efficiency. As OFDM technology demonstrated some benefits over the DS technique, IEEE802.11g was introduced, also using OFDM in the 2.4 GHz band. Seeing as both 802.11b and 802.11 g work in the same frequency band and have the same MAC protocol, these two technologies are nowadays often implemented on the same chipset.

For both 802.11a and 802.11 g, the maximum data rate of 54 Mbit/s will only be achieved if the communicating stations have a high signal-to-noise ratio (SNR) on their communication link. Loosely speaking, the SNR decreases with increasing distance between the stations. Other factors such as shadowing, multipath, interference, etc., also play a role, but, to keep things simple, we refer to the distance. Depending on the SNR values, the stations will adapt their modulation and coding scheme. Therefore, the data rate decreases with decreasing SNR, which in turn depends on the distance between the stations.

To help the reader understand what follows, we would like to emphasize the medium access control (MAC) of IEEE802.11 in the distributed coordinating function (DCF). The MAC is based on carrier sense multiple access with collision avoidance (CSMA/CA). This means that all stations sense the medium in order to ascertain whether the medium is already busy. If this is the case, the sensing station will not send at all, to avoid collisions. Collisions occur if more than one station is using the wireless medium, and the sender will receive multiple overlay signals which it cannot receive successfully. Whenever the medium is sensed as free, the station prepares to send on the medium. As there are possibly other stations also waiting to use the medium, each station has to wait for a certain time before transmitting anything. These waiting times are different from station to station. The station with the smallest waiting time will send first. This means that the medium is busy again, and the other stations will freeze at this point in time, waiting for the next free period to come. When a station has sent a packet, it will wait for an acknowledgement from the counterpart communication device. If there is no acknowledgement, then the station will assume that the previous transmission has undergone a collision with at least one other station. Such collisions are still possible, as two or more stations could have had the same random timer. In this case the waiting time for the next packet will be doubled to produce more time diversity. In contrast to Bluetooth, the channel is not equally slotted. A station will occupy the medium as long as it takes to transmit the packet. This time depends on the length of the packet and the supported data rate. In addition to the sending time, the time for acknowledgement needs to be taken into consideration. Between the sending and the acknowledgement there is a small time when the medium is not being used. To prevent other stations from starting to transmit in these pause intervals, 802.11 has introduced different timers. The station responsible for sending the acknowledgement will access the medium immediately after receipt of the packet. Other stations will need to wait a longer time, and, when this timer expires, the acknowledgement will already be on its way, stopping other stations accessing the medium.

As collisions reduce the efficiency of the communication system, in 802.11, ready-to-send (RTS) and clear-to-send (CTS) messages are used to avoid potential collisions. RTS messages are sent out by the sending station to ask the receiver whether it is currently busy with other transmissions of which the sending station is unaware. When the receiving station is ready, it will send the CTS message. After successful receipt of the CTS, the sending station starts to convey its message. The neighbouring stations are also informed by the RTS and CTS messages that the medium will be busy for some time. At the very least, no collisions should occur with those stations that have received either the RTS or the CTS message.

In IEEE802.11, unicast and broadcast messages can be used. Unicast is the communication between two stations, while broadcast describes the communication originated by one station and received by multiple stations. The unicast data rate is determined by the SNR between the communication partners. In broadcast, the data rates should be set according to the link with the weakest signal. Most 802.11 implementations use the lowest possible data rate whenever broadcast messages are used. Only a few chipsets allow the data rate to be set in the case of broadcast. A combination of unicast and multicast transmission is the opportunistic listening approach. Here, two stations are in communication in normal unicast mode, and the neighbouring devices are overhearing the communication. This approach has some advantages over broadcast in that at least one acknowledgement will be received by the sender.

In Chapter 5, WiFi programming examples for the Symbian OS are explained. Moreover, additional information for WiFi technology is given.

1.2.1.3   2G/3G Cellular Communication

Cellular data communication was introduced with the GSM standard as the second generation of cellular systems. Cellular systems cover larger areas. In the case of 2G, nearly the whole of Europe is covered, apart from some very small areas. The first data rate supported, in circuit switch data (CSD) mode, was 9.6 kbit/s. This was increased slightly by high-speed circuit switch data (HSCSD), using a new modulation technique for mobiles placed near the base station. With the introduction of GPRS, the data rate was improved to 114 kbit/s. Both 2G technologies were based on TDMA technology. With the introduction of the third generation of cellular communication, the data rate was increased to 384 kbit/s with UMTS, and later high-speed downlink packet access (HSDPA) offered 1.5 Mbit/s on mobile devices (PCMCIA cards for laptops may achieve higher data rates). In contrast to 2G technologies, 3G is based on WCDMA instead of pure TDMA. The data rates of some 2G and 3G technologies are given in Figure 1.3. For a full explanation of these technologies, see reference [1]. Chapter 6 gives some programming examples using the Symbian OS for cellular communication.

1.2.2 Future Wireless Trends

In the future, the data rates of short-range and cellular systems will be improved. The family of cellular systems will be extended by WiMAX and LTE. These technologies will be available first at some hot spots, such as cities, not covering the same area as 2G and 3G, but will increase their coverage with time. The data rate of WiMAX is 72 Mbit/s per cell, and the data rate of LTE is 100 Mbit/s per cell.

Improvements are also expected for the short-range technologies. As one example, we will look into the evolution of Bluetooth technology. As shown in Figure 1.4, Bluetooth, in its current implementation in version 2.0, will develop in two directions. The first direction will target higher data rates. This will be achieved by ultra-wideband (UWB) Bluetooth, with more than 400 Mbit/s between two peers over a very short range. The other direction will focus more on connectivity than on data rate. As already explained, the service discovery may take some time if multiple peers are involved. With ultra-low-power (ULP) Bluetooth, this problem is tackled (the term 'ultra-low-power Bluetooth' is still under discussion and may be changed to 'ultra-low-energy (ULE) Bluetooth'). The idea

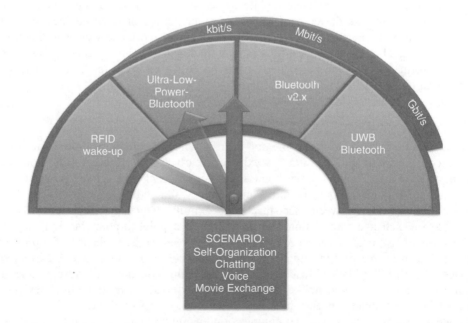

Figure 1.4 Possible Bluetooth evolution

is to find a solution to bundle peripherals such as watches with mobile phones. Watches have only a small energy budget, and the information they want to exchange is very small. WiBree was introduced for such cases, and was taken over by Bluetooth SIG as ULP Bluetooth. A further step in this direction is the use of near-field communication to bundle Bluetooth devices. This is already being implemented in Bluetooth version 2.1. In this case, the bundling of Bluetooth devices is realized by bringing the devices very close together (a maximum distance of 2 cm). This kind of bundling is very quick, but needs more user interaction. In the future, this will be realized even by RFIDs. As the current implementation in Bluetooth version 2.1 is based on UHF and therefore on active elements, RFID could be done in a total passive way. The passive way would have many advantages. Besides being very cheap, RFID technology could offer improvements in the area of energy savings.

1.3 Mobile Architectures

Here, the different architectures will be described, namely cellular networks, point-to-point networks, meshed networks, and cooperative networks. We will focus mainly on networks built by mobile devices, but the most prominent network candidates will also be introduced briefly.

1.3.1 Cellular Networks

In Figure 1.5 a cellular system is shown. These networks cover a larger area through multiple base stations having a fixed frequency plan assigned to avoid interference. Each mobile device will be connected only to one base station at a time, with potential handovers to other base stations if the mobile device starts to move. Being connected to a base station, the mobile device can connect to other mobile or fixed devices, using the base station as relay. Furthermore, the core network can also offer services that the mobile device can use. The core network differs in its implementation, be it a 2G or a 3G system. As this information will not be needed in this book, we refer the reader to other books in this area [2, 3].

1.3.2 Short-range Point-to-Point Networks

Point-to-point communication was the first form of wireless communication demonstrated by Marconi's experiments in 1895. As explained earlier, point-to-point radio communication, as shown in Figure 1.6, has some limitations in range for a fixed power margin. One example of point-to-point communication is the walkie-talkie, a means of half-duplex voice communication between users in close proximity. Nowadays, mobile devices are also able to exchange information and pure data in a point-to-point fashion, but such actions are always user driven (e.g. exchange of business cards, exchange of mp3 songs, etc.). This can be realized by in-built technologies such as infrared (IRDA), Bluetooth, ZigBee, or IEEE802.11b/g. Most consumers are using Bluetooth because it does not require direct line of sight, unlike IRDA, it can be found on most mobile devices, in contrast to ZigBee, and it is easy to set up, in contrast to IEEE802.11.

However, mobile peer-to-peer communication has much more potential than just point to point, and different possibilities will be presented below. Peer-to-peer technology is

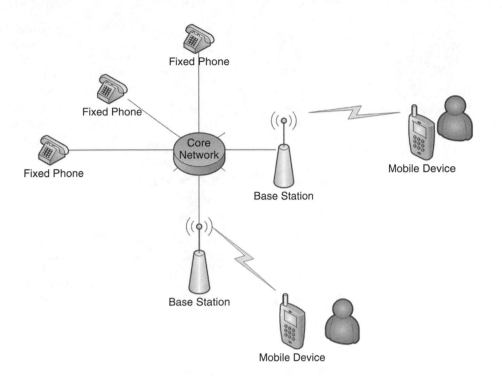

Figure 1.5   Fixed network with wireless extension

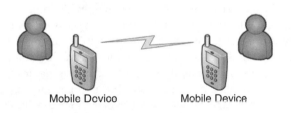

Figure 1.6   Point-to-point communication between two mobile devices

already gaining a lot of ground in fixed communication networks, and will probably also spill over to the wireless world, as laid out in this book, which advocates mobile peer to peer (P2P).

1.3.3 Meshed Networks

Meshed networks are an extension of point-to-point communication. In meshed networks, information is not always sent directly from the origin to the destination but forwarded by intermediate nodes (other mobile devices). This could be for several reasons. A first reason might be that the origin and the destination cannot communicate directly with each other. In such a case an information packet will be forwarded by the other mobile devices until it reaches the destination, as shown in Figure 1.7. Such a case is also referred

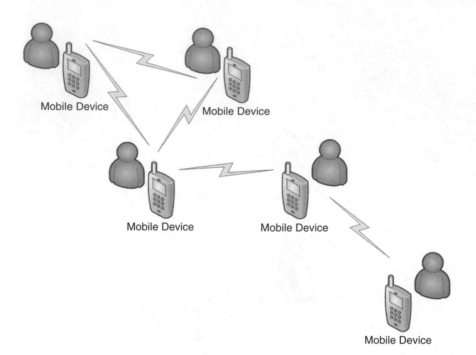

Figure 1.7   Mesh networking with four mobile devices

to as multihop. A second reason might be that, from a network perspective and maybe even from a mobile device perspective, it is more bandwidth and energy efficient to take intermediate hops instead of one hop. Whether this is true or not depends on the underlying wireless technology that is used for multihopping and the scenario. However, if we take one simple example of IEEE802.11g with rate adaptation, a single hop would use 6 Mbit/s for the transmission owing to the long distance between originator and destination. In the case of multihop, each hopping distance would be shorter and higher data rates could be used for each hop. Assuming 54 Mbit/s for every short hop, multihopping would be beneficial if less than nine hops were needed to reach the destination. This brief example demonstrates the complexity for any general architecture. Furthermore, whenever multihop is used, routing schemes are needed.

1.3.4   Cooperative Networks

A hybrid form of meshed networking and the cellular concept is the cooperative wireless network [4]. The main idea is that mobile devices within each other's proximity use their short-range technology to communicate directly with each other (as with meshed networks). In addition to this, each mobile device is connected to the overlay cellular or centralized network, as shown in Figure 1.8.

Using short-range technology, the mobile devices span a so-called *wireless grid*. The idea behind the wireless grid is that a single mobile device does not need to carry the full set of functionalities to retrieve the best possible service. Such services can be realized because the wireless grids accumulate the data rates of the participating mobile devices.

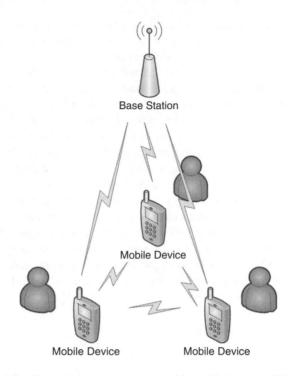

Figure 1.8   Cooperative wireless networking with three mobile devices

The alternative would be a stand-alone mobile device with high data support. However, such high data rates do not come for free. The cellular communication technology will consume more energy, which in turn will drain the battery and may lead to a heating problem of the device. The cooperating devices will only retrieve partial information from the cellular network and therefore will not drain the battery too much. The missing information will then be exchanged over the short-range links among the cooperating devices. The energy consumption will still be lower, as the energy per bit ratio on the short-range communication will be much better than on the cellular link. The cooperative concept for wireless networking was described in detail in references [4] and [5].

1.4   Mobile Scenarios and Business Cases

1.4.1   Social Mobile Networks

Social mobile networks are inspired by the established social networks found on the Internet. Social networks try to connect people who are known or unknown to each other with different goals. Social networks such as LinkedIn focus more on business-oriented people trying to extend their network for business reasons such as those given in Chapter 2. Facebook, on the other hand, focuses more on friendship-oriented networks. Finding old friends or creating new relationships is the most important part of it. Of course, these social networks can be used on any mobile devices with a web browser. However, social mobile networks are more than just a wireless extension.

Social mobile networks connect people who are within each other's proximity. The short-range technology is used to discover other mobile phones in the range. First solutions are on their way, such as aka-aki [6], which enriches a social network such as Facebook with collected information by short-range technology. Users can look at different profiles on the web and add connections they have made in their mobile life. The connections are collected by a mobile application running on mobile phones. The application uses Bluetooth technology to identify known or new Bluetooth contacts. Mobile users can use the application to get in contact right away or to connect up later on the web.

A similar approach is the spider application by Aalborg University [7]. As shown in Figure 1.9, the mobile user can look at a virtual world where his/her own character is moving around. As soon as Bluetooth detects other mobile phones in its proximity that are also running the spider application, more characters fill the room. Each mobile user can now steer his/her own character close to other characters and start actions such as chatting, exchanging profiles, or just looking at the real photo image. The spider approach is based on a concept developed some years ago at Aalborg University called SMARTEX [8]. The idea behind SMARTEX is to exchange digital content among mobile phones, introducing a new concept of digital ownership [9]. Again, Bluetooth technology is used here to form the mobile peer-to-peer network.

1.4.2 Cooperative Wireless Networks

Cooperative wireless networks are being realized at the moment. A very simplistic approach of cooperative access is realized by Jaikoo. The idea is that a mobile device that has flat-fee cellular access opens that connection to other users in its proximity. A mobile device would act as an access point to the neighbouring mobile devices, offering to share the cellular bandwidth with others. The question is: why should a user share

Figure 1.9   Spider screenshot

his/her cellular connection with others? If the other users are unknown, such an act of altruistic behaviour would use up energy and cellular bandwidth that the user of the offering device would like to use for him/herself. However, such an approach could work for devices where the users know each other, for example colleagues working for the same company, friends, family members, etc. The main problem with this approach is that one user carries the entire burden while the others exploit his/her kindness.

Therefore, real cooperative wireless access has been introduced by Aalborg University. Cooperation can be realized by unknown users following the two main rules of cooperation, namely reciprocity and the detection of cheats. The idea is that multiple users will share their cellular access given a need for a cooperative cluster. Here, only two examples will be given.

In cooperative web browsing [10], the activity factor for web browsing is exploited. As the time for reading is 4 times longer than the download phase, the cellular air interface is not used most of the time. However, when it is used, the capacity of the cellular link is not fast enough. The main idea now is to bundle multiple cellular air interfaces together. Whenever a mobile device wants to download a web page, it will contact those devices that are inactive at that moment (the user is reading) to download the content of the web page in a cooperative manner. By this kind of cooperation, the download time will be reduced significantly and the cooperation will be strengthened, as all cooperating devices will be able to gain without an individual device being exploited.

The second example – the cooperative file download – will be explained in detail later in this book with code examples. If mobile users are interested in the same content, such as movies or music, they can download the content in a cooperative manner, i.e. each mobile device can download partial information of the overall information file over the cellular air interface, which can then be exchanged among the devices using short-range technology. In Chapter 7 we will explain the implementation of this idea in full.

The two business cases, cooperative wireless networking and social mobile networking, are closely related. As soon as users start to cluster for whatever reason, these two approaches can be applied. Perhaps users will start to use social mobile networks to find friends in close proximity. Once those friends are found, the mobile devices can also use this clustering to form a mobile cooperative cluster. This cluster could then offer better performance to all connected devices.

References

[1] Fitzek, F.H.P. and Reichert, F. (eds), *'Mobile Phone Programming and its Application to Wireless Networking'*, No. 10.1007/978-1-4020-5969-8, ISBN 978-1-4020-5968-1, Springer, Dordrecht, The Netherlands, June 2007.

[2] Eberspächer, J., Vögel, H.-J., and Bettstetter, C., *'GSM Switching, Services, and Protocols'*, John Wiley & Sons, Ltd, Chichester, UK.

[3] Kaaranen, H., Ahtiainen, A., Laitinen, L., Naghian, S., and Niemi, V., *'UMTS Networks: Architecture, Mobility and Services'*, John Wiley & Sons, Ltd, Chichester, UK.

[4] Fitzek, F.H.P. and Katz, M. (eds), *'Cooperation in Wireless Networks: Principles and Applications – Real Egoistic Behavior is to Cooperate!'*, ISBN 1-4020-4710-X, Springer, Berlin–Heidelberg–New York, April 2006.

[5] Fitzek, F.H.P. and Katz, M. (eds), *'Cognitive Wireless Networks: Concepts, Methodologies and Visions Inspiring the Age of Enlightenment of Wireless Communications'*, ISBN 978-1-4020-5978-0, Springer, Dordrecht, The Netherlands, July 2007.

[6] aka-aki, http://www.aka-aki.com

[7] Sapuppo A., *'Spider Application'*, Aalborg University, http://mobiledevices.kom.aau.dk/projects/
student_projects/spring_2007/social_network/

[8] Pedersen, M. and Fitzek, F.H.P., *'Mobile Phone Programming – SMARTEX: the SmartME Application'*, ISBN 978-1-4020-5968-1 11, Springer, Dordrecht, The Netherlands, 2007, pp. 271–274.

[9] Stini, M., Mauve, M., and Fitzek, F.H.P., 'Digital Ownership: from Content Consumers to Owners and Traders', *IEEE Multimedia – IEEE Computer Society*, **13**(5), October–December 2006, 4–6.

[10] Perrucci, G.P., Fitzek, F.H.P., Boudali, A., Canovas Mateos, M., Nejsum, P., and Studstrup, S., 'Cooperative Web Browsing for Mobile Phones', Proceedings of the International Symposium on Wireless Personal Multimedia Communications (WPMC'07), Jaipur, India, December 2007.

2

The Evolution of Social Interactions in Networked Space

Lara Srivastava
Aalborg University, ls@es.aau.dk

Frank H. P. Fitzek
Aalborg University, ff@es.aau.dk

2.1 Connectivity Takes on a New Dimension

The rapid development of information and communication technologies, and in particular the Internet and the mobile phone, has transformed the way people interact with each other and connect with the environment around them. Over the last few years, a plethora of new applications have sprung up, enabling a whole new dimension of social interaction, on an unprecedented scale.

The mobile phone has been revolutionary in enabling people to communicate anywhere and at any time: people answer their phone calls and texts in restaurants, in class, in meetings, on buses, and even in the toilet. Mobiles now dominate voice communications: there are 3 billion mobile phones worldwide and in the developed world; mobile penetration has reached 97% (see Figure 2.1). The rise in the quantity of mobiles has been correspondingly matched by a significant qualitative evolution: the mobile has shifted from a mere technical device to an important 'social object' present in every aspect of a user's life [1].

The enhanced connectivity afforded by mobile phones has facilitated the creation and maintenance of social networks. There is a subculture of norms underlying mobile phone use, and the device has instilled a new sense of identity and self-assertion for various groups of people – teenagers [2] being a particularly good example. A mobile phone – its look, its feel, its ringtone – can say a lot about the personality and preferences of its user. It has transformed group dynamics and the sense of belonging. Mobile phones are intensely personal. Many people are reluctant to show the contents of their mobile phones, even to

Mobile Peer to Peer (P2P)   Edited by Frank H. P. Fitzek and Hassan Charaf
© 2009 John Wiley & Sons, Ltd

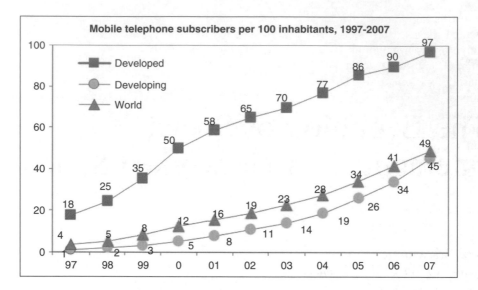

Figure 2.1   Mobile telephone subscribers. Reproduced from © International Telecommunication Union (ITU)

friends or loved ones, for they may contain, photos, diary dates, received calls and stored and/or MMS messages. Put together, all of these clues may reveal the activities of users over a period of time (private and public), their preferences, their social group, and so on. The mobile has become intimate to a person's sense of self. It has also changed the dynamics of wider social interaction. Groups of people are often seen interacting with each other and simultaneously texting third parties that are not present. As such, there is a form of (intentional or unintentional) mingling between the 'copresent' and the 'remote'. There is always the potential for any face-to-face conversation to be interrupted – in fact it has almost become expected. Moreover, when fixed-line phones were the only option, initiators of calls often had to go through an intermediary before reaching the party they wished to call: this could be a parent, a sibling, a friend, or a spouse. With the mobile, the recipient of a call or text is reached directly, without any intermediary. In fact, when others answer, it causes surprise and in some cases may even be disturbing. This direct accessibility has obvious advantages, but it also reduces the presence of spontaneous connectivity and unplanned spin-off conversations with others in a larger family or social network. For parents, in particular, it reduces the possibility of speaking to friends or classmates who might be phoning for their children.

The mobile phone has transformed the way people communicate and interact, mainly because it has become the most intimate technical device we have ever used. It is vital to our daily activities, and its loss, even temporary, causes panic and distress. People are also getting physically closer to their mobile phones at all times of the day, using it as an alarm clock and a source of light in the dark. Beyond the physical, the mobile also acts as a source of comfort when in a queue, an awkward situation, or as a method to ward off unwanted attention, particularly for women.

Just as important as the mobile phone, so-called 'web 2.0' [3] applications have augmented the use and import of digital networks through the incentives they provide for active user participation. Web 2.0 refers to new collaborative and interactive uses of the Internet, and in particular the World Wide Web. It has been driven by notions of trust, sharing, and creativity. First used in a marketing context, the term 'web 2.0' has now gained wide acceptance and can even be said to boast an Internet subculture of its own. When it first hit the mass market, the Internet was used primarily as a mechanism for information retrieval or consultation, and for asynchronous communication (i.e. email). But on today's Internet, information is not only being retrieved by users but increasingly supplied by them. The web is no longer a mere repository of information, but a growing user-driven platform for open and dynamic collaboration, socialization, and knowledge-sharing. A good illustration of this evolution is the difference between the Britannica online [4] service, which provides access to a wealth of encyclopaedic information, and Wikipedia [5], which in many cases has become the favoured Internet stop for general knowledge information. Wikipedia has been written exclusively by everyday Internet users and is managed by a team of editors. Would Pliny or Diderot have imagined such a future for their encyclopaedias – a future of knowledge by popular vote, 'democratic knowledge'? The web 2.0 approach lies at the core of a future digital universe of 'meta-content' – a universe that would be easily searchable, indexable, adaptable, and perpetually updated (e.g. semantic web), not only providing users with a sense of ownership of the network but also enabling knowledge-sharing and collaborative thinking on an unparalleled scale.

This new second-generation approach to the Internet not only has spurred user-generated content but also is at the heart of the phenomenon of online social networking. A 'social network' is defined in Wikipedia as a 'social structure made of nodes (which are generally individuals or organizations) that are tied by one or more specific types of interdependency, such as values, visions, ideas, financial exchange, friendship, kinship, dislike, conflict, or trade' [6]. Services such as Bebo, Facebook, and MySpace exploit the notion of social networks to build online communities of like-minded people. These people can share interests and activities actively, or they may simply be interested in looking at other people's activities and interests. With social networking, the notion of connectivity and communications between people is transformed, as is the very concept of personal identity. An individual's home page has become their main credential in the offline world too. Teenagers who do not have a website where they post information, pictures, and daily musings may be left out of social circles in their daily lives.

However, social networking is not the only application that has revolutionized identity and interaction online. As shown in Figure 2.2, the growth of massive multiplayer online games (MMOGs) and virtual worlds, such as Second Life [7], has been just as significant, enabling interaction between virtual projections of identity – avatars. By some estimates, MMOGs are set to grow from around 16 million in 2008 to 2 million in 2009 (pred. 2006) and 30 million in 2012 (source: Bruce Sterling Woodcock, 'An Analysis of MMOG Subscription Growth', MMOGChart.com). SPORE, a game that was released in the second half of 2008, is an interesting example, as it is intended to 'mimic' real life from its very inception through open-ended game play (e.g. from unicellular organism to a space exploring the social creature). As it has been recently released, categorizations of this

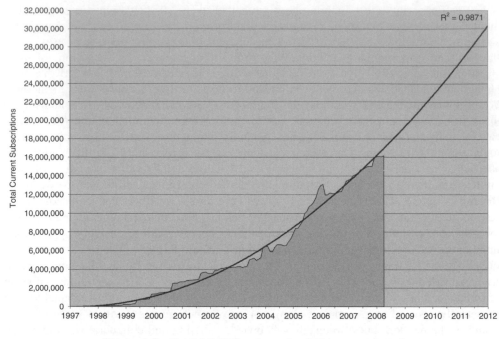

Figure 2.2 Total MMOG active subscriptions – projected

game range from real-time strategy to a life simulation. Spore itself labels its game as an ecosystem in the control of the user: 'It's a bit like the present you imagine a god might get on their first birthday: a mini universe of creation in a box' (source: Spore home page at http://eu.spore.com/whatisspore/ and Wikipedia, Entry for Spore, available at http://en.wikipedia.org/wiki/Spore_(computer_game)#cite_note-origin01-2).

Applications such as these allow users to create representations of themselves that can be as close to or as removed from reality as they wish. They can even build entire environments, including houses, gardens, and businesses, entirely in the digital space. In some sense, the web 2.0 approach makes everyone an Internet celebrity. In fact, having public status, i.e. as well-known digital personae in a particular group or groups, has become desirable if not expected. Digital voyeurism and exhibitionism has become part and parcel of today's web 2.0.

Important trends such as increased mobility, always-on connectivity, social networking, and web 2.0 applications have important consequences for social structures and social behaviour, and these, in turn, affect the development and take-up of emerging technologies and applications. As a result, an understanding of social contexts must play an increasingly important role in the process of technology design.

2.2 The Principle of Sharing

Cooperation is the result of the evolution process. In evolution, the fitness of an individual is tested against others, and its chance of survival becomes better the fitter it is [8]. The only way out of this is the cooperation of multiple individuals. By cooperation, the individuals accumulate their strength and in effect increase their fitness; e.g. ants, which are much smaller than cockroaches, are able to defend their territory against cockroaches very effectively by cooperation. Our human society is also based on cooperation. First forms of cooperation were hunting strategies or defending strategies. Later on, the cooperation became more complex with behaviour such as pay-off relaxation [9].

One component of cooperation is the capability of sharing things and goods. This is not only present in humans. Monkeys are also able to share, and they do a pretty good job [10]. Nevertheless, humans like to collect and to share things. The reason for this lies in our history. With the Neolithic revolution, humans were able to produce more products than they could consume by themselves, and they started to share or trade those extra items.

In the digital world, sharing is still hip. With the introduction of peer-to-peer networks, users were able to share whatever content without central servers. This kind of sharing was very popular, as the content was interesting to the users, but also the way the sharing took place contributed to the success. The idea of peer-to-peer networking is that users share their own content with others. In the optimal case, the amount of give and take is the same. But it is also known that only a minority of users are contributing to the peer-to-peer network, while the majority are just exploiting it (this has also to do with legal issues in some countries, where downloading of illegal content is not illegal, but uploading is). The next generation of peer-to-peer networks came along with new strategies to enforce the cooperativeness of the users. Based on a tit-for-tat mechanism, studied in depth by Robert Axelrod in the 1980s, users could only download the amount of information that they had contributed to the network beforehand. Peer-to-peer technology is still interesting to the users, and it is used quite frequently – eDonkey or BitTorrent.

As this book is about mobile peer to peer (P2P), we will focus on the sharing behaviour on mobile devices. Let us make it loud and clear right at the beginning – sharing on mobile devices is very limited nowadays compared with its potential. To the best of our knowledge, the only commercial sharing among mobile devices is that of ringtones, i.e. if one user wants to share (this means to give away) a ringtone it can be sent to another person. However, this interaction takes place via the overlay cellular network (GSM or UMTS), whereas non-commercial sharing among mobile devices takes place only by certain groups such as teens exchanging video content over Bluetooth. This exchange is based on the manual operation of the users, who need to be at least familiar with the functionality of Bluetooth.

The goal of this book is to advocate a wider use of mobile peer-to-peer networks for sharing digital content among mobile devices. Sharing mobile content in this way can help in two ways. The first way is based on the content distribution. Although the content could also be sent over the cellular network, the advantage in sharing over a mobile peer-to-peer network is that the exchange with other mobile devices uses less energy, as explained later in the book, and may result in less cost, as short-range technologies operate in license-free bands. The second reason is that the local exchange can be used as a sort of filter. Even with free cellular access, the question for the user is what to download. Pages like YouTube (http://www.youtube.com/) already have an overwhelming amount of videos. But local exchange will be based on recommendation and therefore give even more relevant content. Using *collective intelligence*, it should be possible for software to determine which users are likely to have relevant content.

2.3 Transspatial and Transtemporal Perspective

The evolution of mankind was boosted by the capability to exchange information between humans. Conveying information between two human beings allows them to share knowledge. The exchange of knowledge was originally based on sign language, and, later on, speech was developed. With the start of the Neolithic revolution some 10,000 years ago, speech became more complex and richer in syntax and semantics.

Even animals learn from each other. Animals observe others and start to learn how things are done. But never has one animal shown another animal how to do certain things. Planned communication, with the goal of exchanging information, allows knowledge to be exchanged beforehand, before an event takes place, and can be handed down over generations. This last point in particular shows the importance of the exchange and storage of information within a group. Individuals do not have to learn everything from scratch, but they will gain from the experience of their ancestors.

Later in time it became important to convey information over long distances, between different groups. By using messengers and, later, written text, information was not geographically confined. The only limitation was that, the greater the distance between sender and receiver, the more time was needed to deliver the message. This limitation was eliminated by the introduction of the telegraph and the phone. Wireless technology even allowed information to be conveyed over the oceans. At that point in time, spatial and time constraints were totally obsolete. However, as revealed in the *Wall Street Journal* [11], instant and constant access also had a downside, as in the case of Mr James Rothschild:

> In the 1850s, James Rothschild complained that it was a 'crying shame that the telegraph has been established' because suddenly anyone 'can get the news.' The Rothschild banking empire was built through private couriers who ponied from one European trading center to another, profiting from market-moving news about business and trade. The telegraph ended such exclusive access. Almost as annoying, information became a constant.

With the introduction of the Internet, the access of information has become even easier – worldwide access to newspapers, satellite pictures of the globe, etc. However, the Internet has also reversed the way we communicate in terms of the transspatial and transtemporal perspective. With the introduction and widespread usage of emails, the temporal dimension has been relaxed. Thus, information can be conveyed and consumed whenever the receiver is ready to do so. The next step is relaxation of the space domain. As information is becoming more and more accessible, the individual is prone to information overload. To prevent this kind of information overload, information filtering is needed. One way of filtering information is based on *collective intelligence*. Another way is to restrict the information to a certain location (this is also known as *location-based services*), i.e. to give information related to a certain location. For example, if a user is visiting a city and is searching for restaurants, it would not be helpful to get a list of all restaurants around the world. When you are hungry, the closer the restaurant the better.

Figure 2.3 shows the evolution of information exchange among people over the past, starting from the Neolithic revolution. After the development of complex languages, messengers were used to bring information over long distances (we use a triangle here to show that very long distances were less frequently served than short distances). With the beginning of the telegraph, the world was more or less connected. The phone granted access

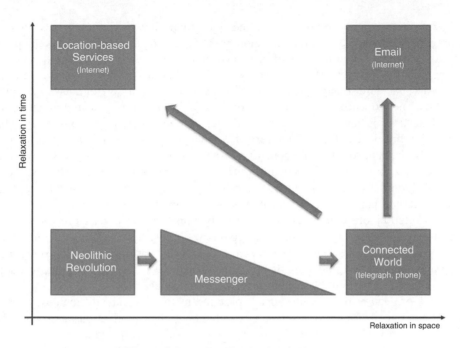

Figure 2.3   Relaxation in time and space

to the connected world for the mass market. The Internet completed the connected work idea and brought about different forms where relaxation was consciously diminished.

2.4   Socialization in the Mobile Digital Age

Technology mediates most forms of human relationship today, be it the mobile phone, SMS, chat, email, social networking spaces, gaming sites, or even a virtual world. Continuous and uninterrupted communications, always-on access to information, and perpetual connectivity are now possible. In some sense, we have attempted to maximize time and minimize space. Although there may be a death of distance in the physical sense, human or personal distance should not be similarly affected.

Human relationships today are increasingly transient and ephemeral. People not only travel more, they tend to change social circles and interests frequently. Technology has afforded the power to stay in touch, but also the power to stay out of touch. There is a growing trend towards 'communication on my own terms', that is to say, people are increasingly self-centred in the way they initiate or respond to communication, even though the essence of human interaction is bidirectional. For example, there is a growing use of mechanisms such as voice messaging and asynchronous text messaging. In instant messaging spaces, users can appear in 'stealth' mode, invisible to other users. As a result, they can observe other users coming on and off line, without revealing their own presence. They are therefore hard to reach, but can, if they wish, reach out to others – another example of 'communication on my own terms'.

The opposite also exists – users who wish to reveal all about themselves at all times (perhaps using falsified information). These users are always on and always reachable, and they respond quickly to posts or comments on their sites or chat messages. In social networks, they may serve as communication brokers, forging connections between people and creating a mass social network of their own. In this sense, the online world is not that different from the offline world: it is 'who you know' that matters. However, in the online world, it is also 'how many' you know. Moreover, there is a sort of 'class system' in online social networks that rates the level of friendship or intimacy with a given person. On MySpace, for instance, users can 'rank' their friends, thereby demonstrating which friends enjoy privileged status. Teenagers often change this status information on a daily or weekly basis, depending upon popularity, disagreements, and so on. Others may simply use the ranking tool once and disregard it. This runs the risk that relationships can often seem 'undifferentiated' and 'ambiguous': a drinking buddy might appear just as important on a user's home page as a close relative or loved one. This stems partly from the fact that it can often be difficult to refuse a request by someone who wishes to add you as a friend: it may seem rude in some cases, as you may actively have to 'reject' an invitation. This may later raise questions if that person is known in the offline world. Many avoid this by accepting most invitations. It becomes even more difficult, therefore, to qualify these relationships, particularly by those viewing home pages.

This lack of nuance in the online social space means that it can be difficult to gauge the nature of a potential 'friend' or acquaintance online, e.g. their motivations and aspirations, and their way of life. Many users even falsify their profiles, either in an obvious manner or in a manner that is harder (and sometimes impossible) to detect. For example, some use the digital space to take on characteristics they may not have in the real world, or to hide aspects of their personality that have been unsuccessful for them in the past.

Nuance is also lacking in the form that communication might take. The mass-scale adoption of, *inter alia*, text messaging, chats, email, and voice messaging has led to a great deal of asynchronous communication and, as a result, prerehearsed communication. This means that thoughts and feelings are more often contrived, while gut reactions and spontaneity take a back seat, not to mention true facial expressions, non-verbal sounds, and body language. This has advantages, in that it enables people who may generally be more shy or inhibited in face-to-face situations to open up and make connections. However, this form of communication is missing an important set of clues that individuals require to build relationships and establish trust.

In this context, the use of digital gesturing is worth a mention. Although popular and often intended as humorous, the overuse of emoticons, such as smiley faces and hearts, can become a simplistic mechanism to express feeling and may be used to hide or mask true feeling more easily than textual communication. Even more ambiguous is the instant messaging 'poke' or 'nudge'. These are signs that can take the form of a shaking or a noise on a recipient's screen. Of course, this may express a desire to be noticed or to be in touch, but not much more. It is unclear whether social interaction is truly desired, indefinitely postponed, or just not required. The social meaning may be unclear to the sender too, leaving the communication open-ended and ambiguous.

Like the Internet, the use of the mobile phone has also affected norms of social behaviour considerably, given its constant presence in daily activity. For instance, owing to the use of SMS, people are often more reluctant to commit to precise meeting times or places, preferring rather to SMS at the last minute. Approximate meeting times are commonplace, and punctuality is no longer as necessary, with the possibility of sending a text message announcing a tardy arrival. Some people also prefer to write SMS rather than initiate a voice call – in some circles, it is considered appropriate to text rather than phone first. Similarly, informal mechanisms such as the use of missed calls are being used to indicate meaning, i.e. one ring for 'call me back' or two rings for 'I'm running late'. This method can be extended to transmit real bit streams by missed calls, as explained in reference [12].

Another important effect of the mobile phone, not unlike social networking, is the blurring of boundaries between public and private spaces. On social networking sites, a large amount of private information is displayed. With the mobile phone, public spaces are increasingly being filled with private conversations. Often, this is unintentional, but in some cases a form of 'stage phoning' [13] is done by users who wish to use the mobile to increase their social status or make themselves noticeable in a crowd.

Always-on digital spaces enable us, as individuals, to connect anywhere and at any time, but this power is also available to commercial entities. This has advantages, in terms of customer relationship management, but also important disadvantages. Unsolicited marketing efforts are already a significant problem online, and will only rise if proper measures are not taken. Moreover, fraudulent activity (which already poses a significant threat online) will have more environments in which to proliferate.

The fervour of innovation underlying today's growth in information and communication technologies has been accompanied with its own set of changing social norms and etiquette. These are affecting the way in which technology is used, but also the way we interact and lead our daily lives. More thinking and analysis is required to understand better the nexus between technology and society, not only for a better grasp of user demand and design-winning products but also for the public interest as a whole.

2.5 Future Perspectives

In spite of some of the adjustments that may be required, digital spaces hold countless possibilities for greater user convenience and the overall enhancement of quality of life. Today, the mobile phone and web 2.0 dominate our attention. The vision of the future network may take us a step further, by connecting not only anyone at any time and anywhere, but anything too. In this future 'Internet of things' [14], the world's objects could be mapped in a virtual world, through emerging technologies such as RFID and sensors [15]. Each object may be tagged with a wealth of readable and updatable data – it would in a sense have its own web page that could contain a wealth of information about its history (e.g. date of manufacture, origin), current status (e.g. location), and future status (e.g. date of expiry, destination). Imagine a world in which the mobile phone and web 2.0 meet the Internet of things. It would mean that social networking and knowledge-sharing tools could be combined with objects in our environment, and therefore become increasingly context aware. In public places, we could use mobile phones to read tags on specific objects to find out more about them, but also to find out what others have said about them, or which of our friends have recently passed by. Citizen comments, recommendations, and virtual tours may become commonplace. This has great advantages for lifelong learning, community living, and knowledge-sharing. The blind, for instance, could more easily navigate the environment around them if they could interact with objects in their vicinity, and derive location or terrain information, e.g. through their walking aid. In this future context, there would be a mapping of the real world in the virtual world, as services become truly portable between devices, people, environments, things, and, indeed, each and every 'node' in the global digital network.

References

[1] Srivastava, L., 'Mobile Phones and the Evolution of Social Behaviour', *Behaviour and Information Technology*, **24**(2), March–April 2005, 111–129.

[2] Lorente, S., 'Youth and Mobile Telephones: More than a Fashion', in '*Juventud y Teléfonos Móviles*', ed. by Lorente, S., Ministerio de Trabajo y Asuntós Sociales, Injuve, 2002.

[3] Web 2.0 is a marketing term first used by O'Reilly Media for a 2004 conference. See O'Reilly, T., '*What is Web 2.0: Design Patterns and Business Models for the Next Generation of Software*', September 2005, available at: http://www.oreillynet.com/pub/a/oreilly/tim/news/2005/09/30/what-is-web-20.html [accessed 21 April 2008].

[4] See http://www.britannica.com/ [accessed 21 July 2008].

[5] See http://www.wikipedia.org/ [accessed 21 July 2008].

[6] See http://en.wikipedia.org/wiki/Social_network [accessed 21 July 2008].

[7] See http://secondlife.com/ [accessed 22 July 2008].

[8] Rechenberg, I., '*Evolutionsstrategie '94*', ISBN-13: 978-3772816420, Frommann Holzboog, Stuttgart, Germany, 2004.

[9] de Waal, F., *et al*., '*Our Inner Ape*', ISBN-13: 978-1573223126, Riverhead Hardcover, New York, NY, 2005.

[10] de Waal, F., *et al*., 'Monkeys Know It's Smart to Share', *ScienceNOW*, 6 April 2000, 3.

[11] Crovitz, L.G., 'Optimism and the Digital World', *Wall Street Journal*, 21 April 2008, A15.

[12] Fitzek, F.H.P., 'The Medium is the Message', in Proceedings of IEEE International Conference on Communication (ICC), 2006.

[13] Plant, S., '*On the Mobile: the Effects of Mobile Telephones on Social and Individual Life*', Motorola, 2003.

[14] ITU Internet Report 2005: '*The Internet of Things*', ed. by Srivastava, L., ITU, 2005, available at: http://www.itu.int/osg/spu/publications/Internetofthings/ [accessed 23 July 2008].

[15] Srivastava, L., 'RFID: Ubiquity for Humanity', *INFO*, **9**(1), 2007.

Part Two

Basic Functionalities for Mobile P2P

3

The Symbian C++ Programming Environment

Morten V. Pedersen
Aalborg University, mvpe@es.aau.dk

Frank H. P. Fitzek
Aalborg University, ff@es.aau.dk

3.1 Introduction

In this chapter we will introduce the programming environment that is used in the subsequent chapters. This will allow readers unfamiliar with the particular tool chain used here to set up a similar environment for testing code and running the code examples found in this book. In the following, a step-by-step description will be given of the installation process and the tools that have been used. After setting up the development environment, we will test the set-up by building a helloworld application and then run it using the emulator and device. If you already have a similar running development environment, or if you are already familiar with the Symbian C++ development environment and the application build process, you may skip this chapter and proceed to the following chapters. New developers of Symbian OS applications may also find more extensive and in-depth getting started guides in, for example, references [1] and [2].

3.2 Tools Overview

In order to get started, we need a couple of tools installed on our PC. These include an integrated development environment (IDE) for building our applications and a suitable software development kit (SDK). The SDK contains libraries, application programming interface (API) documentation, example code, and a number of development tools,

Mobile Peer to Peer (P2P)   Edited by Frank H. P. Fitzek and Hassan Charaf
© 2009 John Wiley & Sons, Ltd

including an emulator for testing and debugging our application before actually deploying it on the target phone.

The recommended IDE by Symbian and Nokia is currently the Eclipse-based Carbide.c++. The Carbide.c++ IDE is available in four different versions from www.forum.nokia.com/carbide:

- Carbide.c++ Express – free version, well suited for non-commercial developers;
- Carbide.c++ Developer – additional capabilities for commercial developers, e.g. on device debugging;
- Carbide.c++ Pro – for advanced commercial development, includes, for example, code profilers;
- Carbide.c++ OEM – for device manufacturers.

Note that other IDEs supporting Symbian OS application development are also available. For example, if you prefer using Microsoft Visual Studio, this is possible using Carbide.vs plug-ins for Visual Studio 2003 and 2005. In the following, we will be using the free Carbide.c++ Express IDE, as it provides all the basic functionalities we need in order to get started. It is recommended that you have a fairly fast development PC. For running the Carbide.c++ Express edition, the following configuration is recommended: Windows XP (SP2) or Windows 2000 (SP4), 1800 MHz processor, 1024 MB RAM, and enough free hard drive space for the IDE and a SDK – typically around 650 MB (additional installs such as Java Runtime Environment and Perl are not included in the 650 MB). At the time of writing, development on Windows Vista is possible, but your mileage may vary. The latest version Carbide.c++ (v1.3) has been reported to work. However, some SDK versions are still not fully functional, and others may require patches (for more information, see wiki.forum.nokia.com/index.php/Moving_to_Windows_Vista).

Every Symbian handset on the market has an SDK version associated with it. Developing an application with a particular SDK allows you to target a range of devices based on that SDK.

The S60 SDKs are listed below (most recent first):

- S60 3rd edition feature pack 2 – Symbian OS v9.3;
- S60 3rd edition feature pack 1 – Symbian OS v9.2;
- S60 3rd edition – Symbian OS v9.1;
- S60 2nd edition feature pack 3 – Symbian OS v8.1;
- S60 2nd edition feature pack 2 – Symbian OS v8.0a;
- S60 2nd edition feature pack 1 – Symbian OS v7.0s enhanced;
- S60 2nd edition – Symbian OS v7.0s;
- S60 1st edition – Symbian OS v6.1.

As of S60 3rd edition, Nokia has pledged to make subsequent releases binary compatible, which means that applications compiled against the S60 3rd edition SDK should run unaltered on feature pack 1 and feature pack 2 devices.

There is a significant difference between 2nd edition and 3rd edition, as Symbian OS v9.1 introduced an intentional binary compatibility break owing to a change in compiler and the introduction of a capability-based platform security system. Although the source changes are usually small, projects built for the 2nd edition must be ported to the 3rd edition, and vice versa.

Symbian maintains a mapping of SDK to handsets at http://developer.symbian.com/main/tools/sdks/s60/, which you can use, in case you are in doubt which one to download for your phone. Do not be afraid to install the wrong SDK. The development tools support multiple SDKs, and you can easily switch between them when building and testing applications.

In addition to the S60 UI platform, some other Symbian smartphones, such as those from Sony Ericsson and Motorola, use the UIQ UI. UIQ is also available in a number of revisions:

- UIQ 3.3 – Symbian OS v9.3;
- UIQ 3.1 – Symbian OS v9.2;
- UIQ 3.0 – Symbian OS v9.1;
- UIQ 2.1 – Symbian OS v7.0;
- UIQ 2.0 – Symbian OS v7.0.

Similarly to S60, Symbian also maintains a list of phones using the UIQ SDKs at developer.symbian.com/main/tools/sdks/uiq/. Even though any newer Symbian-based phone should use one of the two above-mentioned SDKs, a number of SDKs exist for older phones not using the S60 or UIQ SDKs. In that case, visit the phone manufacturer's web page to find the suitable SDK.

3.3   Installing the IDE

In order to download the Carbide.c++ IDE, you need a Forum Nokia account. If you are not yet a registered member, go to www.forum.nokia.com to create an account first. You will also need to register to download and use the SDK, so, if you do not have an account, now is a good time to get one. In addition to allowing you to register the IDE and SDK for free, you will also get access to the development community forums at Forum Nokia. The Carbide.c++ IDE can be downloaded from www.forum.nokia.com/carbide. In subsequent chapters we have used Carbide.c++ v1.3. Download the set-up file and start the installation process. During the installation process you will be prompted to select the IDE variant Express, Developer, Professional, or OEM. Here, you should choose the free Express version. Note that the other variants are not free but can be used for a limited trial period.

3.4   Installing the SDK and Prerequisites

Depending on your target phone, you should now download and install an appropriate SDK. Here we have used the S60 3rd edition FP1 SDK. This and the other S60 SDKs can be found on the Forum Nokia home page (www.forum.nokia.com) under Tools and SDKs. If you choose to use a different SDK, be careful to download an SDK compatible with Carbide.c++. You can ensure this by reading the SDK release notes (recommended) and avoiding SDKs with 'WINS' in their name. The SDK package is quite a large download, so, while downloading the SDK installation files, we can install two third-party prerequisites that are required by the SDK tool chain:

- *Perl.* Perl should be installed to run various build scripts used by the SDK. You can download a free version from www.activestate.com. Note that Symbian requires that we use version 5.6.1.
- *Java Runtime.* In order to use the phone emulator fully, you also need a working installation of Java Runtime Environment. Download the latest version from www.java.com/download. To use Java 6 or a newer version, some tweaks are required to make it work (for more information see wiki.forum.nokia.com/index.php/KIS001066_-_%27Cannot_start_ECMT_Manager%27_error_message_in_emulator).

A final tool that is not necessary but will come in handy is the PC Suite from Nokia. Installing the PC Suite will enable us easily to transfer our application to the actual phone via cable or Bluetooth. Nokia PC Suite can be downloaded from www.nokia.com/pcsuite.

After installing these prerequisites, hopefully the SDK download is complete and we can proceed with the installation of the actual SDK. The SDK is delivered in a zip package that you must extract to run the set-up file, which will guide you through the rest of the installation process.

This completes the installation of IDE and SDK. We should now be ready to build and deploy Symbian applications. The following section will give a small introduction to the features of the Carbide.c++ IDE.

3.5   Using the Carbide IDE

If you have just installed Carbide.c++ you should be able to launch it from the Windows start menu *Start → Programs → Carbide.c++ v1.3*. After launching Carbide.c++, we will be greeted with a welcome screen as shown in Figure 3.1.

The welcome screen contains shortcuts giving us different possibilities to explore the features of Carbide.c++, e.g. through tutorials or the platform overview documentation. It contains a detailed explanation of how to use the advanced features of the IDE. The actual development and project management is done in the workbench window, which can be accessed by pressing the switch to workbench icon in the top right corner. You can always return to the welcome screen by using the *help → welcome* menu option. The workbench window shown in Figure 3.2 is where we create our applications and will spend most of our time; this can be broken down into several important elements:

- Project Explorer. This shows the folder structure of our current projects and allows us to navigate the different project files.
- Editor. Here we can edit our source files.
- The toolbar, among others containing:
  - the build button, which allows us quickly to build our projects;
  - the debug button, which launches application in debug mode;

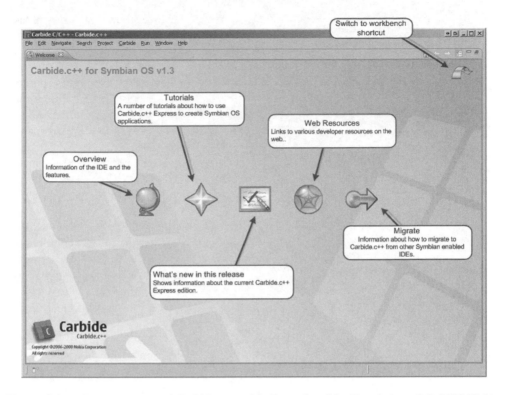

Figure 3.1 Welcome screen of Carbide.c++ v1.3. Reproduced by Permission of © 2009 Nokia. All rights reserved

- the run button, which launches the application for functional testing.
- The tools tabs, which allow us to access a number of other views useful when building and debugging applications.

You can learn more about the Carbide.c++ UI and how to use it in the Carbide.c++ help. This can be accessed though *Help → Help Content → Carbide Help → Carbide.c++ User Guide* which contains a tour of the UI.

The easiest way to ensure that everything is working is to create a simple helloworld test application. Carbide.c++ includes an application wizard that enables us quickly to create a project and get the application directory structure in place. To create a new application project, select the *File → New* option from the menu bar and select *Symbian OS C++ Project*. The application wizard will now ask you to select the project template. Select *3rd-Future Ed. GUI Application* and press *Next*. Now fill in a project name, e.g. *helloworld*, and choose *Next*. The application wizard will now show a dialog containing a list of SDKs and build configurations that we can use for our project. The list depends on the SDKs that we have installed, and in our case this means that the S60 3rd edition feature pack 1 SDK will be listed, as can be seen in Figure 3.3.

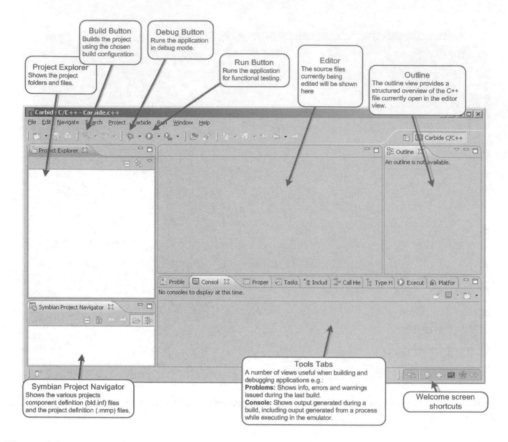

If you expand the tree view of the build configurations, you will see that for each SDK you have a number of target types supported by each build configuration:

- Emulator Debug (WINSCW). This build configuration is used when building our application for execution in the emulator on our PC. This is very useful in the development phase.
- Phone Release (GCCE). This build configuration is used to create binaries suitable for execution on the phone.

You may also have other options available here, depending on the compilers installed on your development PC. Click the *Finish* button, and the application wizard will create the project.

In order to build and run the application, we can either right-click our project and select the *Run As → Run Symbian OS Application* option or click the *Run* icon in the toolbar. This will build and start the application in the emulator, as shown in Figure 3.4. Starting the emulator for the first time can take quite a while, so you will need to be patient.

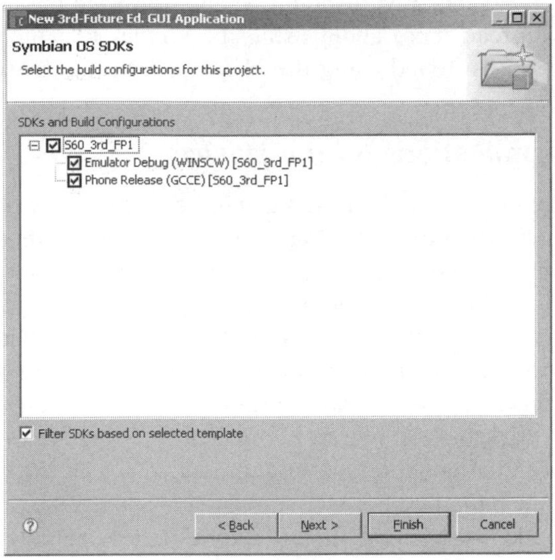

Figure 3.3 The Carbide.c++ SDK and build configuration selection dialog. Reproduced by Permission of © 2009 Nokia. All rights reserved

Figure 3.4 S60 Emulator running the helloworld application. Reproduced by Permission of © 2009 Nokia. All rights reserved

Once the emulator is launched, you should be able to locate the helloworld application and launch it. You can read more about using the emulator in the SDK documentation and in the Carbide.c++ help found using the *Help → Help Contents* menu option.

3.6 Installing Applications on the Device

Most application functionality can be tested using the emulator. However, to ensure fully that our applications are working, we may wish to install them on an actual device. Carbide.c++ can be configured to create a. sis and signed .sisx file automatically when building for the phone. When using the application wizard to create our project, this is done automatically for us, and all we have to do to build the installation files is to change the build configuration. This can be done in several ways. We will do it by selecting the *Project → Build Configuration → 2 Phone Release (GCCE)* option. The new active build configuration is now marked as shown in Figure 3.5.

To start a build using the new build configuration, select the *Project → Build Project* menu option or press the build button in the toolbar. This builds the project and creates two new files in the \sis folder found in the Project Explorer view, namely the unsigned. sis and self-signed .sisx installation files. Note that the individual phone manufacturer determines the security policy mandating what level of signing is needed to install an application on a particular device. However, most devices will install a self-signed application without any problems.[1] The easiest way to install the application on a phone is to use the Nokia PC Suite application installer and a Bluetooth dongle or USB cable connector. If Nokia PC

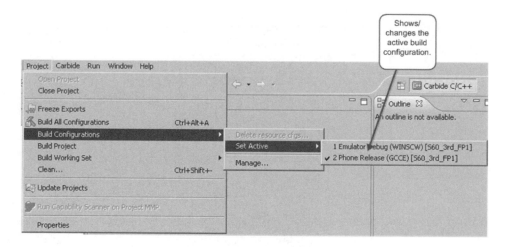

Figure 3.5 Selecting the active build configuration. Reproduced by Permission of © 2009 Nokia. All rights reserved

---

[1] The Nokia E Series devices do not allow self-signed applications to be installed by default. This can, however, be enabled from the phone menu, going to *Application Manager → Options → Settings → Software Installation*. Change the setting from *Signed* to *All*, if needed.

Figure 3.6 The Nokia application installer dialog. Reproduced by Permission of © 2009 Nokia. All rights reserved

Suite is connected to your phone, you can simply double-click the .sisx file in Carbide.c++ Project Explorer, and the PC Suite application installer seen in Figure 3.6 will be activated and allow you to install our application on the phone.

Complete the installation on the phone. You should now be able to find and run the application on the phone.

3.7 Quick Resource Overview

Table 3.1 gives an overview of the links presented here, with a couple of additional links to helpful resources.

Table 3.1 The links discussed, plus two additional links to helpful resources

Overview of phone models and SDK versions:

- S60 phones: http://developer.symbian.com/main/tools/sdks/s60/
- UIQ phones: http://developer.symbian.com/main/tools/sdks/uiq/

S60 SDK and Carbide downloads:

- Carbide.c++ IDE and Visual Studio plug-ins: www.forum.nokia.com/carbide
- SDKs by following the link on www.forum.nokia.com/tools

UIQ SDK (note Carbide.c++ also supports UIQ SDKs):

- http://developer.uiq.com/devtools_uiqsdk.html

SDK prerequisites and additional installs:

- Perl v5.6.1 from www.activestate.com
- Jave Runtime Environment: www.java.com/download
- PC Suite: www.nokia.com/pcsuite

Developer resources such as forums, tutorials, and example code:

- Forum Nokia: www.forum.nokia.com
- Forum Nokia Wiki: http://wiki.forum.nokia.com/
- Symbian Developer Network: http://developer.symbian.com

References

[1] Aubert, M., *et al.*, *'Quick Recipes on Symbian OS – Mastering C++ Mobile Development'*, ISBN-10: 0470997834, John Wiley & Sons, Inc., Hoboken, NJ, 2008, 9–28.
[2] Pedersen, M.V. and Fitzek, F.H.P., *'Mobile Phone Programming – Symbian/C++'*, ISBN 978-1-4020-5968-1 4, Springer, Dordrecht, The Netherlands, 2007, 95–138.

4

Introduction to Bluetooth Communication on Mobile Devices

Morten V. Pedersen
Aalborg University, mvpe@es.aau.dk

Frank H. P. Fitzek
Aalborg University, ff@es.aau.dk

4.1   Introduction

In this chapter we will describe the different Symbian OS C++ Bluetooth APIs available to a developer. The goal is to enable mobile application developers to write Symbian C++ Bluetooth-enabled applications in order to increase the usability of their applications. We will describe how to perform the basic operations such as discovering other Bluetooth devices, advertising Bluetooth services, establishing connections between devices, and transferring data. In the following, we will assume that the reader is familiar with the fundamental Symbian C++ development techniques and has some knowledge of Bluetooth technology. For more information about Symbian C++, we suggest you consult the books and booklets available from Symbian Press (at developer.symbian.com/books). More information about Bluetooth on Symbian OS can be found in *Symbian OS Communications Programming*, 2nd edition, by Iain Campbell, and in articles published on the Symbian Developer Network, for example reference [1]. This chapter has been written on the basis of the APIs available in S60 3rd edition, and application developers targeting S60 2nd edition devices should check that the APIs are available or seek alternative APIs.

Mobile Peer to Peer (P2P)   Edited by Frank H. P. Fitzek and Hassan Charaf
© 2009 John Wiley & Sons, Ltd

4.2   Turning Bluetooth On/Off

When developing Bluetooth-enabled applications, we want to ensure that the Bluetooth
radio is powered up. In some cases we might also wish to turn the Bluetooth power off,
but bear in mind that this may affect other Bluetooth applications running on the device.
Inspecting the power state of the Bluetooth radio can be achieved through the Central
Repository API. The Central Repository allows applications to query and set various
shared or application-specific settings. In the following code example we will use the
Central Repository API to retrieve the Bluetooth power state:

```
#include <centralrepository.h>
#include <btserversdkcrkeys.h>
// Link against centralrepository.lib
TBool BluetoothPowerStateL()
    {
    CRepository* repository = CRepository::
        NewLC(KCRUidBluetoothPowerState);
    TInt state;
    User::LeaveIfError(repository->Get(KBTPowerState, state));
    CleanupStack::PopAndDestroy(repository);
    return (state == EBTPowerOn);
    }
```

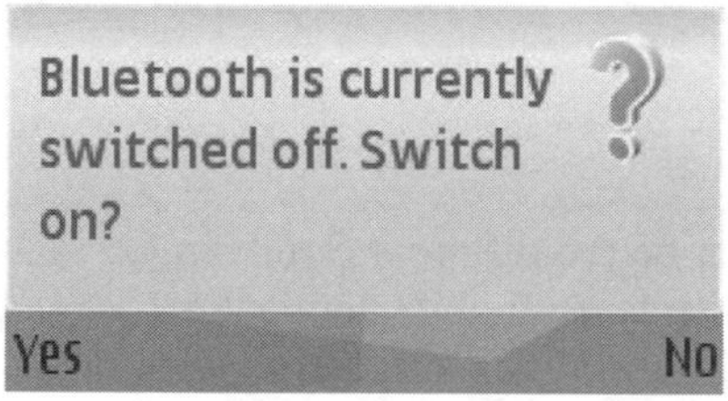

Figure 4.1   Using the RNotifier API to remind the user to turn on Bluetooth

The above function will return ETrue if the Bluetooth power is turned on. Unfortunately,
it is currently not possible to change the Bluetooth power state using the CReposi-
tory::Set() function.[1] Some of this functionality can, however, be achieved through
the RNotifier API, as shown in the following. The notifier will check whether the Bluetooth power is off. If that is the case, it will query the user via a pop-up dialog to turn
on Bluetooth, as shown in Figure 4.1.

```
#include <btnotifierapi.h>

TBool TurnBluetoothOnL()
```

---

[1] For further information, see Known Issue KIS000704, which can be found on http://wiki.forum.nokia.com/
index.php/KnowledgeBase

```
{
RNotifier notifier;
User::LeaveIfError( notifier.Connect() );
TPckgBuf<TBool> dummy(ETrue);
TPckgBuf<TBool> reply(EFalse);
TRequestStatus status; // Should be avoided in
    production code
notifier.StartNotifierAndGetResponse(status,
    KPowerModeSettingNotifierUid, dummy, reply);
User::WaitForRequest(status);
notifier.CancelNotifier(KPowerModeSettingNotifierUid);
notifier.Close();
return reply();
}
```

Note that, in the above code example, we have used a local TRequestStatus object to avoid wrapping the asynchronous call in an active object. This should be avoided in production code, where an active object would be the correct solution. For more information about active objects, see references [2] and [3].

Unfortunately, the RNotifier API cannot be used to turn the Bluetooth power off. This functionality can be achieved via the Bluetooth Engine API, which can be installed as an SDK API plug-in. Plug-in packages for all 3rd edition SDKs can be downloaded from wiki.forum.nokia.com/index.php/SDK_API_Plug-in.

To use the SDK plug-in, it must be installed into your Symbian SDK folder. Note that Nokia does not give any binary compatibility promises with regard to the SDK plug-in APIs, and they can therefore not be guaranteed to work on all devices. The Bluetooth Engine API exposes a number of other features besides the power control, so, if you have a specific requirement not achievable via the normal APIs, it might be worth checking out. After ensuring that the Bluetooth radio is turned on, we will start using it by performing a device discovery.

4.3 Discovering Bluetooth Devices

A common feature needed when developing Bluetooth-enabled applications is the ability to discover nearby devices. This operation can be performed in two ways, depending on the application requirements:

- The user can select via a pop-up the device to which he/she wishes to connect.
- Background device discovery can be performed without any user interaction.

4.3.1 Using the Bluetooth UI

The Bluetooth UI API allows us to prompt the user to select a remote device. This can be achieved, requiring only a small amount of code, through the RNotifier API. Note that, if we choose to use the RNotifer API, we will not have to check whether Bluetooth is powered on, since this is done by RNotifier internally. In order to use the RNotifier API, we need to familiarize ourselves with two auxiliary classes:

- TBTDeviceSelectionParams. In order to limit the number of search results presented to the user, this allows us to filter devices based on their class of device (CoD). The CoD of a device comprises three fields: the major device class, the minor device class, and the major service class. The device class fields indicate which type of device we are interested in, e.g. smartphones, headset, computer, etc. The major service class field gives an indication of which services a particular device offers, e.g. rendering, object transfer, etc. If we are only interested in a specific type of device or service, we can set up a filter using this class. However, this is currently not supported by S60 devices [4].
- TBTDeviceResponseParams. This class is used to retrieve information about the device selected by the user.

The RNotifier API requires that we package the TBTDeviceSelectionParams and TBTDeviceResponseParams instances in a package buffer, TBTDeviceSelection-ParamsPckg and TBTDeviceResponseParamsPckg respectively, allowing them to be transferred over the client/server boundary to the extended notifier server.

In the following code example, we perform a device discovery using the RNotifier API:

```
#include <btextnotifiers.h>
#include <bttypes.h>
// Link against bluetooth.lib, btextnotifiers.lib

const TBTDevAddr& SelectBluetoothDeviceL()
    {
    RNotifier notifier;
    User::LeaveIfError( notifier.Connect() );
    CleanupClosePushL(notifier);

    TBTDeviceSelectionParamsPckg filter;
    TBTDeviceResponseParamsPckg response;
    TRequestStatus status;
    notifier.StartNotifierAndGetResponse(status,
        KDeviceSelectionNotifierUid, filter, response);
    User::WaitForRequest(status);

        // Check for errors
    User::LeaveIfError(status.Int());

        if(!response().IsValidBDAddr())
        User::Leave(KErrGeneral);
```

```
CleanupStack::PopAndDestroy(1); // RNotifier
return response().BDAddr();
}
```

As can be seen in Figure 4.2, a pop-up is displayed to the user, allowing a specific device to be selected.

When the user selects a specific device, we can extract information about the selected device via functions in the `TBTDeviceResponseParams`. In the above case, we validate and return the Bluetooth address of the selected device. The application can now continue to query the selected device for a specific service, or alternatively, if the service is assumed to exist on the device, simply try to connect. To avoid blocking the main application thread, the `RNotifier::StartNotifierAndGetResponse()` call could be called within the context of an active object.

If we are building an application that should run silently in the background and not disrupt the user, we might want to perform device discoveries without requiring user interaction. This can be achieved using the `RHostResolver` API.

4.3.2 Performing Background Device Search

In Symbian OS, the `RHostResolver` API provides an interface to host name resolution services such as standard domain name system (DNS) inquiries. However, it can also be utilized to create a Bluetooth host resolver. When using the `RHostResolver` for Bluetooth device discoveries, two auxiliary classes are needed: the `TinquirySockAddr`

Figure 4.2   Showing the Bluetooth UI of RNotifier

and `TNameEntry` classes. As with the `RNotifier` API, we can specify a number of options affecting how the device search will be performed. These options can be specified on the used `TInquirySockAddr` object via the following functions:

- `TInquirySockAddr::SetAction()`. This function can be used to set a number of flags governing how the device discovery will be performed. Note that several flags can be combined using a bitwise OR operation:

KHostResInquiry	Retrieve the addresses of remote devices
KHostResName	Resolve the name of the remote device
KHostResIgnoreCache	Ignore the local cache of remote devices previously found, only return devices that are currently discovered
KHostResCache	Use the local cache of previously found remote devices

- `TInquirySockAddr::SetIAC()`. This function is used to specify the inquiry access code (IAC) to be used. The Bluetooth specification specifies two IACs:
  - Limited inquiry access code (LIAC). The LIAC access code is used to find devices configured to use the limited discovery mode. This mode is used by devices that are only discoverable for a limited period of time.
  - General inquiry access code (GIAC). Using this access code will allow us to find devices that are in the general discovery mode, but also devices in the limited discovery mode. General discovery mode is used by devices that are continuously discoverable.

An instance of the `TNameEntry` will contain the Bluetooth address and optionally the name of the discovered device. The following code walkthrough of the RHostResolverExample project, found on the DVD, shows how the `RHostResolver` can be used to find other Bluetooth devices:

```
RSocketServ socketServ;
User::LeaveIfError(socketServ.Connect());
CleanupClosePushL(socketServ);
```

We need an open connection to the Symbian OS socket server:

```
TProtocolDesc protocol;
User::LeaveIfError(socketServ.FindProtocol(_L("BTLinkManager"),
    protocol));
```

The BTLinkManager protocol provides the device resolver service for Bluetooth:

```
RHostResolver resolver;
User::LeaveIfError(resolver.Open(socketServ,
    protocol.iAddrFamily, protocol.iProtocol));
CleanupClosePushL(resolver);
```

```
TInquirySockAddr sockaddr;
sockaddr.SetIAC(KGIAC);
sockaddr.SetAction(KHostResInquiry | KHostResName |
    KHostResIgnoreCache);

TNameEntry nameentry;
TInt res = resolver.GetByAddress(sockaddr, nameentry);
```

We open a connection to the resolver server and use the `TInquirySockAddr` to specify the search criteria. The `TNameEntry` object will contain the result of any found devices:

```
while(res == KErrNone)
    {
    // Extract name and address
    TBuf<KMaxBluetoothNameLen> name;
    name = nameentry().iName;

    TBTDevAddr address;
    address = TInquirySockAddr::Cast(nameentry().iAddr).BTAddr();

    // Next result
    res = resolver.Next(nameentry);
    }

CleanupStack::PopAndDestroy(2, &socketServ);
```

Notice that we start the resolver by calling `RHostResolver::GetByAddress()` after retrieving the first result. We call `RHostResolver::Next()` to get any additional search results. This will continue until the API returns either an error or `KErrHostResNoMoreResults`, which signals that no further results are ready. In this code example we have used the synchronous version of the API, which effectively means that the functions `RHostResolver::GetByAddress()` and `RHostResolver::Next()` will block until a result is ready. To avoid this, asynchronous versions of the functions are available that can be easily wrapped in an active object.

As we now know which Bluetooth devices are in the vicinity, we can now use the Bluetooth service discovery protocol (SDP) to explore the services offered by the individual devices.

4.4   The Service Discovery Protocol

The Bluetooth service discovery protocol resolves the common problem of service advertisement and service discovery in a standardized manner. From a programmer's point of view, the SDP allows us to determine which protocols to use when connecting to a specific service, e.g. OBEX, and in addition the port to which we must connect to utilize the service. Note that the term 'port' in Bluetooth can refer to two different entities depending on the context:

- If the L2CAP protocol is used, the port refers to the protocol service multiplexer (PSM), which is usually a 16-bit integer.[2] The lower range from 0×000 to 0×1001 is reserved by the Bluetooth special interest group (SIG) and cannot be used; PSM values above this range can be used freely.

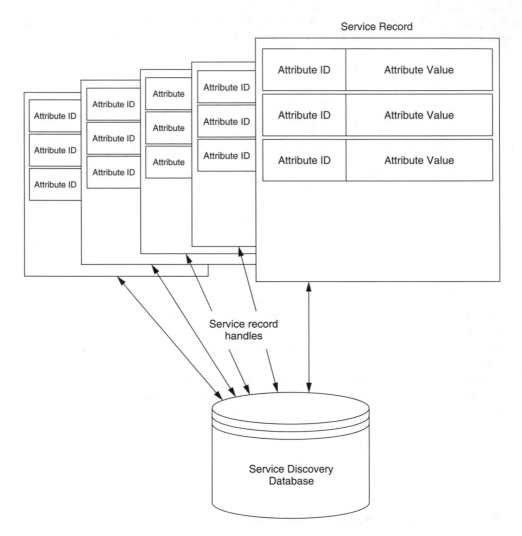

Figure 4.3 The SDP service discovery database contains one service record per service. Each service record consists of a number of attributes describing the properties of the particular service

---

[2] The PSM values must conform to the following rules. The least significant bit of the least significant octet must be '1'. Additionally, the least significant bit of the most significant octet must be '0'. This limits the range of legal values, but still leaves over 16,000 valid values.

- If the RFCOMM protocol is used, the port number refers to the channel number. RFCOMM currently allows 30 different channels.

Unlike many Internet protocols based on user datagram protocol (UDP) and transmission control protocol (TCP), there is no notion of well-known ports such as port 80 for the hypertext transfer protocol (HTTP) defined in Bluetooth. This is quite important, and our Bluetooth services should therefore be assigned a port number dynamically. A programmer must therefore rely on the SDP to discover the port number of a remote service. In the following sections we will go through the Symbian OS APIs exposing this functionality, and see how it can be used in our applications. You will probably notice that the SDP APIs can be a little daunting at first, and it can take a little while until you find your way around the different data structures.

The SDP protocol is fully specified in the Bluetooth core specification [5]. In this section we will give a short overview of the components necessary to understand the Symbian implementation.

4.4.1 Advertising a Service

If we are building an application providing a specific service via Bluetooth, and want to make this accessible to others, we need to advertise its existence. This could be an implementation of one of the standard Bluetooth profiles or our own new service. In order for our service to become accessible to others, we must create a service record in the service discovery database (SDDB).

4.4.2 The Structure of a Service Record

A service record is a key concept in the SDP. All information about a particular service is maintained within a service record. All service records are uniquely identified within a single SDDB using a 32-bit record handle. The record handle is needed if we wish to update information contained in a service record or delete it from the SDDB. The service record consists of a list of service attributes, as shown in Figure 4.3.

Each service attribute contains specific information about the advertised service. An attribute consists of an attribute ID and attribute value. The specific meaning of an attribute value is defined by the 16-bit attribute ID. In Bluetooth, a number of attribute IDs have been predefined, for example:

	Attribute ID	Attribute value
`ServiceClassIDList`	0×0001	A list of universally unique identifiers (UUIDs) specifying the class of the services advertised. The Bluetooth specification contains a list of predefined services classes such as serial port profile, file transfer profile, and headset profile. If we are implementing our own service, we can create a new UUID representing our particular service.

`ProtocolDescriptorList`	0×0004	A sequence of protocols and port numbers that can be used to access the service. The format of the sequence is specified by the particular service class.
`ServiceName`	0×0001^3	The textual name of the service.
`ServiceDescription`	0×0002^3	The textual description of the service.

Applications are allowed to define their own attributes as long as the attribute IDs are outside the reserved attribute ID range, defined as 0×000–0×0200. The SDP supports nine different attribute values, called data elements:

1. Nil, null type.
2. Unsigned integers.
3. Signed integers.
4. Universally unique identifier (UUID).
5. Text strings.
6. Booleans.
7. Data element sequence (DES), a data element whose data field is a sequence of data elements.
8. Data element alternative (DEA), a data element whose data field is a sequence of data elements from which a single element should be selected.
9. Uniform Resource Locator (URL).

4.4.2.1 Creating and Adding a Service Record

In Symbian OS we will be using the following classes to start advertising a new service:

- `RSdp` and `RSdpDatabase`. A session with the SDDB must be established through the `RSdp` which will allow a subsession, `RSdpDatabase`, to be created through which service records can be modified.
- `TSdpServRecordHandle`. This represents a service record handle. We need the handle to apply changes to any of the service records in the SDDB.
- `CSdpAttrValue`. Base class representing an attribute value. A number of concrete attribute instances can be created, e.g. `CSdpAttrValueInt` and `CSdpAttrValueString`. However, the `CSdpAttrValue` allows us to handle these uniformly and extract data correctly by using the `CSdpAttrValue::Type()` function.

The following code, taken from the SdpAdvertiserExample, shows how to advertise our own serial port service. We first need a connection to the service discovery database server:

---

[3] To compute the actual service attribute ID of the service name and service description, a language offset must be added to the base attribute ID. This allows the service name and description to be available in multiple languages. Simply to use the primary language supported by the service record, applications can use the offset 0×0100, which is the primary language offset.

```
RSdp sdpSession;
User::LeaveIfError(sdpSession.Connect());
CleanupClosePushL(sdpSession);

RSdpDatabase sdpDatabase;
User::LeaveIfError(sdpDatabase.Open(sdpSession));
CleanupClosePushL(sdpDatabase);
```

Using the open connection, we can now create a new service record with a specific service class. When the service record is created, we will receive the service record handle which we will use to create and update the attributes of our service record:

```
TSdpServRecordHandle record;

// We use the Serial Port Profile service class UUID
sdpDatabase.CreateServiceRecordL(KSerialPortServiceClass,
    record);
```

In order to maintain interoperability between different SDP implementations, parts of the service record format are mandated by the service class used. In this particular case we are using a serial port service class, which is defined in the serial port profile.[4] The serial port profile specifies the format of the protocol descriptor list (Figure 4.4).

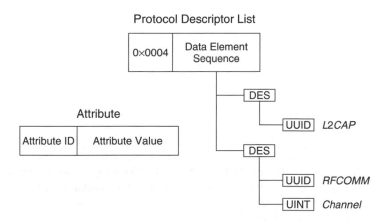

Figure 4.4 The format of the serial port profile protocol descriptor list. The attribute ID is 0×0004; the value is a data element sequence (DES). Each element is another data element sequence, one for each protocol. The protocol data element sequence then contains an UUID representing the protocol, and in this specific case the last protocol specifies the port number on which the service is running

---

[4] A Bluetooth profile is a specification of how to use and communicate with a particular service. The Bluetooth SIG currently maintains a number of profiles, e.g. the file transfer profile, object push profile, and hands-free profile, which ensures interoperability of these services between heterogeneous devices.

This translates into the following code:

```
// The RFCOMM channel where we want other devices
    to connect, note this
// is hardcoded here for illustration purposes only in real code
    this
// should be assigned dynamically.
TBuf8<1> channel;
channel.Append( (TChar) KRfcommPort);

// Using the Serial Port Profile we must create a protocol
    descriptor
CSdpAttrValueDES* protocolDescriptor = CSdpAttrValueDES::
    NewDESL(0);
CleanupStack::PushL(protocolDescriptor);

// Build the protocol descriptor
    protocolDescriptor
        ->StartListL()
            ->BuildDESL()
            ->StartListL()
                ->BuildUUIDL(KL2CAP)
            ->EndListL()
            ->BuildDESL()
            ->StartListL()
                ->BuildUUIDL(KRFCOMM)
                ->BuildUintL(channel)
            ->EndListL()
        ->EndListL();

sdpDatabase.UpdateAttributeL(record,
    KSdpAttrIdProtocolDescriptorList, *protocolDescriptor);
```

In addition to the protocol descriptor list, we would like to provide a textual name and description of our service. This can be done by calling UpdateAttributeL():

```
// Update attribute service name
sdpDatabase.UpdateAttributeL(record,
        KSdpAttrIdBasePrimaryLanguage+
        KSdpAttrIdOffsetServiceName,
        KServiceName());

// Update attribute service description
sdpDatabase.UpdateAttributeL(record,
        KSdpAttrIdBasePrimaryLanguage+
```

```
                KSdpAttrIdOffsetServiceDescription,
                KServiceDescription());
```

We have now successfully created and configured a service record within the SDDB of our mobile device. The final step is to delete it again when our application or service closes. This can be achieved through the `RSdpDatabase::DeleteRecordL()` function, as shown here:

```
TRAP_IGNORE(sdpDatabase.DeleteRecordL(record));
```

Inconveniently, the `RSdpDatabase::DeleteRecordL()` function may leave, which leaves the service record state undefined. You may want to replace the `TRAP_IGNORE()` statement to log the event.

In the following section we will try to find our newly advertised service.

4.4.3   Searching for Services

When a Bluetooth device has been discovered, a common operation is to query that device to determine whether a specific service is available. This functionality is exposed by the Symbian OS implementation via the following classes:

- `CSdpAgent`. The main class needed to utilize and perform queries via the SDP.
- `MSdpAgentNotifier`. A purely virtual interface class. Implementing the functions in this class will allow us to receive event notifications from the SDP agent.
- `CSdpSearchPattern`. A service search pattern is a list of UUIDs used to match service records on the remote device. If any of the service record attributes contains the UUIDs in the search pattern, it is considered a match.
- `CSdpAttrIdMatchList`. When a service record has been found to match the search pattern, this class can be used to specify the attribute IDs that we wish to retrieve from the remote device.

The following code examples are excerpts from the SdpDiscoveryExample on the DVD and show how to use the service discovery API to find a serial port service running on a remote device. The first step is to create a `CSdpAgent` instance using a reference to the `MSdpAgentNotifier` object, which should handle the results of the ongoing service search, and the Bluetooth address of the remote device we wish to query:

```
// The first parameter is a reference to a
    MSdpAgentNotifier object, aAddr is a Bluetooth address
iAgent = CSdpAgent::NewL(*this, aAddr);

// Make the search pattern and attribute match list ready
iSdpSearchPattern = CSdpSearchPattern::NewL();
iMatchList = CSdpAttrIdMatchList::NewL();
```

We are now ready to start the actual service search, but, to avoid receiving too many irrelevant service record results, we create a suitable search pattern and add it to the `CSdpAgent` as a filter:

```
// We look for services with the Serial Port UUID (0x1101)
   in an attribute
// which means we most likely will only find service records on
   PCs
iSdpSearchPattern->AddL( 0x1101 );
iAgent->SetRecordFilterL( *iSdpSearchPattern );

// We also request all attributes of found records
iMatchList->AddL( TAttrRange(0x0000, 0xFFFF) );

// Issue first request
iAgent->NextRecordRequestL();
```

When the `CSdpAgent` discovers a suitable service record or an error occurs, we are notified via the `MSdpAgentNotifier::NextRecordRequestComplete()` callback. If no errors occurred and the `CSdpAgent` found a suitable service record, we initiate an attribute request to retrieve the attributes associated with the service found. When requesting the attributes of a remote service, we can specify a range of attributes that are of interest to us. If, for example, we are only interested in the service name of the different records, this can be specified by adding the service name attribute ID to the `CSdpAttrIdMatchList`:

```
iAgent->AttributeRequestL( aHandle, *iMatchList );
```

When the requested attributes have been found, the `CSdpAgent` notifies us via the `MSdpAgentNotifier::AttributeRequestResult()`. Depending on the attribute ID, we now have to parse the `CSdpAttrValue` to find the value we wish to use. This is quite easy when the attribute only contains one value. However, in the case of, for example, the protocol descriptor list, the `CSdpAttrValue` is more complicated and consists of several sequences of values. To ease parsing, the `CSdpAttrValue` implements the visitor design pattern [6, 7]. The visitor interface is defined in the `MSdpAttributeValueVisitor` class – we will not present the implementation of a protocol descriptor parser here, but an example implementation can be found in the SdpDiscoveryExample example. In most cases we are mainly interested in finding the port number on which the remote service is running, and, when this is known, we are ready to connect to the remote device.

4.5   Connecting and Transferring Data

Following our discussion of how to advertise services and find other devices and services, we are now ready to discuss how we can connect two or more devices and transfer data between them. As with most functionality, Symbian OS provides several APIs through which this can be achieved. We can use the 'low-level' `RSocket` API through which all socket-based functionality can be accessed. The `RSocket` API provides an API similar to the Berkeley Socket API and exposes all protocols available via the Symbian OS socket server, e.g. RFCOMM and L2CAP for Bluetooth specifically.

If you are building an application using several different types of connection, e.g. a wireless local area network (WLAN), a general packet radio service (GPRS), and Bluetooth, the RSocket will provide a consistent interface, and, if carefully implemented, you will only have to change your code slightly to move from one implementation to another. In addition to using the RSocket directly, a developer can choose to use the CBluetoothSocket API which is implemented on top of the RSocket API and exposes a simpler interface to the Bluetooth application programmers.

The implementation of CBluetoothSocket consists of a number of active objects, all with a specific task, e.g. one to send data, one to read data, one to accept new connections, and so on. In order to react to events occurring, we must implement a notifier interface MBluetoothSocketNotifier that can be passed to the CBluetoothSocket object upon construction. In the following, we will go through the parts of the CBluetoothSocket and MBluetoothSocketNotifier needed to create server and client functionality in our application. Finally, we will take a look at how to perform the actual data transfer.

4.5.1 Building a Server

When creating a server application, listening for incoming connections over Bluetooth, and advertising some service for other Bluetooth devices to use, we need to make sure that our code is ready to accept and handle those connections. To achieve this functionality, we need to use the following functions in the CBluetoothSocket API:

- CBluetoothSocket::Bind(). The Bind() function normally specifies on which address and port we want our server to start accepting new connections. However, in the case of Bluetooth sockets, we also use this call to specify the security options that should be active for the service we are creating:

```
// Turn all security off
TBTServiceSecurity security;
security.SetAuthentication(EFalse);
security.SetAuthorisation(EFalse);
security.SetEncryption(EFalse);
security.SetDenied(EFalse);

// Socket object to be used in Bind()
TBTSockAddr addr;
addr.SetPort(KL2CAPPassiveAutoBind);
addr.SetSecurity(security);
  iSocket.Bind(addr);
```

  - enabling authentication means that, if the device connecting has not previously been authenticated, both users will be prompted to authenticate by pairing the devices using a numeric code;
  - enabling authorization will require the user to accept or reject every incoming connection, through a GUI dialog box;

- Enabling encryption will ensure that the data exchange is encrypted;
- enabling the 'denied' is useful temporarily to deny access to a service.
- `CBluetoothSocket::Listen()`. Listen specifies the size of the listening queue, which is the number of new connections that can be held in the queue waiting for the `Accept()` function to be called.
- `CBluetoothSocket::Accept()`. This function accepts a new connection from the listen queue. It takes a blank socket as a parameter. Upon connection, the blank socket will be initialized and may be used to communicate with the connecting device. When a device connects to our service, we receive notification through the `MBluetoothSocketNotifier::HandleAcceptCompleteL()` function.

In the SocketServer code example, we use these functions to set up a simple echo server. In order to connect to our newly created server, we need to program the client functionality.

4.5.2 Building a Client

Implementing the client functionality will allow us to connect to and use remote services. Using the `CBluetoothSocket` API, we only need to use the following function:

- `CBluetoothSocket::Connect()`. This function connects to a remote Bluetooth device. It takes a `TBTSockAddr` that must be constructed using the Bluetooth address of the remote device and the port number of the remote service.

```
TBTSockAddr addr;
// btaddr is of type TBTDevAddr which is returned by e.g. the
    RNotifier
addr.SetBTAddr(btaddr);

// port number should be found using SDP, for pure testing
    purposes
// hard coded port numbers can be used.
addr.SetPort(port);
```

Notification about connection failures or successes are delivered through the `MBluetoothSocketNotifier::HandleConnectComplete()`. The SocketClient code example shows the usage of the two functions. Assuming that a connection has been successfully established either via the server socket or via the client, we are now ready to start transferring data between the two connected devices.

4.5.3 Transferring Data

The data transfer functionality of the `CBluetoothSocket` is provided by a number of functions. In the SocketServer and SocketClient examples using the L2CAP protocol, this is achieved using `CBluetoothSocket::Write()` and `CBluetoothSocket::Recv()` functions:

- **Receiving data**

```
// iRecvBuffer is a TBuf8 which must stay valid until the
// MBluetoothSocketNotifier::HandleReceiveCompleteL()
    function is called.
TInt recverr = iSocket->Recv(iRecvBuffer, 0);

if(recverr != KErrNone)
  {
  // Handle error
  }
```

- **Sending data**

```
// iSendBuffer is a TBuf8 which must stay valid until the
// MBluetoothSocketNotifier::HandleSendCompleteL()
    function is called.
_LIT(KHello, "Hello");
iSendBuffer.Copy(KHello());
TInt err = iSocket->Write(iSendBuffer);
if(err != KErrNone)
  {
  // Handle error
  }
```

Note, that the behaviours of these functions are slightly different, depending on which Bluetooth data transfer protocol we are utilizing. Using the RFCOMM protocol, which is a basic RS232 serial connection, we have a stream-based interface, as known from TCP sockets. In contrast, L2CAP provides a datagram-oriented interface. Unlike UDP, L2CAP does, however, guarantee correct packet ordering. L2CAP additionally enforces a maximum transfer unit (MTU) and maximum receive unit (MRU) specifying the maximum number of bytes that can be transmitted in one datagram (the default is 672 bytes). If sending larger packets, the application must provide segmentation and assembly, change the MTU and MRU, or alternatively rely on RFCOMM.

4.6   Summary

In this chapter we have discussed most aspects of Bluetooth application development, in particular:

- turning the power of the Bluetooth radio on/off;
- discovering other Bluetooth devices;
- advertising our own service;
- discovering Bluetooth services advertised by other Bluetooth devices;
- transferring data between two devices.

References

[1] developer.symbian.com/main/downloads/papers/bluetooth/Rock_Paper_Scissors_over_Bluetooth. pdf
[2] Stichbury, J., '*Symbian OS Explained*', Symbian Press, October 2004.
[3] Harrison, R. and Shackman, M., '*Symbian OS C++ for Mobile Phones, Vol. 3*', Symbian Press, June 2007.
[4] '*S60 Platform: Bluetooth API Developer's Guide*', available at: sw.nokia.com/id/ac4b09b2-519a-4285-be28-1c19ed9028b9/S60_Platform_Bluetooth_API_Developers_Guide_v2_1_en.pdf [accessed 27 June 2008].
[5] Bluetooth Core Specifications, www.bluetooth.com [accessed 26 July 2007].
[6] Gamma, E., Helm, R., Johnson, R., and Vlissides, J., '*Design Patterns: Elements of Reusable Object-Oriented Software*', Addison-Wesley Longman Publishing Co., Inc., Boston, MA, 1995.
[7] Issott, A., '*Common Design Patterns for Symbian OS*', John Wiley & Sons, Ltd, Chichester, UK, October 2008.

5

Introduction to WLAN IEEE802.11 Communication on Mobile Devices

Károly Farkas
University of West Hungary, farkas@inf.nyme.hu

Gergely Csúcs
Budapest University of Technology and Economics, gergely.csucs@aut.bme.hu

5.1   IEEE802.11 Architecture Components

An 802.11 wireless local area network (WLAN), also known as Wi-Fi, is based on the IEEE802.11 standard family [1, 2]. Such an LAN follows a cellular architecture. Each cell, called a basic service set (BSS), consists of mobile nodes (MNs) and is controlled by a base station, or access point (AP). Most WLANs are formed by several cells where the access points are connected through some kind of backbone, or distribution system (DS). This backbone is typically wired, using e.g. Ethernet technology, but can itself be wireless. The whole interconnected WLAN, including the different cells, their respective access points, and the distribution system, is known as an extended service set (ESS) and is also referred to as a service set identifier (SSID). Figure 5.1 depicts the components of a typical IEEE802.11 WLAN.

5.2   IEEE802.11 Layers

The 802.11 protocol covers the physical and medium access control (MAC) layer. The original standard defines a single MAC layer that interacts with three physical layers (later on this was revised and extended by additional physical layers).

Mobile Peer to Peer (P2P)   Edited by Frank H. P. Fitzek and Hassan Charaf
© 2009 John Wiley & Sons, Ltd

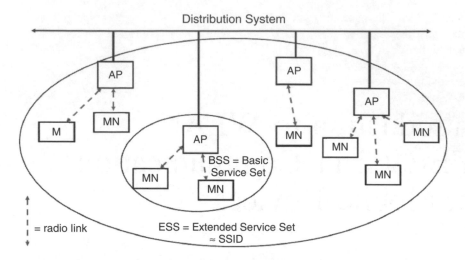

Figure 5.1   Components of a typical IEEE 802.11 WLAN (AP, access point; MN, mobile node)

5.2.1   The Physical Layer

In the initial version of 802.11, three physical layers were standardized: frequency hopping spread spectrum (FHSS), direct sequence spread spectrum (DSSS), and infrared light (IR). Later, three major revisions were added that are mostly commonly used today: 802.11a, 802.11b, and 802.11g. These standards use different frequency bands and radio modulation techniques, resulting in different data rates and interoperability. The physical layer specified by 802.11a works in the 5 GHz frequency band, and, as 802.11b/g standards specify the 2.4 GHz frequency band for operation, 802.11a devices cannot interoperate with 802.11b/g devices. Moreover, 802.11b uses DSSS as the radio modulation technique and supports bandwidth speeds of up to 11 Mbps, whereas 802.11a/g use orthogonal frequency division multiplexing (OFDM) for modulation and support speeds of up to 54 Mbps.

5.2.2   The MAC Layer

The MAC layer defines two different access methods, the distributed coordination function (DCF) and the point coordination function (PCF).

   The basic access method is the DCF, which is basically a carrier sense multiple access with collision avoidance (CSMA/CA). This method uses a collision avoidance mechanism together with a positive acknowledgement scheme. The station desiring to transmit first senses the medium. If the medium is busy (i.e. some other station is transmitting), then the station delays its transmission. If the medium is sensed free, then the station is allowed to transmit. The receiving station checks the cyclic redundancy check (CRC) (used for error detection) of the received packet and sends an acknowledgement packet (ACK). Receipt of the acknowledgement indicates to the transmitter that no collision occurred. If the sender does not receive the acknowledgement, then it retransmits the fragment until it receives acknowledgement or the fragment is dropped after a given number of retransmissions. Beyond the basic DCF, there is an optional PCF, which may be used to implement time-sensitive services such as voice or video transmission. This PCF makes use of higher-priority access, and the AP issues polling requests to the stations for data transmission, hence controlling medium access. In order still to enable regular stations to access the medium, there is a provision that the AP must leave enough time for distributed access, too.

In order to reduce the probability of two stations colliding because they cannot hear each other, a virtual carrier sense mechanism is used. A station wanting to transmit a packet first transmits a short control packet called a request to send (RTS), which includes the source, destination, and the duration of the following transaction (i.e. the packet and the respective ACK). The destination station responds (if the medium is free) with a response control packet called a clear to send (CTS), which includes the same duration information. All stations receiving either the RTS and/or the CTS set their virtual carrier sense indicator, or network allocation vector (NAV), for the given duration. This mechanism reduces the probability of a collision on the receiver area, and the duration information on the RTS also protects the transmitter area from collisions during the ACK.

To resolve contention between different stations wanting to access the medium, a back-off method is used. This method requires each station to choose a random number n between 0 and a given number, and wait n slots before accessing the medium, always checking if a different station has accessed the medium before. The slot time is defined in such a way that a station will always be capable of determining if another station has accessed the medium at the beginning of the previous slot. This reduces collision probability by half. The 802.11 standard defines an exponential back-off algorithm. This means that, each time the station chooses a slot and collision occurs, it will increase the maximum number for the random selection exponentially.

5.3 Joining the WLAN

When a station wants to join an existing BSS, the station needs to get synchronization information from the AP. The station can get this information through either passive scanning or active scanning. In the former, the station just waits to receive a beacon frame from the AP. The beacon frame is a frame sent out periodically by the AP and containing synchronization information. In the latter case the station tries to locate an AP by transmitting probe request frames, and waits for probe response from the AP. Once the station has located an AP and decides to join its BSS, it goes through the authentication process. This is the interchange of information between the AP and the station, where each side proves the knowledge of a given password. When the station is authenticated, it then starts the association process, which is the exchange of information about the stations and BSS capabilities and which allows the APs to know about the current position of the joined station. A station is capable of transmitting and receiving data frames only after the association process is completed.

5.4 Handover

Handover is the process of moving from one cell to another without losing connection. This function is similar to cellular phone handover. However, on a packet-based LAN system the transition from cell to cell may be performed between packet transmissions. On a voice system, a temporary disconnect may not affect the conversation, while in a packet-based environment it can significantly reduce performance owing to the retransmissions. The 802.11 standard does not define how handover should be performed, but defines the basic tools. These include active/passive scanning and a reassociation process, where a station which is switching from one AP to another becomes associated with the new one.

5.5   Synchronization

Stations need to be synchronized. On an infrastructure BSS, this is achieved by all the stations updating their clocks according to the AP clock. The beacon frames transmitted by the AP periodically contain the value of the AP clock at the moment of transmission. The receiving stations check the value of their clocks at the moment the signal is received, and correct it to keep in synchronization with the AP clock. This prevents clock drifting, which could cause loss of synchronization after a few hours of operation.

5.6   Security

The WLAN lacks even the minimal privacy provided by a wired LAN because the medium can be accessed easily by anybody. The 802.11 wired equivalent privacy (WEP) mechanism provides protection at a level that is felt to be equivalent to that of a wired LAN. Data frames that are encrypted are sent with the WEP bit in the frame control field of the MAC header set. The receiver decrypts the frame and passes to the higher-layer protocols. Only the frame body is encrypted, which leaves the complete MAC header of the data frame unencrypted and available even to casual eavesdroppers. The encryption algorithm used is RSA's RC4, which is a symmetric stream cipher that supports a variable key length (a 40-bit key length is chosen in 802.11). It is symmetric because the same key and algorithm are used for both encryption and decryption. The standard describes the use of the RC4 algorithm and the key in WEP, but key distribution or key negotiation is not specified. It is important to mention that WEP provides only minimal protection to frames in the air, and it is not too difficult for a casual attacker to decrypt the frames. In order to increase the security level in wireless communication, stronger protection mechanisms must be used, such as Wi-Fi protected access preshared key (WPA-PSK).

5.7   Multihop Networks

As opposed to single-hop networks, where the terminals have direct connection to the nodes in the network, a multihop network consists of common nodes that also relay traffic of other nodes. The two types of multihop network are mobile mesh networks, which are often called mobile ad hoc networks (MANETs), and infrastructure mesh networks.

5.7.1   Mobile Ad Hoc Networks

In certain circumstances the users may wish to build up WLAN networks without an AP, e.g. when two notebook users want to establish direct file transfer between their

Figure 5.2   Mobile ad hoc network

computers, thus forming an ad hoc network. A mobile ad hoc network (see Figure 5.2) is a kind of short-lived wireless self-organized network built of a collection of diverse nodes (users) [3]. The nodes are basically hosts and at the same time mobile routers that are connected by wireless links and communicate spontaneously, and that form a multihop network with an arbitrary network topology without relying on any pre-existing infrastructure or central administration. These routers are free to move randomly (they can even appear or disappear at any time) and organize themselves in a self-configuring manner, and thus the network's wireless topology may change rapidly and unpredictably. Such a network may operate in a stand-alone fashion, or may be connected to the Internet.

There is no restriction with regard to the wireless link technology to be used between the nodes. Today, the most popular solution is Wi-Fi because it is cheap, license free, simple to install/use, and provides broadband communication possibilities. The 802.11 standard specifies an ad hoc mode of operation, in which case there is no AP and part of its functionality is performed by the end-user stations, such as beacon generation or synchronization.

To make the multihop communication possible in a MANET, the mobile routers have to implement a common ad hoc routing protocol. Unfortunately, there are hundreds of ad hoc routing protocol proposals, and a common consensus has not been reached. This and the lack of pre-existing infrastructure and central administration make the practical implementation of MANETs a challenging task.

Typical usage scenarios of mobile ad hoc networks cover the military domain (e.g. implementing a spontaneous communication infrastructure on a battlefield), collaborative working (e.g. during a project meeting), or entertainment (e.g. playing a multiplayer game during a train trip).

5.7.2   Infrastructure Mesh Networks

An infrastructure wireless mesh network (see Figure 5.3) is a communication network built
of static radio nodes organized in a mesh topology [4]. It can be considered as a type
of wireless ad hoc network where all radio nodes are static and do not experience direct
mobility. The coverage area of the radio nodes working as a single network is sometimes
called a mesh cloud. End-hosts can access this mesh cloud via the radio nodes, which
serve also as APs. The radio nodes act as routers to transmit data from nearby nodes to
peers that are too far away to be reached in a single hop, resulting in a network that can
span larger distances. Thus, mesh architecture sustains signal strength by breaking long
distances into a series of shorter hops. Intermediate nodes not only boost the signal but
also cooperatively make forwarding decisions based on their knowledge of the network,
i.e. perform routing.

A mesh network is reliable, can self-form and self-heal, and offers redundancy. It has
a relatively stable topology, except for the occasional failure of nodes or addition of new
nodes. The traffic, being aggregated from a large number of end-users, changes infre-
quently. When a node can no longer operate, the rest of the nodes can still communicate
with each other, directly or through one or more intermediate neighbours.

The choice of the radio technology for wireless mesh networks is crucial. The popularity
of Wi-Fi makes it possible to build wireless mesh networks quickly and cost efficiently.
There are three options to create Wi-Fi mesh networks, using single, dual, and multiple
radios.

In a single-radio mesh, each mesh node acts as an AP that supports local Wi-Fi client
access and forwards traffic wirelessly to other mesh nodes. The same radio (usually
802.11b/g) is used for access and wireless backhaul. This is a cheap solution, but it offers
only limited capacity.

In a dual-radio mesh, the APs have two radios operating on different frequencies. One
radio is used for client access, and the other provides wireless backhaul. The radios operate

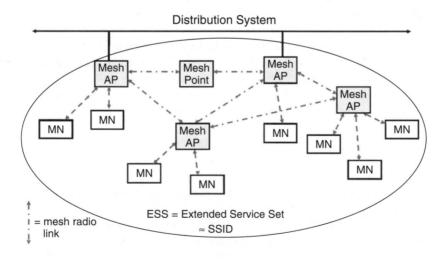

Figure 5.3   Infrastructure wireless mesh network

in different frequency bands, so they can run in parallel with no interference. A typical configuration is 2.4 GHz Wi-Fi (802.11b/g) for local access and some flavour of 5 GHz wireless (802.11a) for backhaul. This solution already separates the access and backbone traffic, but the network's capacity is limited in this case by the shared backbone.

Like a dual-radio wireless mesh, a multiradio wireless mesh separates access and backhaul. However, in a multiradio wireless mesh, multiple radios in each mesh node are dedicated to backhaul. The backhaul mesh is no longer a shared network, since it is built from multiple point-to-point wireless links and each of the backhaul links operates on a different independent channel (typically using 802.11a technology). Owing to the dedicated links in the backbone, this structure provides increased capacity compared with the previous solutions.

Nonetheless, Wi-Fi is not the only possibility to establish wireless links in mesh networks. As the penetration of WiMAX[1] devices increases, Wi-Fi technology is expected to be combined with and later on replaced by WiMAX.

Typical application scenarios for wireless mesh networks include voice over IP (VoIP), surveillance applications, and the implementation of wireless community networks.

5.8 Building Blocks for S60 Ad Hoc WLAN Networking

Although the statement 'Ad hoc networking is quite a new area in the field of networking applications' [6] already appears in a document released more than 3 years ago, it is still true. Ad hoc WLAN networks are rarely used in a PC-based environment, and almost never used in mobiles.

In this chapter, some clues are going to be provided to how easy it is to use (mainly ad hoc) WLAN networks with S60 devices. Together with the fundamentals, the experimental code of a mobile ad hoc Monitor program will be presented, which displays an estimated graph of the participating nodes in an ad hoc network on the basis of the signal strengths of the links.

5.8.1 Enumerating Nearby WLAN Networks

Prior to doing anything actively in a WLAN environment, it can be useful simply to look around and scan for available WLAN networks. In the world of secure WLANs, mere scanning usually does not allow connections to be made (configuring security requires user interaction in many cases, and, if the user has to configure anything manually, the Settings application of the device provides a more familiar way in comparison with a third-party solution), but such information can still be useful for slightly unrelated tasks such as WLAN-assisted localization.

5.8.1.1 Method 1

The S60 platform has been offering `RConnectionMonitor` API for quite a long time (published in S60 2nd edition feature pack 2), and apparently this API is

---

[1] WiMAX (Worldwide Interoperability for Microwave Access) is another emerging wireless technology and a flexible telecommunication architecture based on the family of IEEE802.16 standards [5].

capable of monitoring and controlling currently active connections via a series of
`Get/Set<type>Attribute` methods such as

```
IMPORT_C void GetPckgAttribute( const TUint aConnectionId,
                                const TUint aSubConnectionId,
                                const TUint aAttribute,
                                            TDes8& aValue,
                                TRequestStatus& aStatus ) const;

IMPORT_C TInt SetBoolAttribute( const TUint aConnectionId,
                                const TUint aSubConnectionId,
                                const TUint aAttribute,
                                const TBool aValue ) const;
```

For example, later in this chapter, `RConnectionMonitor::GetIntAttribute` is going
to be used to retrieve the signal strength of an active connection.

However, `rconnmon.h` (`RConnectionMonitor` has no other documentation effectively) contains some interesting sections such as

```
// Bearer specific general connection id
enum TConnMonBearerId
  {
  EBearerIdAll           = 0,
  EBearerIdGPRS          = 2000000, //covers internal and
                                            GPRS and EdgeGPRS
  (...)
  EBearerIdWLAN          = 2000004,
  EBearerIdLAN           = 2000005,
  (...)
  };
```

and

```
// TPckgBuf Attributes
// Used by GetPckgAttribute
const TUint KStartTime         =400; // TTime
const TUint KClientInfo        =401; // TConnMonClientEnum
                                            (connections only)
const TUint KNetworkNames      =402; // TConnMonNetworkNames
const TUint KIapAvailability   =403; // TConnMonIapInfo
```

where the last two constants (`KNetworkNames` and `KIapAvailability`) can be
easily combined with `EBearerIdWLAN`. In the former case, the resulting `TConn-
MonNetworkNames` package buffer will contain up to 10 entries of SSID–signal

strength–network mode (infrastructure/ad hoc, secure/unsecure) triplets of nearby WLAN networks:

```
// Package class definition for getting network names
const TUint KConnMonMaxNetworkCount=10;

class TConnMonNetwork
  {
public:
  TBuf8< 32 >  iName;
  TInt8        iType; // see TConnMonNetworkMode (0 - Infra,
                      //             1 - Ad Hoc, 2 - SecureInfra
  TUint8       iSignalStrength;
  };

class TConnMonNetworkNames
  {
public:
  TUint             iCount;
  TConnMonNetwork   iNetwork[ KConnMonMaxNetworkCount ];
  };

typedef TPckgBuf< TConnMonNetworkNames > TConnMonNetworkNamesBuf;
```

KIapAvailability works in a similar way: TConnMonIapInfo can hold the identifiers of up to 25 Internet access points (IAPs) considered currently available. Since it contains simple identifiers, it can only refer IAPs already configured in the device. Ad hoc WLAN access points are always reported to be available.

A strange non-trivial effect is that using 0 (EBearerIdAll) as connection identifier usually results in no WLAN networks reported by these two requests.

A 'tweaked' solution is as follows:

```
RConnectionMonitor conmon;
conmon.ConnectL();
CleanupClosePushL(conmon);

TRequestStatus stat;

TConnMonNetworkNamesBuf names;
conmon.GetPckgAttribute(EBearerIdWLAN,0,KNetworkNames,
    names,stat);
User::WaitForRequest(stat);

if(stat==KErrNone)
  for(TInt i=0;i<names().iCount && i<10;i++)
```

```
        {
        ... // use names().iNetwork[i].iName/iType/iSignalStrength
        }


TConnMonIapInfoBuf iaps;
conmon.GetPckgAttribute(EBearerIdWLAN,0,KIapAvailability,
        iaps,stat);
User::WaitForRequest(stat);


if(stat==KErrNone)
    for(TInt i=0;i<iaps().iCount && i<KConnMonMaxNetworkCount ;i++)
        {
        ... // use iaps().iIap[i].iIapId
        }


CleanupStack::PopAndDestroy(); // conmon
```

The code snippet above contains `User::WaitForRequest` solely for improving readability. In live code, the above service invocations should be properly wrapped into an active object, since they are rather slow, causing a detectable pause in application responsibility; even ViewSvr 11 panics sometimes.

5.8.1.2 Method 2

A dedicated WLAN scanning API also exists, starting from S60 3rd edition, athough it is not part of the SDK itself. SDK API plug-ins can be downloaded from Forum Nokia Wiki (wiki.forum.nokia.com). SDK extensions come with no compatibility guarantees, either for existing or for future devices. The extension packs are available for all S60 3rd edition releases (initial, feature pack 1, and feature pack 2).

From the WLAN point of view, the SDK API plug-in provides three API packages:

- WLAN Info API: Publish and Subscribe keys for retrieving the WLAN MAC address (the one displayed after *#MAC WLAN# – *#62209526#), and for checking the WLAN indicator status (off/available/active/active + secured).
- WLAN Settings UI API: This provides an API for launching the WLAN page of the Settings application directly. It also provides the table and column names for WLAN security settings in the communications database (CommsDb).
- WLAN Management API: This offers similar functionality to `RConnectionMonitor`, but it is obviously WLAN specific, and provides more detailed information.

The most interesting one is the WLAN Management API: scan results still contain the RX level, and theoretically the whole IEEE802.11 management frame is accessible. In particular, BSSID, beacon interval, capability, and security mode fields are provided directly. The rest can be accessed after requesting pointers to them using the proper element ID. The API apparently removes quantity limitations; the result of the network scan is accessible via a simple enumerator interface, while identifiers of available IAPs are provided in a dynamic RArray. Practically the same data is provided for the currently active WLAN connection:

```
CWlanMgmtClient *client=CWlanMgmtClient::NewL();
CleanupStack::PushL(client);

CWlanScanInfo *info=CWlanScanInfo::NewL();

TInt err=client->GetScanResults(*info);

if(err==KErrNone)
  for(info->First();!info->IsDone();info->Next())
    {
    ... // use info->Bssid()/RXLevel()/SecurityMode()/
              BeaconInterval()/Capability()
    ... // - least significant bit of info->Capability():
              0 - Ad Hoc, 1 - Infra
    ... // use info->InformationElement() for IEs, 0th is the SSID
for example
    }

delete info;

RArray<TUint> iaps;

err=client->GetAvailableIaps(iaps);

CleanupStack::PopAndDestroy(); // client

if(err==KErrNone)
  {
  ... // use iaps
  }

iaps.Close();
```

The default refresh rate for both S60 specific methods is 15 s. According to reference [7], it can be modified in certain configurations via an undocumented route.

5.8.2   Enumerating WLAN Access Points Configured in the Device

Besides knowing about nearby accessible WLAN networks, it also matters what kind of access points have already been configured in the device. S60 offers an access point engine wrapper around the communications database. This API supports a fairly complete set of AP-related operations:

• CApDataHandler. Creating–modifying–removing–prioritizing individual IAPs.

- CApSelect. This provides a filtered, sorted list of access points. Filtering can be done by Internet/wireless application protocol (WAP) capability and bearer. Either the result can be accessed in an array or the iterator interface can be provided by CApSelect itself. The list contains pairs of displayable names and WAP uids and is thus usable for picking IAPs both with and without user interactivity.
- CApUtils. Utility methods for accessing a selected set of attributes of an IAP. It also provides means for ensuring name uniqueness, checking if mandatory fields are filled properly, checking if an IAP/WAP uid refers to an existing IAP, and converting between IAP and WAP uids (CApSelect reports WAP uid, but the IAP uid is actually necessary for using the given access point).
- CApAccessPointItem. This class wraps all possible CommsDb fields for an access point, providing a really simple collection of read/write methods, where the CommsDb fields are addressed by a single enumeration, and thus tables and especially the intertable relations are completely hidden from the developer.

```
CCommsDatabase *db=CCommsDatabase::NewL();
CleanupStack::PushL(db);


CApSelect                                              *select=
    CApSelect::NewLC(*db,KEApIspTypeAll,EApBearerTypeWLAN,
        KEApSortNameAscending);

CApUtils *utils=CApUtils::NewLC(*db);
CApDataHandler *handler=CApDataHandler::NewLC(*db);
CApAccessPointItem *item=CApAccessPointItem::NewLC();

if(select->MoveToFirst())
  do
    {
    ... // use select->Name()/Uid()/...
    ... // use utils->IapIdFromWapIdL(select->Uid())
            for getting IAP id
    ... // - RConnection requires IAP id for connecting
    ... // use handler->AccessPointDataL(select->Uid(),*item)
            to retrieve complete data
    ... // - item->ReadTextL(EApWlanNetworkName,text)
            retrieves SSID
    ... // - item->ReadUint(EApWlanNetworkMode,uint)
            retrieves network mode (0 -Ad Hoc)
    }
  while(select->MoveNext());

CleanupStack::PopAndDestroy(5); // item, handler, utils, select,
                                  db
```

5.8.3 Connecting to the Network

When developing WLAN applications, sooner or later everyone wants actually to connect to a given network. From the user's point of view there are numerous possible ways of establishing and re-establishing connections, ranging from manually picking an IAP every time the application needs the network to the completely automated solution where the application automatically selects an IAP, perhaps even creating an application-specific ad hoc IAP if it is not configured.

The behaviour also depends on the device family: upon the first occurrence of outgoing activity (practically, `RSocket::Connect/SendTo` for TCP/UDP) on a socket without an associated network connection, S60 devices automatically bring up the IAP selection dialog, while UIQ devices pick an access point based on the preferences configurable in the settings. However, when expecting incoming activity (`RSocket::Accept/RecvFrom`), no Symbian device connects to the network automatically, which necessitates explicit usage of the `RConnection` class.

`RConnection` can be used for both manual and automated/preconfigured IAP selection, the difference lying in the arguments supplied for `RConnection::Start`, such as:

```
class RConnection : public RSubSessionBase
  IMPORT_C void Start(TRequestStatus& aStatus);
  IMPORT_C void Start(TConnPref& aPref, TRequestStatus& aStatus);
  IMPORT_C TInt Start();
  IMPORT_C TInt Start(TConnPref& aPref);
```

`TRequestStatus` does not change what the method does, only that it is performed asynchronously. `TConnPref` makes the difference. This is actually a parent class. `TCommDbConnPref` is the useful derived class for WLAN networking:

```
class TCommDbConnPref : public TConnPref
  IMPORT_C void SetIapId(TUint32 aIapId);
  IMPORT_C void SetNetId(TUint32 aNetId);
  IMPORT_C void SetDialogPreference(TCommDbDialogPref
      aDialogPref);
  IMPORT_C void SetDirection(TCommDbConnectionDirection
      aDirection);
  IMPORT_C void SetBearerSet(TUint32 aBearerSet);
```

5.8.4 Manual IAP Selection

On S60 devices, a call to `RConnection::Start` automatically brings up the IAP selection dialog if no `TConnPref` argument is supplied, although the list is going to contain every access point configured in the device (regardless of bearer or even availability):

```
// RSocketServ iSockServ;
// RConnection iConnection;
```

```
User::LeaveIfError(iConnection.Open(iSockServ));
User::LeaveIfError(iConnection.Start());
```

TCommDbConnPref can be configured in order to display WLAN access points only:

```
TCommDbConnPref pref;
pref.SetBearerSet(KCommDbBearerWLAN);
pref.SetDialogPreference(ECommDbDialogPrefPrompt);
pref.SetDirection(ECommDbConnectionDirectionOutgoing);
User::LeaveIfError(iConnection.Start(pref));
```

5.8.5   Selecting the IAP Programmatically

Programmatic IAP selection can be either fully automated (application enumerates and evaluates access points, creating a new one if necessary) or via some kind of setting, where actually the user picks the IAP but it happens separately from using the given IAP. Both approaches can be easily implemented using the access point engine already introduced.

Showing a filtered IAP selection dialog can be done via CApSettingsHandler::RunSettingsL, for example:

```
CActiveApDb* db = CActiveApDb::NewL();
CleanupStack::PushL(db);
CApSettingsHandler* settings = CApSettingsHandler::NewLC(*db,
                                             ETrue,
                              EApSettingsSelListIsPopUp,
                            EApSettingsSelMenuSelectOnly,
                                          KEApIspTypeAll,
                                        EApBearerTypeWLAN,
                                   KEApSortNameAscending,
                                                       0,
                                          EVpnFilterNoVpn,
                                                 EFalse);
TInt result = settings->RunSettingsL(0, iIap);
CleanupStack::PopAndDestroy(2); // settings, db
```

There are numerous CApSettingsHandler::NewLC overloads. The one in the code above is special because of the last two arguments: VPN access points and 'Easy WLAN' are going to be hidden. Otherwise, a pop-up dialog is constructed that supports selecting an access point with WLAN bearer. If the full menu were enabled, the dialog would provide the same functionality as the Connection page in the Settings application, including creating–editing–deleting access points, which is obviously not necessary now. iIap is going to contain the identifier of the selected IAP, given that the result is KApUiEventS-elected.

If this kind of list does not fulfil the needs, or the whole IAP selection process has to be done from code, CApSelect and CApAccessPointItem provide support for low-level IAP selection, as described in Section 5.8.2.

Having an IAP identifier, a TCommDbConnPref can be configured with SetDialog-Preference(ECommDbDialogPrefDoNotPrompt) and SetIapId.

5.8.6 Communication

Sockets in Symbian are capable of sending and receiving 8-bit descriptors. It does not really matter if the WLAN interface is used or something else. Since usage of RConnection is fairly inevitable (especially if server sockets are necessary), RSocket::Open(RSocketServ &aServer, TUint addrFamily, TUint sockType, TUint protocol, RConnection &aConnection) should be used in almost all cases.

5.8.6.1 TCP/IP

In an ad hoc WLAN environment, naming service is usually not present, and thus manual input of the IP address of the server might be necessary on the client side. Otherwise, everything proceeds in the normal way.

Client

```
// RSocket iSocket;
// TInetAddr iAddr;

User::LeaveIfError(iAddr.Input(aSomeAddress));
iAddr.SetPort(8877);
User::LeaveIfError(
iSocket.Open(iSocketServ,KAfInet,KSockStream,KProtocolInetTcp,
    iConnection));
iSocket.Connect(iAddr,iStatus);
SetActive();
```

Typical Symbian TCP client code, it preferably resides inside an active object. The question of getting aSomeAddress is discussed later in this chapter.

Address and port are packaged into a TInetAddr (IP-specific descendant of the generic TSockAddr type) object. TInetAddr::Input expects a numeric IP address in a common 16-bit descriptor. Owing to the need for RConnection, the only choice is the three-specifier variant of RSocket::Open as mentioned above. The address family is Internet, the socket type is stream, and the protocol is TCP/IP.

Since all actors in an asynchronous request (arguments and obviously the request provider itself) should be available and intact during the whole request, everything is a member variable of the containing active object.

Server

```
// RSocket iServerSocket;

User::LeaveIfError(iServerSocket.Open(iSocketServ,KAfInet,
    KSockStream,KProtocolInetTcp,iConnection));
User::LeaveIfError(iServerSocket.SetLocalPort(8877));
iServerSocket.Listen(1);
User::LeaveIfError(iSocket.Open(iSocketServ));
iServerSocket.Accept(iSocket,iStatus);
SetActive();
```

This code snippet could be typical, too, although, in 'traditional' mobile networks, mobile devices can rarely act as a TCP server owing to addressing issues and sometimes operator policy to prevent all listening for inbound connections. Since ad hoc WLAN networks really behave like LANs, they are not affected by such issues.

Otherwise, on the server side the requirement for the communication socket is that it should be open, while the acceptor socket should be initialized as in any other environment (listen, bind). RSocket::SetLocalPort is equivalent to RSocket::Bind with an empty (or KInetAddrAny) address.

Transferring Data Using TCP

In the case of stream sockets, RSocket::Write and RSocket::Send (if modifier flags are required) provide an easy way of sending the content of an 8-bit descriptor over the net. The accessibility requirement still applies; the data itself should also be available and intact during the request being served.

```
iSocket.Write(iData,iStatus);
SetActive();
```

Received data also lands in 8-bit descriptors. The direct counterparts of the sender methods are RSocket::Read and RSocket::Recv. However, it is an important aspect that, while sending sends the data actually present in the descriptor, these two receiver methods fill the descriptor to its maximum length. The operation does not succeed until the descriptor is full, which can be a problem in the case of stream-like protocols or in protocols using varying message sizes.

```
iSocket.Read(iData,iStatus);
SetActive();
```

When the size of expected incoming data is not known, RSocket::RecvOneOrMore can help. This method completes when it can provide at least one byte of data. For example, if some amount of data is already pending, the request completes immediately, otherwise it waits. Then messages or message fragments can be collected into a dynamic buffer (CBufBase derivatives) until the data can be recognized and processed.

5.8.6.2 UDP/IP

UDP is a rather convenient choice for ad hoc WLAN networks, especially if UDP multi- or broadcast is employed. In the 'traditional' mobile environment, usage of UDP suffers from more or less the same limitations as TCP does, and interesting datagram features like multi-/broadcast do not work at all. The ad hoc WLAN setting eliminates these difficulties, and multi-/broadcast actually works, sparing the effort of finding and propagating network addresses and even conserving energy.

Transferring Data Using UDP

UDP sockets SendTo and RecvFrom 8-bit descriptors. The 'to' and 'from' parts denote a TSockAddr argument; every outgoing datagram has to be addressed individually, and inbound datagrams are paired with the address of their originator:

```
User::LeaveIfError(iSocket.Open(iServ,KAfInet,KSockDatagram,
    KProtocolInetUdp,iConnection));
iSendAddr.SetAddress(KInetAddrAny);
iSendAddr.SetPort(5566);
User::LeaveIfError(iSocket.Bind(iSendAddr));
iSendAddr.SetAddress(KInetAddrBroadcast);
```

and then

```
iSocket.SendTo(iData,iSendAddr,0,iStatus);
SetActive();
```

or

```
iSocket.RecvFrom(iData,iRecvAddr,0,iStatus);
SetActive();
```

Receiving a datagram is a one-step operation; the passed descriptor is not filled prior to completion. In fact, it is a problem if a datagram does not fit into the descriptor: the remaining part is going to be lost by default.

Packaging Data into 8-bit Descriptors

8-bit descriptors are byte arrays and are thus obviously suitable for representing any kind of data. However, it matters how that representation is managed.

It is always possible to hack through the whole descriptor concept and use TPtr8::Set with the memory address of arbitrary structures (practically, T-classes) and their size. However, this should be avoided, because Symbian provides its own, friendly utilities for that.

TPckg and TPckgBuf provide access to wrapped structures in a bidirectional (read-write access) way, while TPckgC packages data into a constant descriptor.

The example ad hoc Monitor program uses the `TRxElement` structure for communication:

```
class TRxElement
   {
public:
   TUint32 iSrcAddr;
   TUint32 iDstAddr;
   TUint8 iRxLevel;
   };
```

Since data is both sent and received, two `TPckgBuf` s are used, obviously as member variables:

```
TPckgBuf<TRxElement> iSendElement;
TPckgBuf<TRxElement> iRecvElement;
```

After that, `iSendElement` and `iRecvElement` are `TBuf8s`, completed with an extra `operator()` allowing access to the packaged `TRxElement` structure: `iSendElement().iRxElement = 0;` is a valid statement.

`TPckg` and `TPckgC` packaging descriptors are `TPtr8` and `TPtrC8` descriptors, and thus they do not allocate memory; instead, they have to be initialized with an already existing object of the appropriate type.

Packaging descriptors are fairly comfortable to use, but they are subject to platform-dependent alignment issues, which can easily cause compatibility problems in a multiplatform environment, or even between different releases of the same platform. Do not rely on descriptor packaging to read and write binary data in generic network protocols. If byte-level control is required, `RDesReadStream` and `RDesWriteStream` can help.

In the case of text-based protocols, unicode descriptors are UTF-8 encoded/decoded via the `CnvUtfConverter` class. By converting the 16-bit descriptor to UTF-8 format, the result is going to be an 8-bit descriptor suitable for handling by such methods as `RSocket::Write`.

5.8.7 Advanced Tasks

Some interesting possibilities are addressed in this subsection. The following uses of WLAN are seldom necessary in day-to-day usage of WLAN APIs, but they can be used in the creation of novel applications/'cool stuff'.

5.8.7.1 Creating IAPs Programmatically

The access point engine also supports the creation of a new access point. Via the 'traditional' CommDb approach, creating an access point would require synchronized update of 10+ database tables. Completed with the slightly underdocumented CommsDat API, which is CommDb embedded into the central repository, things get a little more complicated.

On the other hand, the access point engine requires only a couple of lines of configuration in order to create a non-secured ad hoc WLAN access point with an automatically associated link local IP address (169.254/16):

```
CApAccessPointItem *item=CApAccessPointItem::NewLC();
item->SetNamesL(_L("Amorg Ad-Hoc"));
item->SetBearerTypeL(EApBearerTypeWLAN);
item->WriteTextL(EApWlanNetworkName,_L("AmorgNet"));
item->WriteUint(EApWlanNetworkMode,0);
CCommsDatabase *db=CCommsDatabase::NewL();
CleanupStack::PushL(db);
CApDataHandler *handler=CApDataHandler::NewLC(*db);
handler->CreateFromDataL(*item);
CleanupStack::PopAndDestroy(3); // handler, db, item
```

These lines create a WLAN access point `Amorg Ad-Hoc` (the name itself appears in the LANService, WLANServiceTable, Network, IAP, and WAPAccessPoint tables of CommDb), with SSID `AmorgNet` ad hoc mode.

5.8.7.2   Finding Our IP Address

`RSocket::LocalName` and `RSocket::RemoteName` report addresses of the two endpoints of a connection. Unfortunately, when there is no connection, neither are there any addresses. The server socket itself has no associated address until a client connects to it. However, versatile methods `RSocket::SetOpt` and `RSocket::GetOpt` make it possible to enumerate all Internet interfaces of the device and obtain the addresses associated with them.

Enumeration of interfaces requires the `TSoInetInterfaceInfo` type

```
class TSoInetInterfaceInfo
   {
   (...)
   TName       iName;
   TInetAddr   iAddress;
   (...)
   };
```

and three constants: `KSolInetIfCtrl` is the necessary option level, `KSoInetEnumInterfaces` starts enumeration, and `KSoInetNextInterface` steps enumeration:

```
TSoInetInterfaceInfo ifinfo;
TPckg<TSoInetInterfaceInfo> ifinfopkg(ifinfo);
User::LeaveIfError(iSocket.SetOpt(KSoInetEnumInterfaces,
    KSolInetIfCtrl));
while(KErrNone==iSocket.GetOpt(KSoInetNextInterface,
    KSolInetIfCtrl, ifinfopkg))
   (...)
```

The interface can be recognized via iName (which contains the substring 'WLAN'), and then iAddress contains the IP address.

If the IAP ID is known, it can also be used for recognition at the cost of another GetOpt call with TSoInetIfQuery:

```
class TSoInetIfQuery
  {
  (...)
  TName iName;
  TInetScopeIds iZone;
  (...)
  };
```

It is possible to query information about an interface on the basis of its name (which is known from the interface enumeration above), and, after the query is completed, iZone [1] is going to contain the IAP ID (the second element of the so-called 'scope ID vector'):

```
ifquery.iName = ifinfo.iName;
if(KErrNone!=iSocket.GetOpt(KSoInetIfQueryByName,
    KSolInetIfQuery, ifquerypkg))
  break;
if (ifquery.iZone[1] == iIapId)
  {
  if(ifinfo.iAddress.Address() > 0)
    {
    iLocalAddr = ifinfo.iAddress;
    break;
    }
  }
```

If the IAP ID is not known, because the user chooses it from a list provided by the argumentless RConnection::Start, for example, it can be acquired from the RConnection object itself by requesting the ID field of the associated IAP table as a number:

```
iConnection.GetIntSetting(_L("IAP\\Id"), iIapId);
```

5.8.7.3 Finding the Signal Strength of the Active Connection

The current signal strength of a WLAN connection can be retrieved by using a similar method to that described in Section 5.8.1. Both RConnectionMonitor and CWlanMgmt-Client can request the current signal strength of the active WLAN access point:

```
TInt32 rssi;
User::LeaveIfError(iWlanMgr.GetConnectionSignalQuality(rssi));
```

or via the asynchronous method

```
iMonitor.GetIntAttribute(iConnectionId,0,KSignalStrength,
    iRssi,iStatus);
SetActive();
```

This latter approach requires a connection identifier, which can be acquired via iteration through all connections:

```
iMonitor.GetUintAttribute(iConnectionId,0,KIAPId,iConnectionIap,
    iStatus);
SetActive();
```

When the requested `iConnectionIap` happens to be equivalent to `iIap`, `iConnectionId` can be used to request the signal strength.

As can be seen, a single value for signal strength can be retrieved, which is useful for infrastructure networks but does not give all the information required in an ad hoc environment. The retrieved RSSI value refers to the last packet received via the network, which is not necessarily the same as the last packet handed to the application. Unfortunately, there is a chance of overlapping, even if individual sources transmit sparely, if two of them happen to transmit in a short interval. As a best effort, retrieval of signal strength should be initiated immediately a packet is handed to the code.

5.9 Ad Hoc Monitor Example

The short example code accompanying this chapter is an experimental code displaying an estimated graph of participating nodes in an ad hoc network based on the RSSI values for packets received from the individual nodes (see Figure 5.4). No special transformations are

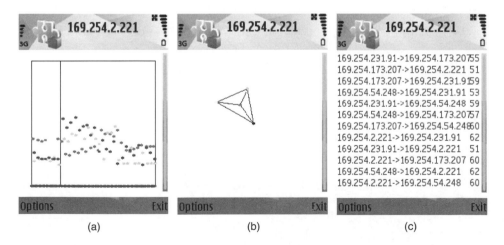

(a)	(b)	(c)

Figure 5.4 Different views of the ad hoc Monitor application: (a) time graph; (b) graph estimation; (c) measurement data

performed, and the RSSI values are treated as directly representing the distance between the nodes. A simple LSE algorithm is applied that tries to move nodes around on a pixel basis, obviously focusing on the graphical representation (as the RSSI values usually vary between 4 and 85, the resulting graph can be easily fitted on the display).

The basic idea is periodically to transmit all known `TRxElement` s (introduced as the example structure in the section discussing packaging descriptors), and update our 'own' `TRxElement` on every receipt. The example is based on the knowledge introduced in this chapter, tries to find or create the `Amorg Ad-Hoc` access point, and uses UDP broadcast (eliminating the need for typing IP addresses). The example (in sis format) and the source code are available, like all other examples, on the web.

References

[1] 'IEEE 802.11 Standard Family'. Available at: http://standards.ieee.org/getieee802/802.11.html [accessed 30 May 2008].
[2] Brenner, P., 'A Technical Tutorial on the IEEE 802.11 Protocol', Alvarion (www.alvarion.com), Tel Aviv, Israel, 1997.
[3] Perkins, C.E. (ed.), 'Ad Hoc Networking', Addison-Wesley, Boston, MA, 2001.
[4] Aggelou, G., 'Wireless Mesh Networking', McGraw-Hill Professional, New York, NY, 2008.
[5] 'IEEE 802.16 Standard Family'. Available at: http://standards.ieee.org/getieee802/802.16.html [accessed 30 May 2008].
[6] 'Series 80 Platform: Ad Hoc Communications Over WLAN', Forum Nokia (http://www.forum.nokia.com), 2005.
[7] 'WLAN Control in S60 APIs', Forum Nokia (http://www.forum.nokia.com), 2007.

6

Developing Network-capable Applications

Péter Ekler
Budapest University of Technology and Economics, peter.ekler@aut.bme.hu

Bertalan Forstner
Budapest University of Technology and Economics, bertalan.forstner@aut.bme.hu

Gábor Zavarkó
Budapest University of Technology and Economics, gabor.zavarko@aut.bme.hu

6.1 Introduction

When we talk about mobile phones and applications for mobile devices, we need to consider the basic architecture of mobile communication. This architecture contains the mobile devices, the wireless network with base stations, and the mobile operators providing several services on the network. These architectural elements have been developed side by side, enabling increasing functionality over time, available to mobile phone users.

As the capabilities of mobile phones increase, the gap between the PC and smartphones has become blurred, but, in terms of networking, there are still differences in network performance, battery life, and billing that must be considered whenever network connections are established on mobile handsets.

The development of the smartphone means that mobile applications can now connect across the Internet in much the same way as applications developed for personal computers. We can browse the Internet from our mobile device, download and upload contents, and even participate in peer-to-peer networks with our mobiles [1]. An important set of peer-to-peer protocols uses some kind of server in order to manage the traffic. For example, in the BitTorrent protocol [2], the tracker is a simple web application and the clients communicate with it via HTTP requests and responses.

Mobile Peer to Peer (P2P)   Edited by Frank H. P. Fitzek and Hassan Charaf
© 2009 John Wiley & Sons, Ltd

In this chapter we focus on network applications and introduce webshop, an example Symbian OS application that presents a simple shop with the goods list populated from a server. The webshop also provides a web interface to upload new content from a handset.

The next section will demonstrate how we can retrieve information about the mobile network with Symbian OS-based applications. Application itself will then be discussed.

6.2 Retrieving Phone Network Data on Symbian OS

Symbian OS v9 supplies APIs to retrieve information about telephony, such as the mobile operator and phone network status. This information is retrieved using the CTelephony class which is provided by the Etel3rdParty.h header and the Etel3rdparty.lib library.

CTelephony provides a simple interface to the telephony subsystem of the mobile phone for third-party developers. It basically provides two main services:

- information about the phone, i.e. phone settings, line information, call functionality, network information, and basic supplementary service settings;
- dialling, answering, and controlling voice calls.

Below we will show the implementation of our CMyPhoneInfo class which is used to retrieve relevant information about the mobile network and also about the device. Firstly, we have to create the header file for the class, which summarizes the functions and variables:

```
#ifndef MYPHONEINFO_H
#define MYPHONEINFO_H

#include <Etel3rdParty.h>

class CMyPhoneInfo: public CActive
  {
public:
  static CMyPhoneInfo* NewL();
  virtual ~CMyPhoneInfo();

protected:
  CMyPhoneInfo();
  void ConstructL();

public:
  TInt GetPhoneId(CTelephony::TPhoneIdV1Pckg& aPhoneIdPkg);
  TInt GetSubscriberId(CTelephony::TSubscriberIdV1Pckg&
    aSubscriberIdPkg);
  TInt GetFlightMode(CTelephony::TFlightModeV1Pckg&
```

```
      aFlightModePkg);
   TInt GetIndicator(CTelephony::TIndicatorV1Pckg&
      aIndicatorPkg);
   TInt GetCurrentNetworkName(CTelephony::TBatteryInfoV1Pckg&
      aBatteryInfoPkg);
   TInt GetSignalStrength(CTelephony::TSignalStrengthV1Pckg&
      aSignalStrengthPkg);
   TInt GetLockInfo(const CTelephony::TIccLock &aLock,
      CTelephony::TIccLockInfoV1Pckg& aIccLockInfoPkg);
   TInt GetLineStatus(const CTelephony::TPhoneLine &aLine,
      CTelephony::TCallStatusV1Pckg& aCallStatusPkg);
   TInt GetNetworkRegistrationStatus(
      CTelephony::TNetworkRegistrationV1Pckg&
      aNetworkRegistrationPkg);
   TInt GetCurrentNetworkInfo(CTelephony::TNetworkInfoV1Pckg&
      aNetworkInfoPkg);
   TInt GetCurrentNetworkName(CTelephony::TNetworkNameV1Pckg&
      aCurrentNetworkNamePkg);
   TInt GetOperatorName(CTelephony::TOperatorNameV1Pckg&
      aOperatorNamePkg);

protected: // from CActive
   void DoCancel();
   void RunL();

private: // data members
   // we are using this to get synchronous-like behaviour in
   // order to make the example clearer
   CActiveSchedulerWait*        iWait;
   CTelephony*                  iTelephony;
   TBool                        iBusy;
   };

#endif // MYPHONEINFO_H
```

Note that the class is an active object (derived from CActive), since many of the calls to CTelephony are asynchronous. The class contains the iTelephony protected variable which we use each time in the various 'getter' methods.

The implementation of the class looks as follows:

```
#include "MyPhoneInfo.h"

CMyPhoneInfo* CMyPhoneInfo::NewL()
```

```
  {
  CMyPhoneInfo* self = new (ELeave) CMyPhoneInfo();
  CleanupStack::PushL(self);
  self->ConstructL();
  CleanupStack::Pop(self);
  return self;
  }

CMyPhoneInfo::~CMyPhoneInfo()
  {
  Cancel();
  delete iTelephony;
  delete iWait;
  }

CMyPhoneInfo::CMyPhoneInfo() : CActive(
  CActive::EPriorityStandard )
  {
  CActiveScheduler::Add(this);
  }

void CMyPhoneInfo::ConstructL()
  {
  iWait = new (ELeave) CActiveSchedulerWait;
  iTelephony = CTelephony::NewL();
  }

void CMyPhoneInfo::DoCancel()
  {
  // no implementation required
  }

void CMyPhoneInfo::RunL()
  {
  iWait->AsyncStop();
  }

TInt CMyPhoneInfo::GetPhoneId(CTelephony::TPhoneIdV1Pckg&
  aPhoneIdPkg)
  {
  if (iBusy) return KErrInUse;
  iBusy = ETrue;
  iTelephony->GetPhoneId(iStatus, aPhoneIdPkg);
  SetActive();
  iWait->Start();
```

```
  iBusy = EFalse;
  return iStatus.Int();
  }

TInt CMyPhoneInfo::GetSubscriberId(
  CTelephony::TSubscriberIdV1Pckg& aSubscriberIdPkg)
  {
  if (iBusy) return KErrInUse;
  iBusy = ETrue;  iTelephony->GetSubscriberId(iStatus,
      aSubscriberIdPkg);
  SetActive();
  iWait->Start();
  iBusy = EFalse;
  return iStatus.Int();
  }

TInt CMyPhoneInfo::GetFlightMode(
  CTelephony::TFlightModeV1Pckg&   aFlightModePkg)
  {
  if (iBusy) return KErrInUse;
  iBusy = ETrue;
  iTelephony->GetFlightMode(iStatus, aFlightModePkg);
  SetActive();
  iWait->Start();
  iBusy = EFalse;
  return iStatus.Int();
  }

TInt CMyPhoneInfo::GetIndicator(
  CTelephony::TIndicatorV1Pckg& aIndicatorPkg)
  {
  if (iBusy) return KErrInUse;
  iBusy = ETrue;
  iTelephony->GetIndicator(iStatus, aIndicatorPkg);
  SetActive();
  iWait->Start();
  iBusy = EFalse;
  return iStatus.Int();
  }

TInt CMyPhoneInfo::GetBatteryInfo(
  CTelephony::TBatteryInfoV1Pckg& aBatteryInfoPkg)
  {
  if (iBusy) return KErrInUse;
  iBusy = ETrue;
```

```
   iTelephony->GetBatteryInfo(iStatus, aBatteryInfoPkg);
   SetActive();
   iWait->Start();
   return iStatus.Int();
   }

TInt CMyPhoneInfo::GetSignalStrength(
   CTelephony::TSignalStrengthV1Pckg& aSignalStrengthPkg)
   {
   if (iBusy) return KErrInUse;
   iBusy = ETrue;
   iTelephony->GetSignalStrength(iStatus, aSignalStrengthPkg);
   SetActive();
   iWait->Start();
   iBusy = EFalse;
   return iStatus.Int();
   }

TInt CMyPhoneInfo::GetLockInfo(const CTelephony::TIccLock
   &aLock, CTelephony::TIccLockInfoV1Pckg& aIccLockInfoPkg)
   {
   if (iBusy) return KErrInUse;
   iBusy = ETrue;
   iTelephony->GetLockInfo(iStatus, aLock, aIccLockInfoPkg);
   SetActive();
   iWait->Start();
   iBusy = EFalse;
   return iStatus.Int();
   }

TInt CMyPhoneInfo::GetLineStatus(const CTelephony::TPhoneLine
   &aLine, CTelephony::TCallStatusV1Pckg& aCallStatusPkg)
   {
   return iTelephony->GetLineStatus(aLine, aCallStatusPkg);
   }

TInt CMyPhoneInfo::GetNetworkRegistrationStatus(
   CTelephony::TNetworkRegistrationV1Pckg&
   aNetworkRegistrationPkg)
   {
   if (iBusy) return KErrInUse;
   iBusy = ETrue;
   iTelephony->GetNetworkRegistrationStatus(
     iStatus, aNetworkRegistrationPkg);
   SetActive();
```

```
     iWait->Start();
     iBusy = EFalse;
     return iStatus.Int();
     }

TInt CMyPhoneInfo::GetCurrentNetworkInfo(
   CTelephony::TNetworkInfoV1Pckg& aNetworkInfoPkg)
   {
   if (iBusy) return KErrInUse;
   iBusy = ETrue;
   iTelephony->GetCurrentNetworkInfo(iStatus,
     aNetworkInfoPkg);
   SetActive();
   iWait->Start();
   iBusy = EFalse;
   return iStatus.Int();
   }

TInt CMyPhoneInfo::GetCurrentNetworkName(
   CTelephony::TNetworkNameV1Pckg& aCurrentNetworkNamePkg)
   {
   if (iBusy) return KErrInUse;
   iBusy = ETrue;
   iTelephony->GetCurrentNetworkName(iStatus,
     aCurrentNetworkNamePkg);
   SetActive();
   iWait->Start();
   iBusy = EFalse;
   return iStatus.Int();
   }

TInt CMyPhoneInfo::GetOperatorName(
   CTelephony::TOperatorNameV1Pckg& aOperatorNamePkg)
   {
   if (iBusy) return KErrInUse;
   iBusy = ETrue;
   iTelephony->GetOperatorName(iStatus, aOperatorNamePkg);
   SetActive();
   iWait->Start();
   iBusy = EFalse;
   return iStatus.Int();
   }
```

The proposed CMyPhoneInfo class provides several functions that we can use to ask for the required information. It is also possible to convert the code to be asynchronous by

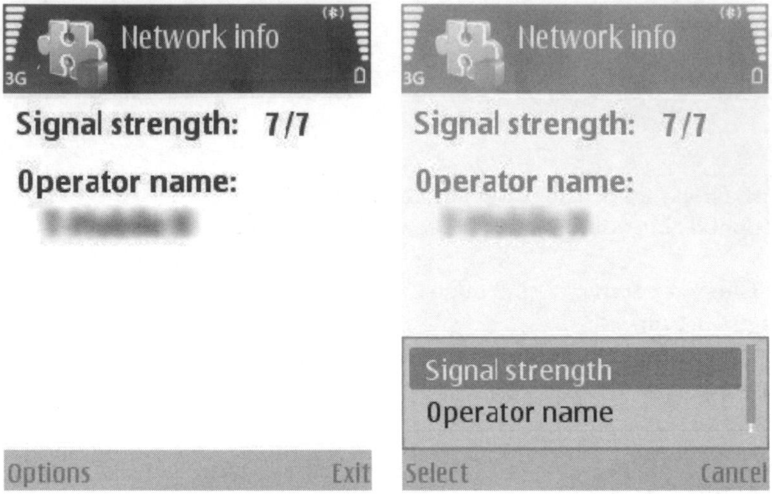

Figure 6.1 Display network information

using an active object (see Chapter 4 in reference [3]). In order to use `CMyPhoneInfo`, we need to create an instance of it first. Then we can call the getter methods and use or display the relevant information. By using this class, we can easily implement an example application that displays network information (Figure 6.1).

The following demonstrates how we can retrieve the signal strength and display it on a label control:

```
TBool CPhoneInfoContainerView::
  HandleSignal_strengthMenuItemSelectedL( TInt aCommand )
  {
  CTelephony::TSignalStrengthV1 signalStrength;
  CTelephony::TSignalStrengthV1Pckg
    signalStrengthPkg(signalStrength);
  TInt result = iMyPhoneInfo
    ->GetSignalStrength(signalStrengthPkg);
  if (result == KErrNone)
    {
    TBuf<10> buf;
    // iBar value is between 0 and 7
    buf.Num(signalStrength.iBar);
    ((CEikLabel*)iPhoneInfoContainer
      ->ComponentControl(CPhoneInfoContainer::
      ELabelSignalStrength))->SetTextL(buf);
    }
  else
    // handle error during request
  return ETrue;
  }
```

The above method is called by the `AppUi`'s event handler (`HandleCommandL`) when the `Signal strength` menu item is selected.

If the `Operator name` menu item is selected, the following method is executed:

```
TBool CPhoneInfoContainerView::
  HandleOperator_nameMenuItemSelectedL( TInt aCommand )
  {
  CTelephony::TOperatorNameV1 operatorName;
  CTelephony::
    TOperatorNameV1Pckg operatorNamePkg(operatorName);
  TInt result = iMyPhoneInfo
    ->GetOperatorName(operatorNamePkg);
  if (result == KErrNone)
    {
    ((CEikLabel*)iPhoneInfoContainer
      ->ComponentControl(CPhoneInfoContainer::
      ELabelOperatorName))->SetTextL(
      operatorName.iOperatorName);
    }
  else
    {// handle error during request}
  return ETrue;
  }
```

As the code above demonstrates, the operator name is retrieved in much the same way as the signal strength, and other interesting methods are called in the same way. By calling `GetFlightMode()`, we can ask whether the phone is in flight mode or not. With the `GetCurrentNetworkName()` the name of the current network can be retrieved, and we can even determine the battery level with the `GetBatteryInfo()` method.

In this section we have introduced the `CTelephony` class, and we have given an example of how we can use this class to retrieve different types of information.

6.3 Mobile Clients in the Context of the Client–Server Architecture

Networked applications can be implemented as thick clients, thin clients, or somewhere in between:

- A thick client does all the processing on the device, perhaps interacting with a server to update/synchronize information.
- A thin client does most of the processing on the server, leaving the client to update the UI and send commands to the server.

One of the main types of mobile application is thick solution. In this case the application on the mobile phone connects to a central server or web application via a wireless network and provides front-end functionality of the server and the content of its database. This solution is becoming popular on mobile phones, since the capabilities, screen size, and controls of the devices are improving. (Thin clients are also becoming popular with things like widgets/web-page-based applications, etc.) The main advantage of using mobile phones to deliver a solution like this is that one device is able to support different types of network connectivity method, such as GPRS, 3G, and even WLAN, and the users are able to decide which connectivity method they wish to use.

In this section we will discuss the connection of a mobile client to a simple webshop.

6.3.1 Main Features of the Example Webshop Client

When creating a mobile client, firstly we have to clarify the architecture of the complete solution. Figure 6.2 shows the high-level client–server architecture in the case of the proposed webshop example.

The architecture contains three main elements: mobile clients, the webshop, and its database. The webshop is a PHP-based web application that connects to the database where the content of the shop is stored. Mobile clients reach the content of the webshop via simple HTTP request–response messages. As we can see in Figure 6.2, the webshop is able to serve multiple clients simultaneously; it is similar to the case of multiple users browsing a website from web browsers.

The main functions of the mobile client are as follows:

- **Items list**. The client can download the latest list of items currently available in the webshop.

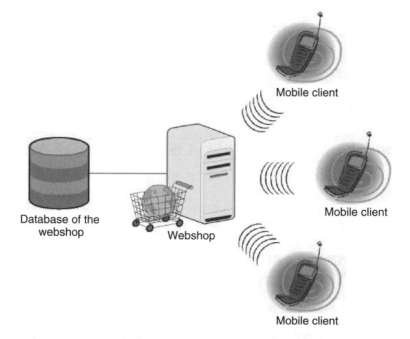

Figure 6.2   High-level architecture of a webshop supporting mobile clients

- **Item detail**. This provides details on an item in the list, including item name, price, and detailed description.
- **Add new item**. This uploads new items to the webshop. Here we can set the name, price, and description of the new item.
- **Settings**. This sets the network address of the webshop; thus, if the shop moves to another server, we must change its address in the mobile client.

After we have designed the architecture and the functions of our webshop, we need the user interface of the application. In this section we will show only the user interface of our solution, which can be used as a general example for similar mobile clients.

Figure 6.3 shows the main view, the menus, and the settings view of our application.

We can see from Figure 6.3 that, from the main menu, we can reach the main features of the application. In the case of mobile phone programming, it is always a good design plan for the main view to show the main functions of the application, and from here we can reach these functions easily.

Figure 6.4 illustrates three other views where we can see (from left to right) the list of items, the details of the selected item, and the new item upload form.

Generally, we can say that this sort of client–server arrangement works very well on mobile phones. The phone is always with us, and we can reach the content of central applications easily. In addition, we are also able to upload new content to the website, which will become immediately visible to others accessing the service.

In the following section we will discuss the connection of the mobile shop client and deal with network-handling issues.

6.3.2   Connecting a Mobile Client to a Webshop

In order to connect to the webshop from a Symbian OS-based mobile client, we have to use the RConnection class [4].

Figure 6.3   Main view and settings view of the proposed mobile client

Figure 6.4 Webshop-related views

Symbian R classes represent different types of resource; typically, they are proxies for objects owned elsewhere. R classes are opened using an open method, and closed using a close method. An R object must be closed once if it has been opened. Generally, the resource associated with an R object is closed automatically if the thread that opened the object terminates.

The `RConnection` class is a management interface for a network connection. To use this class, firstly we have to open the connection by using the following open function:

```
TInt Open(RSocketServ &aSocketServer,
        TUint aConnectionType=KConnectionTypeDefault);
```

The first parameter of the open method is a connected `RSocketServ` object, and the second parameter is reserved and defaults to IP connection.

The next step is to start the connection. We can start it in synchronous or asynchronous (with an active object) mode:

```
//Synchronous
TInt RConnection::Start();
//Asynchronous
void RConnection::Start(TRequestStatus &aStatus);
```

We can also pass a connection preference object, i.e. `TCommDbConnPref` to the `Start()` method, to change default connection settings, for example which IAP to start and whether to prompt the user with connection preferences.

Finally, when the connection is no longer required, we can close it by calling the `Close()` method.

The following example shows how to use the `RConnection` class in asynchronous mode with a wrapper class. The header file looks as follows:

```
#ifndef CONNECTION_H_
#define CONNECTION_H_

#include <in_sock.h>

class MConnectionObserver
  {
public:
  virtual void ConnectingFinished(TInt aError) = 0;
  };

class CConnection: public CActive
  {

public:
  static CConnection* NewL(RSocketServ& aSockServ,
    MConnectionObserver& aObserver);
  ~CConnection();

private:
  CConnection(RSocketServ& aSockServ,
    MConnectionObserver& aObserver);
  void ConstructL();

public:
  /** Connects to the given IAP. Callback
      MConnectionObserver:: ConnectingFinished()
      will be called when the operation ends. */
  void Connect(TInt32 aIap);

  void Close();

  inline RConnection& Connection() { return iConnection; }

protected:
  virtual void RunL();
  virtual void DoCancel();

protected: // data members
  RSocketServ&            iSockServ;
  MConnectionObserver&    iObserver;
  RConnection             iConnection;
  };

#endif /*CONNECTION_H_*/
```

Note that the header contains the declaration of the `MConnectionObserver` class which will be used to get notification about the state of the connection. The implementation of the `CConnection` class is as follows:

```cpp
#include <CommDbConnPref.h>
#include "&Connection.h"

CConnection* CConnection::NewL(RSocketServ& aSockServ,
    MConnectionObserver& aObserver)
  {
  CConnection* self = new (ELeave) CConnection(aSockServ,
    aObserver);
  CleanupStack::PushL(self);
  self->ConstructL();
  CleanupStack::Pop(self);
  return self;
  }

CConnection::CConnection(RSocketServ& aSockServ,
    MConnectionObserver& aObserver)
 : CActive(EPriorityNormal),
  iSockServ(aSockServ),
  iObserver(aObserver)
  {
  }

void CConnection::ConstructL()
  {
  CActiveScheduler::Add(this);
  User::LeaveIfError(iConnection.Open(iSockServ));
  }

CConnection::~CConnection()
  {
  Cancel();
  Close();
  }

void CConnection::Connect(TInt32 aIap)
  {
  TCommDbConnPref pref;
  pref.SetIapId(aIap);
  pref.SetDialogPreference(ECommDbDialogPrefDoNotPrompt);
  pref.SetDirection(ECommDbConnectionDirectionOutgoing);
  iConnection.Start(pref, iStatus);
```

```
  SetActive();
  }

void CConnection::Close()
  {
  iConnection.Close();
  }

void CConnection::RunL()
  {
  iObserver.ConnectingFinished(iStatus.Int());
  }

void CConnection::DoCancel()
  {
  Close();
  }
```

In order to illustrate how we can use the CConnection class, let us assume that we have a CMyClass implementing the MConnectionObserver. Firstly, we need a connected RSocketServ. Thereafter, we can create the CConnection class, as shown in the StartConnectingL() function:

```
void CMyClass::StartConnectingL()
  {
  if (iConnection)
    return; // connection already started
  //iSocketServer is a RSocketServ type object
  iSocketServer.Connect();
  iConnection = CConnection::NewL(iSocketServer, this);
  iConnection->ConnectL(0); // when aIap is 0, preference
    // dialog is prompted to user
  }

void CMyClass::ConnectingFinished(TInt aError)
  {
  //Called when asynchronous connecting finished
  //aError parameter is equal to KErrNone, when no error
  //occurred during connection
  }

void CMyClass::Disconnect(TInt aError)
  {
  delete iConnection;
```

```
    iConnection = NULL;
    iSocketServer.Close();
    }
```

We can see that the `CMyClass` contains the `ConnectingFinished()` function, which is called via the observer when the connection succeeds.

In the case of our proposed webshop solution, we connect to a simple website and pass the parameter application requests as URL parameters. The following example shows how to produce the URL. String parameters should be escaped by using the `EscapeUtils::EscapeEncodeL()` function:

```
_LIT8(KScheme, "http");
_LIT8(KHost, "example.com");
_LIT8(KPath, "/example.php");

CUri8* url = CUri8::NewLC();
//set the scheme component
url->SetComponentL(KScheme, EUriScheme);
//set the host component
url->SetComponentL(KHost, EUriHost);
//set the path component
url->SetComponentL(KPath, EUriPath);

HBufC8* utf;
HBufC8* escaped;
// for simpleness allocate 1024 byte length buffer
HBufC8* query = HBufC8::NewLC(1024);

utf = EscapeUtils::ConvertFromUnicodeToUtf8L(stringParam);
CleanupStack::PushL(utf);
escaped = EscapeUtils::EscapeEncodeL(*utf,
  EscapeUtils::EEscapeUrlEncoded);
CleanupStack::PushL(escaped);
query->Des().Append(_L8("?string="));
query->Des().Append(*escaped);
CleanupStack:: PopAndDestroy(2); // escaped, utf

query->Des().Append(_L8("&number="));
query->Des().AppendNum(numParam);

url->SetComponentL(*query, EUriQuery);
```

```
//send the request with url: url->Uri().UriDes()

CleanupStack::PopAndDestroy(2); // query, url
```

By using this solution, we can easily set up different URL addresses. In order to send data to the URL, we can use the built-in `CHttpTransport` class to send our request via HTTP protocol. The constructor of the `CHttpTransport` class requires an `RSocketServ` handle and an `RConnection`; both of them can be found in our previously introduced `CConnection` class. After the object has been created, we have to set which class implements the `MHttpTransportObserver` interface, which contains the methods that will be called when the response for our request arrives. An example for creating the `CHttpTransport` is as follows:

```
iTransport = CHttpTransport::NewL(iSocketServ.Handle(),
   reinterpret_cast <TInt> (&iConnection->Connection())));
iTransport->SetListener(this);
```

In the following section we will discuss the server side of the webshop.

6.3.3 *Implementing a Webshop to Serve Mobile Clients*

Our client application communicates via HTTP protocol with the server application. (If the application requires security, we have to consider using HTTPS.) Within the server, there are two separate bits of logic to deal with the request for the shop item's list and the new product data to be uploaded.

We start with upload.php. This handles the storage of item details, such as product name, description, and price, in a text file. The fields are separated by a semi-colon, and the products are separated by new-line characters.

In order to upload an item, the item name and details are part of the URL. An example URL looks as follows:

http://example.com/upload.php?itemname=bicycle&description=red&
price=120&currency=EUR

```
<?PHP

writedata(str_replace(";",",",$_GET["itemname"]).";".
str_replace(";",",",$_GET["description"]) .";".
   str_replace(";",",",$_GET["price"])." ".
str_replace(";",",",$_GET["currency"]);

function writedata($aString)
{
```

```
    $handle = fopen("productlist.txt", 'a');
    // the example do not care with duplicate items
    fwrite($handle, $aString."\n");
    fclose($handle);
}


?>
```

The other file, productlist.php, is a simple one that sends back the content of the productlist file:

```
<?php

if (@$handle = fopen("productlist.txt", "rb")) {
  $contents = '';
  while (!feof($handle)) {
    // in order to make the example clearer we not prepare for
    // thousands of products
    $contents .= fread($handle, 8192);
  }
  fclose($handle);
  echo $contents;
}

?>
```

6.4 Summary

As mobile phones are supporting more and more networking technology, the need for different kinds of mobile client is increasing. The category of mobile client is very wide; it includes email clients, applications that download news or RSS from a special website, and also webshop-like applications, which we have discussed in the previous section.

In this chapter we have described two important topics related to applications that use mobile networks. The first example demonstrates how we can retrieve information related to the current mobile network, such as signal strength, operator name, etc. We have shown the complete implementation of our CMyPhoneInfo class, and we have also described how we can use this class in Symbian OS-based applications.

The second example describes a complete webshop supporting mobile clients. We have discussed the architecture of the implementation, and also the relevant bits of source code from both the mobile client and the server-side application.

This chapter has discussed how we can implement applications for mobile phones that use mobile networks. We have given general examples; more advanced examples can be found in reference [4]. We sincerely hope that, by studying the examples, it will become easier to create similar applications to the webshop.

References

[1] Ekler, P., Nurminen, J.K., and Kiss, A.J. 'Experiences of Implementing BitTorrent on Java ME Platform', *CCNC'08, 1st IEEE International Peer-to-Peer for Handheld Devices Workshop 2008*, Las Vegas, NV, to be published.

[2] '*BitTorrent Specification*'. Available at: http://wiki.theory.org/BitTorrentSpecification [accessed 8 October 2008].

[3] Aubert, M., *et al.*, '*Quick Recipes on Symbian OS*', ISBN-10: 0470997834, John Wiley & Sons, 2008.

[4] Campbell, I., *et al.*, '*Symbian OS Communications Programming*', 2nd edition, ISBN: 978-0-470-51228-9, John Wiley & Sons, 2008.

Part Three

Mobile P2P Examples

7

SymTorrent and GridTorrent: Developing BitTorrent Clients on the Symbian Platform

Imre Kelényi
Budapest University of Technology and Economics, imre.kelenyi@aut.bme.hu

Bertalan Forstner
Budapest University of Technology and Economics, bertalan.forstner@aut.bme.hu

7.1 Introduction

At the point of writing, the BitTorrent protocol is one of the most popular alternative file transfer technologies on the Internet. In contrast to centralized solutions, such as HTTP or FTP, the BitTorrent protocol aims to transfer the data in a completely distributed way by dividing files into smaller pieces that can be retrieved from several locations. The other sources are BitTorrent users who have already downloaded all or part of the file. In return, the user's BitTorrent client may upload part of a file that has been previously downloaded. The key to scalable distribution is cooperation. Those who get a file use their own upload capacity to give the file to others at the same time. The greater the number of users downloading, the greater is the number of users uploading as well. This is the essence of BitTorrent, but more details will be given in the next section.

Having this technology on mobile phones was not always possible earlier for several reasons. BitTorrent requires maintaining several network connections simultaneously and accessing multiple files at a time. However, with the introduction of powerful mobile hardware and open software platforms, which provide free development tools and enable third-party applications to be created, the time has come to bring peer-to-peer (P2P) file-sharing to mobile phones.

Mobile Peer to Peer (P2P)   Edited by Frank H. P. Fitzek and Hassan Charaf

This chapter discusses two implementations of a BitTorrent client on Symbian OS, SymTorrent and GridTorrent. Both projects share the same code base.

SymTorrent was the first BitTorrent client for mobile phones. It was released in 2006 as an open-source project, and has since been downloaded more than half a million times. SymTorrent uses the standard BitTorrent protocol and so allows the downloading of any content shared with BitTorrent from the Internet in the same way as a desktop client.

GridTorrent is a specialization of SymTorrent that allows the users to form local clusters ('mini-networks' or 'grids', hence the name) and download files in a cooperative way, saving both bandwidth and energy.

The aim of this chapter is to give an insight into how complex P2P applications can be created on Symbian OS. Since SymTorrent and GridTorrent are quite large projects with thousands of lines of code and organized into several libraries, we cannot have a full coverage of the source code, but instead focus on the architecture, the key concepts, and the difficulties we faced during the development. This book is about programming, so, after giving an overview on the projects and how BitTorrent works, we jump right into writing code. We also discuss network interfaces, sockets, and Symbian's HTTP framework, so this chapter will be of interest to any developers interested in networking-based application and not just peer to peer.

BitTorrent is a peer-to-peer file-sharing protocol that was designed by Bram Cohen [1, 2]. After releasing the first fully functional version in 2003, it became an immediate success, and by 2004 the client software had been downloaded more than 10 million times. The key concepts are dividing the data into small pieces and transferring these between the participants in both directions. This means that, when one of the users has downloaded a piece, it can immediately start uploading it to another user. The pieces are not downloaded from a central source, but from the users themselves. Of course, an initial source is required, but, after enough users have started downloading, the number of requests to the original source reduces, to the point where it becomes redundant. BitTorrent also features an intuitive tit-for-tat mechanism that prevents free riding (downloading but never uploading) by giving more bandwidth to those peers that upload data at a higher rate. Both the content provider and the user benefit from using BitTorrent, since the load on the servers is much lower, while the transfer speeds can be higher than with a central server. BitTorrent provides excellent redundancy, since it distributes data networkwide, limiting the problems caused by a central server going down.

In general, BitTorrent can be used to replace any centralized file transfer protocol, such as the FTP and HTTP protocols built into browsers, but at the moment BitTorrent clients are not as widespread.

To be able to understand the following parts of this chapter and the architecture of SymTorrent and GridTorrent, you must get familiar with the basics of the BitTorrent protocol.

When we refer to a *torrent*, we mean the file or files to be downloaded or shared. BitTorrent allows a single file or multiple files organized into directories (similar to a zip file) to be shared. After the creator of the torrent (the initial source of the data) has selected the files to be shared, there is no way of changing them. From this point in time, the torrent is a closed entity, and files cannot be added or removed. However, some BitTorrent clients allow only selected files to be downloaded from a multifile torrent. We often refer to the peers downloading and sharing a particular torrent as a *swarm*. Everybody who is in a swarm exchanges the pieces of a particular torrent.

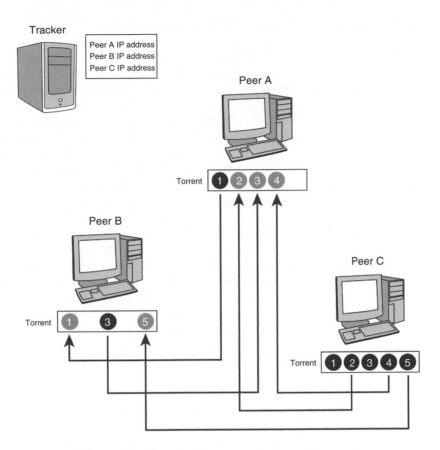

Figure 7.1 Transferring a torrent between three peers

To gain a better understanding of how data transfer works in BitTorrent, we will show a snapshot of the process of transferring a torrent between three peers. Figure 7.1 illustrates an example scenario. Peers are marked with letters A, B, and C. The bars under the peer icons show the status of the torrent. In this example, the torrent consists of five pieces. Real-life torrents usually have several hundreds or even thousands of pieces. The pieces are numbered from 1 to 5. Black filled circles denote pieces that have been downloaded, while grey circles mark the pieces that are being downloaded. As you can see, one of the peers, peer C, has already downloaded the whole torrent and is acting as a *seeder*, a peer that only uploads. Peer A has one piece downloaded (piece 1) and is downloading three other pieces: one from peer B and two from peer C. Peer B has also finished one piece and is downloading two pieces, one from each of the other peers. As time progresses, peers A and B will have more and more pieces downloaded, which they can upload to each other, taking the load from peer C. This is just a simple example with three peers, but the same mechanism also works with thousands of clients. The inclusion of the tracker in the picture is to emphasize that it does not participate in the data transfer. The tracker does not have the torrent, and it only hosts the list of addresses of peers in the swarm.

Some of the most important terms of BitTorrent are as follows:

- *Tracker*. A central server whose task is to coordinate the peers that are participating in a swarm. The tracker itself does not share any data, it only maintains the list of peers that are downloading and sharing the torrent. Every torrent must have a tracker. Each time a peer starts downloading a torrent, it connects to the tracker, which provides it with the list of peers in the swarm. This procedure is referred to as *announcing*, for the peer also announces its own address to the tracker. The tracker is a fundamental component of BitTorrent: if it is not available, new peers cannot join the swarm. The peers communicate with the tracker via standard HTTP GET requests. It should be noted that a tracker can host several torrents, and a torrent is often registered in several trackers in order to achieve some level of redundancy. Although the newest version of BitTorrent supports *trackerless* torrents [3], which store and retrieve peer addresses from a distributed hash table (DHT), this is mainly used only if the tracker is unavailable. Hence, in this chapter we focus on the standard tracker solution only.
- *Torrent file*. A binary[1] file that contains all the required information to download a torrent (join the swarm). It contains a link (a URL) to the tracker and the list of files in the torrent, along with the hash values of the pieces of the torrent. These SHA-1 hash values allow the integrity of the downloaded data to be checked. Other metadata, such as the creator of the torrent, can also be added when the torrent file is created. As mentioned earlier, a torrent cannot be changed after it has been created. In practice, this is achieved by using the hash of the torrent file as the ID for the torrent. This ID is used in several protocol messages, and thus it cannot be changed. Since changing the torrent file would change its ID as well, this is not possible without violating the protocol. It is important to understand that the *torrent file* is not synonymous with the *torrent*. The former is just a reference to the swarm, while the latter is the swarm itself.
- *Peers (leechers and seeders)*. Users (computer, mobile phones, etc.) running an instance of a BitTorrent client. Peers are the source of data, and they are also the downloaders. If there are no peers available, the torrent cannot be downloaded. The protocol that peers use to communicate with each other is referred to as the *peer wire*. It defines a set of messages, such as REQUEST (requests a block of a piece) or PIECE (sends a block of a piece). The peers are often divided into two categories:
  - *Leechers*. Peers that have not downloaded the full torrent yet. They are both uploading and downloading.
  - *Seeders*. Peers that have the full torrent. They are not downloading any more, but keep uploading the torrent. When the torrent is created, an initial seeder is required to host the shared data until it is spread in the network. Seeders have a positive effect on the overall available bandwidth of the torrent.

To summarize how the protocol works, here are the steps for creating a new torrent and starting to share it:

1. The files that will be shared are selected.
2. Using a special application, the *torrent maker*, the torrent file, is created. The files that are shared and the address of the tracker must be given.

---

[1] The data in torrent files is in a format referred to as *bencode*.

3. The torrent is registered in the tracker whose address was encoded into the torrent file.
4. The initial seeder starts sharing the torrent by announcing to the tracker.

After the initial source has started sharing the torrent, any peer can join the swarm, provided it possesses the torrent file. Without the torrent file, theoretically, it is not possible to join a torrent, since it is the only source from where the torrent's ID and the address of the tracker can be obtained. After the peer has announced to the tracker and received the list of some other peers, it can start establishing connections to them and transfer pieces of the torrent.

7.2 SymTorrent

SymTorrent is a complete BitTorrent client for Symbian OS. Currently, it is released for the S60 3rd edition platform, but most of the code is platform independent, and only the UI layer is specific to S60. SymTorrent features a multiview user interface, allows multiple torrents to be downloaded at a time, and can resume torrents after exiting the application. A screenshot of the application is shown in Figure 7.2. At the point of writing, torrents must be added manually in SymTorrent (via the 'Add torrent' dialog). Compared with a PC client, SymTorrent lacks some of the more advanced features, such as peer exchange, NAT traversal, scheduling, etc. However, in terms of downloading, SymTorrent performs reasonably well. The source code is freely available under the terms of the GNU General Public License at http://symtorrent.aut.bme.hu.

SymTorrent was written entirely in Symbian C++ using the S60 3rd edition SDK MR. It does not use the recently introduced Open C/C++ framework, nor any other add-on

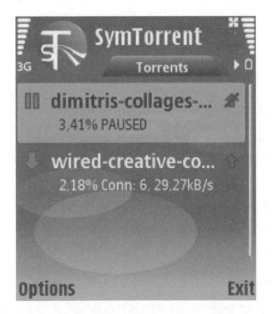

Figure 7.2   A screenshot of the main view of SymTorrent, showing two loaded torrents: the first is paused, the second is being downloaded from six peers

libraries. In terms of the architecture, when the first public version was released, Sym-Torrent consisted of a single executable only. Later, as the application was developed and the source code became larger and larger, the code was divided into several components. After putting the UI layer into a separate DLL, we also started dividing the 'engine' part into several libraries that can be maintained more easily. At this point, SymTorrent consists of the following subprojects:

- *SymTorrent*. The name might be a bit misleading, but this is only the UI-dependent part of SymTorrent. This project is responsible for creating the different UI views, initializing the engine, and processing the user inputs. Practically, this project creates the executable that starts when the application is selected in the phone's menu.
- *SymTorrentEngine*. This is the essence of SymTorrent that does all the non-UI-dependent tasks. The engine is responsible for implementing the BitTorrent protocol, including parsing torrent files, announcing to the tracker, and establishing peer-wire session with the other peers. Technically, SymTorrentEngine is a DLL. Any third-party application can use it, provided that it implements a couple of predefined interfaces.
- *LibBencode*. A DLL implementing BitTorrent bencode decoding and encoding. Bencode is the binary format of torrent files and the tracker requests.
- *KiNetwork*. Since SymTorrent depends heavily on networking, we decided to create a separate DLL that is responsible for almost all networking tasks, such as initializing the network interfaces, handling sockets, and accepting incoming connections. KiNetwork provides base classes for objects using UDP, TCP, or even Bluetooth sockets. These classes make Symbian socket programming much easier by providing simple methods for writing to the socket and receiving data. KiNetwork can also be used to initialize the network interface of HTTP sessions.
- *KiLogger*. A simple set of classes that allow the creation and manipulation of log files. Generally, log files are used for debugging purposes. Many parts of the code of SymTorrent contain logging calls, which write debugging information into a text file.
- *SymTracker*. Since SymTorrent was started as a research project, we wanted to experiment with several scenarios, including having a separate tracker on the phone itself. SymTracker is a very simple tracker that can host a list of peers and provide them to the announcing peers. However, it also has a built-in torrent maker function, which allows torrents to be created and hosted in a few steps on the device. Since SymTracker is an optional component and not a fundamental part of SymTorrent, it can be ignored if you are not interested in hosting a separate tracker on the device.

When you build SymTorrent using the SDK's development tools, all of these projects are compiled, linked, and, in the final phase, if you build for the device, combined into an installable SIS file. In this chapter we mainly focus on certain parts of SymTorrentEngine and KiNetwork.

7.3   GridTorrent

GridTorrent uses the same engine as SymTorrent. The newest versions of SymTorrent and GridTorrent both build on top of SymTorrentEngine, which also contains the application logic of GridTorrent. The differences are only in the main UI projects. As it can be seen

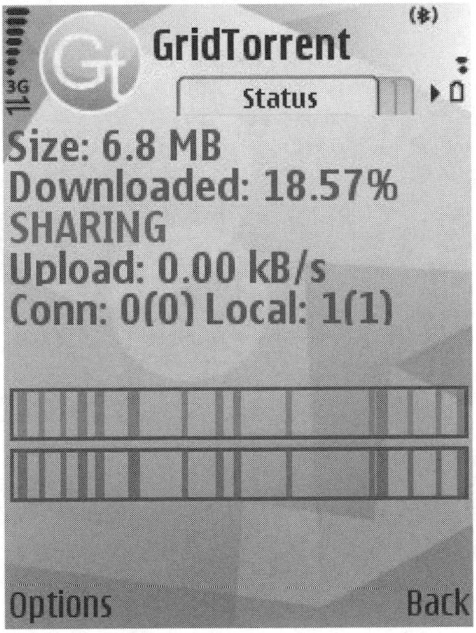

Figure 7.3 A screenshot from GridTorrent, showing the status of a torrent being transferred from one local peer

in Figure 7.3, GridTorrent has a different download status view, with statistics on the local connections. It also shows a special status bar that displays which pieces have been downloaded from the local network.

Otherwise, GridTorrent is very similar to SymTorrent. It is a BitTorrent client that enables local cooperation in downloading torrents. This means that users can form small local networks (clusters, grids) that are connected via WLAN or Bluetooth and cooperate to download torrents more efficiently. The peers in the local network download pieces both from each other and from peers on the Internet. Downloading via the local links can be faster and more efficient; thus, downloading pieces from local peers is preferred. The locally connected peers share extra information on their status with each other. The goal is to minimize data traffic with peers connected over the long-range links and obtain as much data as possible from the local cluster. This is how cooperating GridTorrent peers conserve both energy and data traffic.

The topology of a network with GridTorrent peers is illustrated in Figure 7.4. The peers using GridTorrent, which are marked with the phone icon, are connected over short-range links, typically over Bluetooth. They form the local cluster, which is marked with a cloud. Besides the locally connected peers, GridTorrent clients also establish connections with peers on the Internet, over a long-range network interface, which can be HSDPA, GRPS, or even WLAN.

GridTorrent can be used as a standard BitTorrent client, and torrents can be added and downloaded from the Internet without using any of the added features. However, there are a couple of new options in the menus that enable us to establish local connections between the devices. By selecting 'Start local listening', a phone starts listening via the

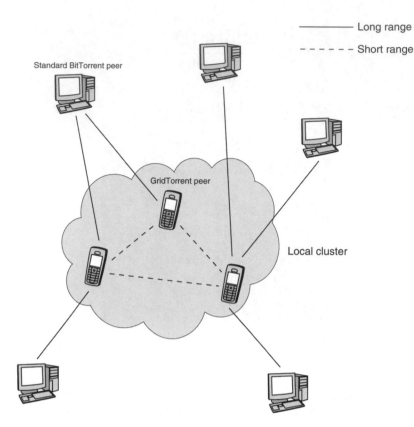

Figure 7.4   Topology of a GridTorrent-based network

selected network interface, which can be Bluetooth or WLAN. If we want to make a
connection to a local device that is already listening, this can be done by selecting the
'Add local peer' option. Here, the IP address of the device can be given, or, in case of
Bluetooth, a device discovery dialog is shown. After the local links have been established,
the devices download pieces from the Internet and from each other in a cooperative way.
Pieces that are available locally are downloaded from the local peers.

   At the point of writing, GridTorrent has not been released to the public, but we are
planning to make it open source. Generally speaking, GridTorrent is currently a research
project, but we think that any developer can benefit from our experiments with creating
the application.

7.4   Developing a BitTorrent Client

Designing and implementing a P2P client on Symbian OS is a demanding task. The
application logic is complex and the programmer must be familiar with many advanced
features of the platform. This chapter aims to give you some tips, ideas, and code fragments that will help you take the first steps. In accordance with the topic of this book, we
focus on the networking aspects of the application. We do not go into the implementation

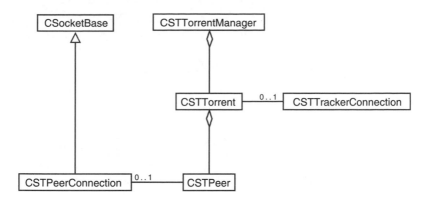

Figure 7.5   The simplified class diagram of the engine of SymTorrent

of the BitTorrent protocol, and most of the topics covered here can be reused in any application using networking. The code snippets are based on the engine of SymTorrent and GridTorrent; however, they are not simply copied and pasted code. The classes are greatly simplified. For example, we have removed parts of the code that are considered less significant, and, to simplify the code, we have left out NewL() and NewLC() methods and some other definitions.

Nevertheless, you can always refer to the full open-source version of SymTorrent and GridTorrent [4]. We try to point out the projects in which you can find the associated source files. From now on we will use SymTorrent when we refer to the complete mobile application. The header files for the Symbian-based classes used can be found by searching the help file of the SDK. All of the source code in this chapter was tested with the S60 SDK 3rd edition MR (Maintenance Release).

Figure 7.5 shows the simplified class diagram of the engine of SymTorrent. It does not include the user interface classes, and several lower-level classes are also omitted.

7.4.1   Creating the Network Manager

Before moving on to the BitTorrent-related classes, we are going to implement a simple networking framework that makes network and socket programming simpler. This is the lowest level of the application, where network connections are created and sockets are read and written; thus, these code snippets can be utilized in almost any application that uses networking. The full source code can be found in the KiNetwork subproject of SymTorrent. Figure 7.6 shows the classes of the networking framework that we are going to implement.

The network manager is responsible for starting and maintaining the active network connection, providing a socket server session and listening for incoming connections. These are implemented by a single class referred to as CNetworkManager. This is a singleton class, which means that only one instance of it can exist at any time, and this instance can be accessed globally. Traditionally, singletons are implemented using static class members; however, in Symbian OS, it is not preferred to use global writable static data in DLLs [5]. Instead, thread-local storage (TLS) is used. TLS is a single machine word of static memory whose scope is the thread in which the code of the DLL is running.

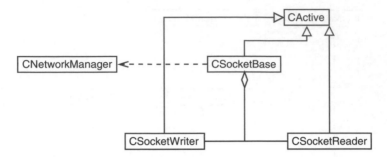

Figure 7.6   The simplified class diagram of the networking layer

In a DLL that uses multiple singleton classes, the TLS has to be set to some container class that manages the singletons. In this example, however, we are going to use only one singleton class per DLL. Thus, the TLS can be safely set to the address of this singleton. The declaration of the class is as follows:

```
class CNetworkManager : public CBase
   {
public:
   static CNetworkManager* Instance(); // Singleton access
   static void InitializeL(); // Singleton initialization
   static void Free(); // Singleton cleenaup

   ~CNetworkManager();

   void StartNetworkConnectionL(
     MNetworkConnectionStarterObserver* aObserver = NULL);

   TBool IsNetworkConnectionStarted() { return
       iNetworkConnectionStarted; }

   void StartListeningL(TUint aPort, MSocketListenerObserver*
       aObsever);
   void StopListening();

   RSocketServ& SocketServ() { return iSocketServer; }
   RConnection& NetworkConnection() { return iConnection; }

private:
   CNetworkManager() : CCoeStatic(KUidNetworkManagerSingleton) {}
   void ConstructL();
   void GetIapNamesAndIdsL(RArray<TUint32>& aIds, CDesC16Array&
       aNames);
   TUint32 QueryIapIdL();
```

```
private:
  TBool iNetworkConnectionStarted;
  RConnection iConnection;
  RSocketServ iSocketServer;
  CSocketListener* iSocketListener;
  TInt iReferenceCount;
  };
```

Before any access can be made to CNetworkManager, the static method InitializeL() must be called. It creates the singleton instance if it is not initialized yet, and increments a reference counter, which is used during clean-up to ensure that the object is not cleaned up while it is still in use:

```
void CNetworkManager::InitializeL()
  {
  // Get TLS
  CNetworkManager* instance = (CKiLogManager*)Dll::Tls();

    if (instance == 0)
      {
      instance = new (ELeave) CNetworkManager();
      CleanupStack::PushL(instance);
      instance->ConstructL();
      CleanupStack::Pop();

      Dll::SetTls(instance); // Set TLS to the singleton
      }

    instance->iReferenceCount++;
  }
```

Every call to InitializeL() must be paired with a call to the static method Free(), which cleans up the object. Reference counting enables the singleton to be used in a shared DLL. The reference counter is decreased each time Free() is called. When the counter reaches zero, the singleton is cleaned up. For debug purposes, a panic is raised if the singleton is freed up too many times:

```
void CNetworkManager::Free()
  {
  CNetworkManager* instance = (CNetworkManager*)Dll::Tls();

  if (instance)
    {
    instance->iReferenceCount--;

    if (instance->iReferenceCount == 0)
```

```
      {
      delete (CNetworkManager*)Dll::Tls();
      Dll::SetTls(NULL);
      }
    }
  else
    User::Panic(KLitNetworkManagerPanic,
        ENetworkManagerFreedUpTooManyTimes);
}
```

Accessing the singleton is performed by calling the static Instance() method, which does nothing else but return the content of the TLS:

```
CNetworkManager* CNetworkManager::Instance()
  {
  return (CNetworkManager*)Dll::Tls();
  }
```

To simplify accessing the network manager, we define the inline function NetMgr():

```
inline CNetworkManager* NetMgr()
  {
  return                           CNetworkManager::Instance();
  }
```

The second-phase constructor of CNetworkManager opens a session to the socket server:

```
void CNetworkManager::ConstructL()
  {
  User::LeaveIfError(iSocketServer.Connect(255));
  }
```

The destructor releases the owned resources, namely the socket server handle, the network connection handle, and the socket listener, if it has been initialized:

```
CNetworkManager::~CNetworkManager()
  {
  iSocketServer.Close();
  iConnection.Close();
  delete iSocketListener;
  }
```

7.4.2 Network Connections

We are going to create a P2P application, which means that our program needs access to the Internet. To do so, we must establish a network connection. By network connection we mean the actual network interface, for example WLAN or GPRS. By default, the framework pops up a network connection selection dialog when the network is first accessed, and automatically starts the selected network connection. However, this pop-up can sometimes be annoying, especially if it pops up multiple times. In order to provide a better user experience, the network selection dialog can be avoided by setting up the desired connection directly. Another plus is that, by directly programming the connection, it can be saved and reloaded after the application restarts. Under Symbian OS, each network connection is associated with an access point. An access point is an entry in the communications database. It has several fields, including a name and a unique ID. To start a connection, we must first obtain its ID. In the following example we are going to query all available access points from the framework and display them in a dialog for the user. On the S60 platform, the access point engine can also be used via the `CApSelect` class to access the available access points. However, in this example we are going to extract the access points directly from the communications database. The full process of querying the access point and starting the network connection is illustrated in Figure 7.7.

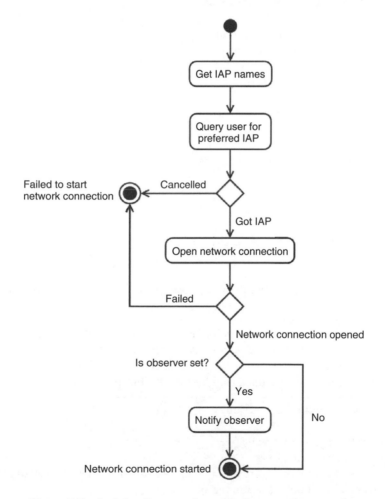

Figure 7.7 Activity diagram of starting the network connection

The first step is to get the names and IDs of the available access points. To do so, we need to access the Internet access point (IAP) table of the communications database and get all of its records. The following method extracts the access point fields into the passed arrays:

```
void CNetworkManager::GetIapNamesAndIdsL(RArray<TUint32>& aIds,
    CDesC16Array& aNames )
    {
    // Open COMM database
    CCommsDatabase* commsDb = CCommsDatabase::NewL();
    CleanupStack::PushL(commsDb);

    // Get the table with the access points
    CCommsDbTableView* view = commsDb->OpenTableLC( TPtrC(IAP) );
    TInt res = view->GotoFirstRecord();

    // Read all the access points
    while (res != KErrNotFound)
      {
      User::LeaveIfError(res);

      TBuf<KCommsDbSvrMaxFieldLength> name;
      TUint32 id;
      view->ReadTextL(TPtrC(COMMDB_NAME), name);
      view->ReadUintL(TPtrC(COMMDB_ID), id);

      aIds.Insert(id, 0);
      aNames.InsertL(0, name);

      res = view->GotoNextRecord();
      }

    CleanupStack::PopAndDestroy(2, commsDb); // view, commsDb
    }
```

With the name and ID of the access points in hand, we are able to display a dialog for the user. `QueryIapIdL()` creates a pop-up list dialog, populates it with the access points, displays it to the user, and returns the ID of the selected item. This dialog is very similar to the one that is automatically displayed by the OS, but it lacks the small icons:

```
TUint32 CNetworkManager::QueryIapIdL()
    {
    RArray<TUint32> idArray;
    CleanupClosePushL(idArray);
    CDesCArrayFlat* namesArray = new (ELeave) CDesCArrayFlat(5);
    CleanupStack::PushL(namesArray);
```

```
// Get access points
GetIapNamesAndIdsL(idArray, *namesArray);

// Create the popup list
CEikTextListBox* list = new (ELeave)
    CAknSinglePopupMenuStyleListBox;
CleanupStack::PushL(list);
CAknPopupList* popupList = CAknPopupList::NewL(list,
  R_AVKON_SOFTKEYS_OK_CANCEL,AknPopupLayouts::EMenuWindow);
CleanupStack::PushL(popupList);

// Initialize the listbox.
list->ConstructL(popupList, CEikListBox::ELeftDownInViewRect);
list->CreateScrollBarFrameL(ETrue);
list->ScrollBarFrame()->SetScrollBarVisibilityL(
                                    CEikScrollBarFrame::EOff,
                                    CEikScrollBarFrame::EAuto);

// Set list items
CTextListBoxModel* model = list->Model();
model->SetItemTextArray(namesArray);
model->SetOwnershipType(ELbmDoesNotOwnItemArray);

// Set title
popupList->SetTitleL(_L("Select connection"));

// Show popup list
TBool changed = popupList->ExecuteLD(); // shows the dialog
CleanupStack::Pop(); // popuplist

TInt iapId = 0;
if (changed)
  iapId = (TUint32)idArray[list->CurrentItemIndex()];

CleanupStack::PopAndDestroy(3, idArray);
return iapId;
}
```

The next step is to define the method that actually starts the network connection. Like many networking function calls, starting the connection is an asynchronous process. Thus, it should be called by an active object [6] so that the thread of the application is not blocked. In this example, however, we use a synchronous `WaitForRequest()` call to make the code more readable. Nevertheless, we show an observer class that could be used if we implemented the asynchronous version. The caller can pass an implementation of the observer whose `NetworkConnectionStartedL()` method is called when starting of the network connection is completed or fails:

```
class MNetworkConnectionStarterObserver
  {
public:
  virtual void NetworkConnectionStartedL(TInt aResult,
    RConnection& aConnection) = 0;
};
```

The `StartNetworkConnectionL()` method calls `QueryIapIdL()` to obtain the access point ID from the user. The network connection is encapsulated by the `RConnection` class, which must be opened before it can be used. Starting the connection is done by configuring the fields of a `TCommDbConnPref` object with the acquired access point and passing it to the `Start()` method of the connection. Since we use a synchronous `WaitForRequest()` call, the thread is blocked at this point until the connection has been started or the operation fails. We can obtain the result from the passed `TRequestStatus` object. Finally, we signal the observer if it is available:

```
void CNetworkManager::StartNetworkConnectionL(
  MNetworkConnectionStarterObserver* aObserver)
  {
  TUint32 iapId = QueryIapIdL(); // Query the access point ID

  if (iapId)
    {
    TCommDbConnPref prefs;
    prefs.SetIapId(iapId);
    prefs.SetDirection(ECommDbConnectionDirectionOutgoing);
    prefs.SetDialogPreference(ECommDbDialogPrefDoNotPrompt);
    prefs.SetBearerSet(KCommDbBearerUnknown);

    User::LeaveIfError(iConnection.Open(iSocketServer));

    TRequestStatus status;
    iConnection.Start(prefs, status); // Start the connection
    User::WaitForRequest(status); // ActiveObject should be used

    if (status.Int() == KErrNone)
      iNetworkConnectionStarted = ETrue;

    if (aObserver)
      aObserver->NetworkConnectionStartedL(status.Int(),
          iConnection);
    }
  }
```

After the network connection has been started, it can be used to initialize sockets, host resolvers, or HTTP sessions. All of these classes have a method that can be used to attach an RConnection instance that encapsulates the started network connection.

7.4.3 Listening for Incoming Connections

In BitTorrent, peers communicate with each other over TCP/IP connections. To accept incoming connections, we need to start listening on a port. If an incoming connection is accepted on the given port, the framework gives us a configured socket that can be used to communicate with the other party. By its nature, listening is an asynchronous process. Symbian OS allows us to do listening synchronously, but it does not make too much sense, since this would block the entire thread. Hence, we show you how to implement listening asynchronously by using active objects.

First of all, we create a callback method encapsulated in an observer class MSocketListenerObserver. This class is responsible for notifying the client when an incoming connection is accepted:

```
class MSocketListenerObserver
    {
public:
    // Called when an incoming connection is accepted, the
        ownership of the socket is passed to the called object.
    virtual void AcceptSocketL(RSocket& aSocket) = 0;
    };
```

We implement listening in the active object CSocketListener. Listening is started by calling StartListening() and specifying a port and an observer. The private fields of the class include two socket handles: iSocketListener is the socket that actively listens and iBlankSocket is the socket that encapsulates the next incoming connection:

```
class CSocketListener : public CActive
    {
public:
    CSocketListener() : CActive(EPriorityStandard) {}
    ~CSocketListener();

    TInt StartListening(TUint aPort, MSocketListenerObserver*
        aObserver);
    void StopListening();

private: // from CActive
    void RunL();
    void RunError();
    void DoCancel();
```

```
private:
  MSocketListenerObserver* iObserver;
  RSocket iSocketListener;
  RSocket iBlankSocket;
  };
```

`StartListening()` begins with checking whether the object has been activated. Before we can start listening, we must make sure that the network connection has been started. If the connection is offline, then we start it through the network manager. Since we implemented `StartNetworkConnectionL()` as a synchronous method, we do not need to pass an observer and wait for the result.

To start listening, the listening socket must be opened first. It is important to pass the started network connection as the fourth parameter of the `Open()` method. Otherwise, the automatic access point selection dialog is displayed. Then we must specify the port on which the socket listens by binding an arbitrary network address with the selected port to the socket. Calling `Listen()` starts listening, but incoming connections are not accepted until `Accept()` is called. `Accept()` is an asynchronous operation. Its first parameter is the blank socket that will be attached to the incoming connection. The asynchronous operation is completed (and the active object event handler method `RunL()` is executed) when an incoming connection arrives:

```
TInt CSocketListener::StartListening(TUint aPort,
  MSocketListenerObserver* aObserver)
  {
  if (IsActive()) User::Panic(...);
  iObserver = aObserver;

  if (!NetMgr()->IsNetworkConnectionStarted())
    {
    TRAPD(err, NetMgr()->StartNetworkConnectionL());
    if (err != KErrNone)
      return err;
    }

  TInt err = iSocketListener.Open(NetMgr()->SocketServ(),
      KAfInet,
    KSockStream, KProtocolInetTcp, NetMgr()->
        NetworkConnection()));

  if (err != KErrNone)
    return err;

  TInetAddr addr;
  addr.SetPort(aPort);
```

```
err = iSocketListener.Bind(addr);
if (err != KErrNone)
  return err;

err = iSocketListener.Listen(5);
if (err != KErrNone)
  return err;

iBlankSocket.Close();
iBlankSocket.Open(NetMgr()->SocketServ());
iSocketListener.Accept(iBlankSocket, iStatus);
SetActive();

return KErrNone;
}
```

We also provide a method to stop the listening process. Two calls are performed: the active object and the asynchronous `Accept()` request are cancelled by calling `Cancel()`, and the resources of the listening socket are released by calling the `Close()` method of the socket handle:

```
void CSocketListener::StopListening()
  {
  Cancel();
  iSocketListener.Close();
  }
```

The last method we need to implement in the socket listener class is the event handler method of the active object. `RunL()` is called when the `Accept()` request is completed. The completion of the request does not necessarily mean that it has been successful. Thus, we need to check the result by accessing the `iStatus` member variable of the active object. If it is set to `KErrNone`, then accepting an incoming connection has been successful, and `iBlankSocket` is attached to it. In this case, we pass the socket to the observer. It should be noted that the observer must take the ownership of the new socket. After passing the socket, a new `Accept()` request can be issued to continue listening. This is done by reinitializing the blank socket, issuing the request, and setting the object to the active state. If the `Accept()` request fails, we stop the listening process:

```
void CSocketListener::RunL()
  {
  if (iStatus.Int() == KErrNone)
    {
    if (iObserver)
      iObserver->AcceptSocketL(iBlankSocket);
```

```
      else
        iBlankSocket.Close();

      // Initialize a new blank socket
      iBlankSocket = RSocket();
      iBlankSocket.Open(NetMgr()->SocketServ());
      iSocketListener.Accept(iBlankSocket, iStatus);
      SetActive();
      }
    else
      StopListening();
    }
```

We also need to implement DoCancel(), the method that cancels the asynchronous request. In our case, it calls the CancelAll() method of the listener socket, which cancels the active Accept() request:

```
void CSocketListener::DoCancel()
  {
  iSocketListener.CancelAll();
  }
```

The destructor cancels the active object and closes both owned socket handles:

```
CSocketListener::~CSocketListener()
  {
  Cancel();
  iBlankSocket.Close();
  iSocketListener.Close();
  }
```

Now that we have defined CSocketListener, we should also add the listening methods to the network manager. In this way, listening for incoming connections can be started by calling a method of the easily accessible singleton network manager. Listening is started by calling StartListeningL(), which creates a new instance of the socket listener and starts listening. Stopping listening is performed by calling StopListeningL(), which deletes the socket listener instance:

```
void CNetworkManager::StartListeningL(TUint aPort,
  MSocketListenerObserver* aObserver)
  {
  if (iSocketListener == NULL)
    iSocketListener = new (ELeave) CSocketListener;

  if (!iSocketListener->IsActive())
```

```
      User::LeaveIfError(iSocketListener->StartListeningL(aPort,
          aObserver));
   }

void CNetworkManager::StopListening()
   {
   delete iSocketListener;
   iSocketListener = NULL;
   }
```

7.4.4   Sending Data Via Sockets

Communicating with the peers is performed via sockets. Reading and writing sockets must be handled asynchronously so that an active operation does not block the entire application. We are going to create a generic socket class that encapsulates a socket handle and can be used to write to the socket and get notifications when data is received from the connected peer. This class is referred to as *socket base* (CSocketBase). Since both sending and receiving are handled asynchronously, both of these functions require separate active objects (CSocketWriter and CSocketReader).

The first class we are going to implement is CSocketWriter, an active object that encapsulates an asynchronous write request to the socket server. The first-phase constructor takes the owner socket class as a reference (CSocketBase); this class will be implemented later. The socket writer does not open a socket or make any connections. Its purpose is to send data via an already initialized and connected socket. The socket writer can only have one active write operation. This means that, if we want to send data when there is already an active request, then we must store the data in a buffer and send it later. This way, an arbitrary number of requests can be issued to the socket writer, and the write operations will be performed in a sequential order:

```
class CSocketWriter : public CActive
   {
public:
   CSocketWriter(CSocketBase& aSocketBase)
     : CActive(EPriorityStandard),
       iSocket(aSocketBase.Socket()), iSocketBase(aSocketBase) {}

   void ConstructL();
   ~CSocketWriter();
   void WriteL(const TDesC8& aBuf);

private:
   void IssueWrite();
```

```
private: // from CActive
  void RunL();
  void DoCancel();

private:
  RSocket& iSocket;
  CSocketBase&        iSocketBase;
  CBufSeg*            iLongBuffer;
  RBuf8               iShortBuffer;
  };
```

In the second-phase constructor we add the active object to the active scheduler and then initiate the two data buffers that are used for sending the data. A shorter buffer is used for the actual write requests, and a longer buffer is used to queue the writable data until a new request can be issued:

```
void CSocketWriter::ConstructL()
  {
  CActiveScheduler::Add(this);
  iShortBuffer.CreateL(16384); // 16 KB

  iLongBuffer = CBufSeg::NewL(256);  // 256 byte for the
      granularity
  }
```

The destructor frees up the resources and cancels the active object:

```
CSocketWriter::~CSocketWriter()
  {
  Cancel();
  iShortBuffer.Close();
  delete iLongBuffer;
  }
```

The WriteL() method puts the writable data into the write buffer and issues a new write operation if the active object is not active. If it is already in the active state, then the data will be sent after the current write request has been completed:

```
void CSocketWriter::WriteL(const TDesC8& aBuf)
  {
  iLongBuffer->InsertL(iLongBuffer->Size(), aBuf);
  if (!IsActive()) IssueWrite();
  }
```

Issuing a new socket write request is performed by filling up the short transfer buffer and calling the asynchronous write operation. The data is read from the long buffer and is deleted immediately from there:

```
void CSocketWriter::IssueWrite()
  {
  if (iLongBuffer->Size() < iShortBuffer.MaxLength())
    iLongBuffer->Read(0, iShortBuffer, iLongBuffer->Size());
  else
    iLongBuffer->Read(0, iShortBuffer);

  iLongBuffer->Delete(0, iShortBuffer.Length());

  iSocket.Write(iShortBuffer, iStatus);
  SetActive();
  }
```

Cancelling the socket writer is performed by calling the `CancelWrite()` method of the socket handle:

```
void CSocketWriter::DoCancel()
  {
  iSocket.CancelWrite();
  }
```

In the event handler method, we get the result of the last write request. If it has been successful, we check whether there is data in the send buffer. If the buffer is not empty, a new write request is issued. If the write request fails, then the `HandleWriteErrorL()` method of the owner socket base is called. This is a virtual method that can be implemented by classes derived from `CSocketBase()` being notified when writing to the socket fails:

```
void CSocketWriter::RunL()
  {
  switch (iStatus.Int())
    {
    case KErrNone: // Writing to socket has been completed
      if (iLongBuffer->Size() > 0) IssueWrite();
    break;

    default: // Write error
      iSocketBase.HandleWriteErrorL();
    break;
    }
  }
```

7.4.5 Receiving Data from Sockets

Similarly to writing data to a socket, reading is also an asynchronous process and must be handled via an active object. We are going to show you how to implement the socket reader class `CSocketReader` which can actively read incoming data from a connected socket. This class will also be owned by the base socket class `CSocketBase`; thus, we pass a reference of the owner to the constructor. A reference to a byte buffer is also passed. The received data will be put into this buffer. We have chosen to use an externally owned buffer, since the received data will not be processed inside the class:

```
class CSocketReader : public CActive
  {
public:
  CSocketReader(CSocketBase& aSocketBase, CBufBase& aLongBuffer)
    : CActive(EPriorityStandard),
      iSocket(aSocketBase.Socket()), iSocketBase(aSocketBase),
      iLongBuffer(aLongBuffer) {}

  void ConstructL();
  ~CSocketReader();

  void StartReading();

protected: // from CActive
  void RunL();
  void RunError();
  void DoCancel();

private:
  RSocket&           iSocket;
  CSocketBase& iSocketBase;
  CBufBase&     iLongBuffer;
  TBuf8<16384> iShortBuffer; // 16 KByte
  TSockXfrLength        iLastRecvLength;
  };
```

We begin defining the methods with the second-phase constructor and the destructor. The constructor only needs to add the active object to the scheduler. The destructor cancels the active object:

```
void CSocketReader::ConstructL()
  {
  CActiveScheduler::Add(this);
  }

CSocketReader::~CSocketReader()
  {
  Cancel();
  }
```

Reading is started by the public method `StartReading()`. This checks the active object's status and, if it is not active, then issues a new request by calling the `RecvOneOrMore()` method of the socket. This method requires a buffer where the received data is stored and a `TSockXfrLength` reference in which the length of the received data is written after the completion of the read request. The `RecvOneOrMore()` request is completed when any data is received. However, it is not specified whether the sent data is received in one larger burst or in more, smaller ones:

```
void CSocketReader::StartReading()
  {
  if (!IsActive())
    {
    iSocket.RecvOneOrMore(iShortBuffer, 0, iStatus,
        iLastRecvLength);
    SetActive();
    }
  }
```

Cancelling the receive request is performed by calling `CancelRecv()`:

```
void CSocketReader::DoCancel()
  {
  iSocket.CancelRecv();
  }
```

In the event handler method, if the receive request has been successful, the received data is appended to the buffer that was given at the construction of the socket reader. This buffer is owned by the socket base class, which is notified by calling its `OnReceiveL()` virtual method. Classes derived from `CSocketBase` can process data by accessing the long buffer. Failure of the receive request is handled by the `HandleWriteL()` virtual method of the socket base class:

```
void CSocketReader::RunL()
  {
  switch (iStatus.Int())
    {
    case KErrNone:
      iLongBuffer.InsertL(iLongBuffer.Size(), iShortBuffer);
      iShortBuffer.SetLength(0); // Reset the short buffer
      StartReading(); // Continue reading

      iSocketBase.OnReceiveL(); // Notify the owner socket base
          object
    break;
```

```
      default:
        iSocketBase.HandleReadErrorL();
      break;
      }
    }
```

7.4.6   The Socket Base Class

The socket base is an abstract class that encapsulates a socket. It allows reading and writing of the socket by using a CSocketWriter and a CSocketReader instance. Its virtual methods, which were also discussed briefly with the code of the socket reader and writer, notify the derived class when incoming data is received or an error occurs. In SymTorrent, this is the base class of the peer connection class. Generally, it can be used wherever a connected socket is needed. We derive the class from CActive so that it can be used to encapsulate other asynchronous requests besides reading or writing the socket. One important use case for this is establishing a connection to another host. Since connecting is also an asynchronous request, the socket base can be used as its active object:

```
class CSocketBase : public CActive
  {
public:
  CSocketBase() : CActive(EPriorityStandard) {}
  void ConstructL();
  void ConstructL(RSocket& aSocket);
  ~CSocketBase();

public:
  void SendL(const TDesC8& aDes);
  inline RSocket& Socket() { return iSocket; }

protected:
  // Called when incoming data is received
  virtual void OnReceiveL() = 0;
  virtual void HandleReadErrorL() = 0; // Called on read error
  virtual void HandleWriteErrorL() = 0; // Called on write error

protected:
  RSocket iSocket;
  CBufFlat* iRecvBuffer; // Buffer passed to the socket reader
  TBool iIncomingConnection;

private:
  CSocketReader* iSocketReader;
  CSocketWriter* iSocketWriter;
```

```
    friend class CSocketReader; // for calling HandleReadErrorL()
    friend class CSocketWriter; // for calling HandleWriteErrorL()
    };
```

The class has two second-phase constructors. The one without parameters is used in the general case when we want to establish the connection to another host. By contrast, the other overload takes an already connected socket handle. This can be used when an incoming connection is accepted (i.e. by using our previously written socket listener). The already connected socket is attached to the socket base instance. There is a protected member variable, iIncomingConnection, that enables us to check whether this socket was initialized with an incoming connection. In the constructor, the network connection is started, the socket is initialized, and then the socket reader and writer instances are created. Reading from the socket is started immediately:

```
void CSocketBase::ConstructL()
  {
  if (!NetMgr()-> IsNetworkConnectionStarted())
    NetMgr()->StartNetworkConnectionL();

  if (!iIncomingConnection)
    iSocket.Open(NetMgr()->SocketServ(), KAfInet,
      KSockStream, KProtocolInetTcp, NetMgr()->
        NetworkConnection());

  // 256 byte granularity of buffer expansion
  iRecvBuffer = CBufFlat::NewL(256);

  iSocketReader = new (ELeave) CSocketReader(*this,
      *iRecvBuffer);
  iSocketReader->ConstructL();
  iSocketReader->StartReading();

  iSocketWriter = new (ELeave) CSocketWriter(*this);
  iSocketWriter->ConstructL();
  }

void CSocketBase::ConstructL(RSocket& aSocket)
  {
  iIncomingConnection = ETrue;
  iSocket = aSocket;

  ConstructL(); // Call the other overload
  }
```

To send data, the socket writer instance can be used. To make the operation simpler, we can create a Send() method that calls the WriteL() method of the socket writer. It should be noted that, since this is an asynchronous operation, the program is not stopped at this point. The `Write()` request is forwarded to the socket server, and sending of data takes place asynchronously in another process. In this implementation, the socket base class is not notified when a write request is completed; however, it is not a difficult task to add such a function to `CSocketWriter`:

```
void CSocketBase::SendL(const TDesC8& aDes)
  {
  iSocketWriter->WriteL(aDes);
  }
```

The socket base can be used for several purposes. The derived classes must implement its three pure virtual methods, most importantly the `OnReceiveL()` method. The example here does not establish a connection. Connecting can be implemented by using the `Connect()` method of the socket handle (`RSocket`).

7.4.7 The Peer Connection

Now that we have a framework that enables us to start network connections, listen for incoming TCP/IP connections, and send/read data on the sockets, we can move on to creating the class that encapsulates a peer connection. In BitTorrent, the content of the torrent is downloaded from the peers. We do not have the space to go into the peer communication protocol specification or the complex logic of the class. Instead, we will show some of the more interesting methods of the class as examples. The peer connections (`CSTPeerConnection`) are associated with a torrent. On the code level, the `CSTPeer-Connection` instances are owned by a `CSTTorrent` instance. The complete version of

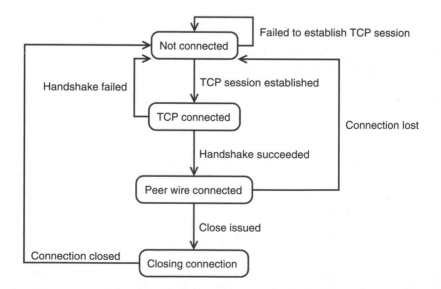

Figure 7.8   State chart of a peer connection

these classes can be found in the project SymTorrentEngine. All the names of the classes in the engine are prefixed with ST, which refers to SymTorrent.

A state chart of a peer connection life cycle can be seen in Figure 7.8. Newly created peer connections are not connected. The current state is stored in the `iState` member variable. This is an enumeration, referred to as `TPeerConnectionState`. The various values it can take are as follows:

- `EPeerNotConnected`: the peer is not connected.
- `EPeerTcpConnecting`: the peer is establishing a TCP connection.
- `EPeerPwHandshaking`: the peer is performing the BitTorrent (peer-wire) handshake.
- `EPeerPwConnected`: the peer is connected (the handshake is complete).
- `EPeerClosing`: the peer is disconnected and freeing up its resources.

As you can see, a newly created, unconnected peer connection enters the listed states in a sequential order. Firstly, it establishes a connection, and then it performs the handshake. If the handshake has been successful, it enters the connected state and exchanges messages until the connection is closed. The protocol of the handshake and the messages are fixed, and its specification can be found at the official BitTorrent site [2]. Without going into such detail, we will investigate the `OnReceiveL()` method of the class, which is called when incoming data is received. If the peer is still in the handshake state, then the size of the received data is checked. If the whole handshake string is received, then parsing the handshake can be performed. You can see that the received data is read from `iRecvBuffer`, the buffer that we also passed to the socket reader. The length of the buffer can be queried, along with the data contained.

Receiving messages in the connected state works similarly. The first step is to check the length of the next message, which is transmitted as a four-byte integer. All of the BitTorrent messages begin with this length prefix. Having at least as many bytes in the receive buffer as the parsed message length means that a new message has been received, and can be parsed. It is very important that, after processing the message, it be deleted from the receive buffer so that the next message can be processed:

```
void CSTPeerConnection::OnReceiveL()
  {
  switch (iState)
    {
    case EPeerPwHandshaking:
      {
      TInt protLength = (iRecvBuffer->Ptr()) [0];
      TInt handshakeLength = protLength + 1 + 48;
      if (iRecvBuffer->Size() >= handshakeLength)
        {
        // Parse handshake...
        }
      }
    break;
```

```
    case EPeerPwConnected:
      {
      while (iRecvBuffer->Size() >= 4)
        {
        TUint messageLength = ReadInt();
        if (TUint(iRecvBuffer->Size()) >= (4 + messageLength))
          {
          // Process incoming message...

          // Delete the processed data from the buffer
          iRecvBuffer->Delete(0, 4 + messageLength);
          }
        else
          break;
      }
    break;
    }
  }
```

We used the method ReadInt() in the implementation of OnReceiveL(). This method shows how a four-byte-long integer can be extracted from the buffer:

```
TUint CSTPeerConnection::ReadInt(TInt aIndex)
  {
  TPtrC8 ptr = iRecvBuffer->Ptr().Right(
    iRecvBuffer->Ptr().Length() - aIndex);

  TUint value = ptr[0] << 24;
  value += (ptr[1] << 16);
  value += (ptr[2] << 8);
  value += ptr[3];

  return value;
  }
```

Sending an integer can be performed by separately sending all of its four bytes:

```
void CSTPeerConnection::SendIntL(TUint32 aInteger)
  {
  TBuf8<4> buffer;
  buffer.SetLength(4);

  buffer[3] = aInteger & 0xFF;
  buffer[2] = ((aInteger & (0xFF << 8)) >> 8);
  buffer[1] = ((aInteger & (0xFF << 16)) >> 16);
  buffer[0] = ((aInteger & (0xFF << 24)) >> 24);
```

```
    SendL(buffer);
    }
```

Closing and deleting a peer connection is performed in two steps. As mentioned earlier, the peer connection instances are created and owned by a CSTTorrent instance. Thus, it is also the owner's responsibility to delete the instances. Also, there are various tasks that have to be performed when a peer is disconnected, such as trying to establish new connections or removing the peer's address if it has failed too many times. To do so, peers close their connection and set the value of the variable that determines the tasks that have to be performed. This variable, which is an instance of the enumeration TConnectionCloseOrder and is referred to as iCloseOrder, can be set to the following values:

- EDeletePeer: the peer has to be deleted.
- EIncreaseErrorCounter: the error counter of the peer has to be increased.
- EDelayReconnect: the peer should be reconnected after a short delay.
- ENotSpecified: no specified order.

After setting iCloseOrder, the state of the peer is changed to closing. After this, the peer is not deleted immediately. Instead, it will be deleted by the CSTTorrent owner when it becomes aware that there is a peer that is closing. CSTTorrent periodically checks its peers to see whether they are closing:

```
void CSTPeerConnection::CloseL(TConnectionCloseOrder aOrder)
    {
    if (iState != EPeerClosing)
       {
       iCloseOrder = aOrder;

       iSocketReader->Cancel();
       iSocketWriter->Cancel();
       iSocket.Close();

       ChangeState(EPeerClosing);
       }
    }
```

7.4.8 The Tracker Connection

The tracker is a fundamental component of the BitTorrent system. It is responsible for coordinating the whole swarm and supplying the peer addresses to its clients. Each Bit-Torrent client must periodically establish connections to the tracker to obtain new peer addresses and announce its presence to the swarm. The clients communicate with the tracker via standard HTTP GET requests. Fortunately, Symbian OS offers a framework that makes issuing HTTP requests an easy procedure. Here, we show the class CST-TrackerConnection, which is responsible for announcing to the tracker in SymTorrent.

To be able to receive HTTP events, the MHTTPTransactionCallback interface must be implemented. Its methods are called by the framework when an event is received during the HTTP request. This class is also part of the project SymTorrentEngine:

```
class CSTTrackerConnection : public CBase,
                             public MHTTPTransactionCallback
    {
public:
    enum TDownloadResult
      {
      EPending = 0,
      EFailed,
      ESucceeded
      };

    CSTTrackerConnection(CSTTorrent& aTorrent,
      TTrackerConnectionEvent aEvent = ETrackerEventNotSpecified)
    : iTorrent(aTorrent), iEvent(aEvent) {}

    void ConstructL();
    ~CSTTrackerConnection();
    void StartTransactionL();
    void Cancel();
    TBool IsRunning() const;
    TDownloadResult Result() { return iResult; }
    TTrackerConnectionEvent Event() const;

private:
    void SetHeaderL(RHTTPHeaders aHeaders, TInt aHdrField,
      const TDesC8& aHdrValue);
    void SetFailed();
    void CreateUriL();

private: // from MHTTPSessionEventCallback
    void MHFRunL(RHTTPTransaction aTransaction, const
        THTTPEvent& aEvent);
    TInt MHFRunError(   TInt aError,    RHTTPTransaction
        aTransaction,
      const THTTPEvent& aEvent);

private:
    CSTTorrent& iTorrent;
    RHTTPSession iSession;
    RHTTPTransaction iTransaction;
    TDownloadResult iResult;
    HBufC8* iUri;
```

```
HBufC8* iReceiveBuffer;
TTrackerConnectionEvent     iEvent;
};
```

The various states through which the system goes while performing the HTTP transaction are depicted in Figure 7.9.

Starting the actual HTTP transaction is carried out by the method `StartTransactionL()`. The first part of the method might seem to be a little complicated. It is responsible for setting the various parameters of the HTTP session, including the preferred network connection. The result is the same as with the sockets: no network connection selection dialog is popped up, and it uses the network connection we set up before. After setting these basic properties, listening on a socket is started. This step is not required to establish a connection to the tracker, but we should be aware that other peers will try to connect us after we have connected to the tracker. Thus, this is the right point to start listening. The last step is to create the URI (a resource identification string) of the request and configure some basic headers, such as the name of the user agent and the type of acceptable content. Finally, the request is issued by calling `SubmitL()` on the HTTP transaction:

```
void CSTTrackerConnection::StartTransactionL()
  {
  iSession.OpenL(); // Open HTTP session
  RStringPool strP = iSession.StringPool();
  RHTTPConnectionInfo connInfo = iSession.ConnectionInfo();

  // Set the socket server property
  connInfo.SetPropertyL(strP.StringF(HTTP::EHttpSocketServ,
    RHTTPSession::GetTable()), THTTPHdrVal(NetMgr()->
        SocketServ().Handle()) );

  // Set the network connection property
  TInt connPtr = REINTERPRET_CAST(TInt, &(NetMgr()->
      NetworkConnection())));
  connInfo.SetPropertyL(strP.StringF(HTTP::EHttpSocketConnection,
    RHTTPSession::GetTable()), THTTPHdrVal(connPtr));

  // Start listening before connecting to the tracker
  NetMgr()->StartListeningL(0, Preferences()->IncomingPort());

  // Create URI string for the HTTP request
  CreateUriL();

  TUriParser8 uri;
  uri.Parse(*iUri);
  RStringF method = iSession.StringPool().StringF(HTTP::EGET,
```

```
   RHTTPSession::GetTable());
iTransaction = iSession.OpenTransactionL(uri, *this, method);

RHTTPHeaders hdr = iTransaction.Request()
     .GetHeaderCollection();
_LIT8(KUserAgent, "SymTorrent");
SetHeaderL(hdr, HTTP::EUserAgent, KUserAgent);
_LIT8(KAccept, "*/*"); // Accept all content type
SetHeaderL(hdr, HTTP::EAccept, KAccept);

// Submit the transaction.
iTransaction.SubmitL();
iRunning = ETrue;
}
```

After starting the HTTP GET request, events will be received according to the various states of the transaction. These can be handled in the virtual method MHFRunL(). There are several events, the most important of which are as follows:

- THTTPEvent::EGotResponseHeaders: the HTTP headers are received. Here we should check the status code of the transaction, which reflects whether the request has been successful. In the example, we check whether the status code 200 is received. We can also check the various headers that are received in the response.
- THTTPEvent::EGotResponseBodyData: this event is triggered when a part of the body of the response is received. The body can be accessed via the Body() method of

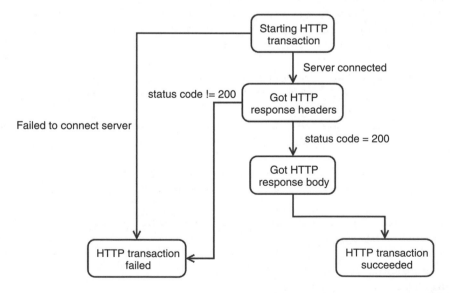

Figure 7.9   HTTP transaction state chart

the transaction. In this example, we create a data buffer and append the received body part to it. After we have processed the received data, it must be released by calling `ReleaseData()` on the body. This event could be triggered multiple times, based on how many parts of the response are received.

- `THTTPEvent::ESucceeded`: this event means that the HTTP transaction has succeeded. Here we can process the received data, in our case the list of peers sent by the tracker. A method of `CSTTorrent` is called that processes the response and registers the received peer addresses.

- `THTTPEvent::EFailed`: this event is triggered if the transaction fails. In SymTorrent, this results in closing the transaction and setting the state of the class to failed.

```
void CSTTrackerConnection::MHFRunL(RHTTPTransaction aTransaction,
  const THTTPEvent& aEvent)
  {
  switch (aEvent.iStatus)
    {
    case THTTPEvent::EGotResponseHeaders:
      RHTTPResponse resp = aTransaction.Response();
      TInt status = resp.StatusCode();

      if (status != 200)
        {
        SetFailed();
        Cancel();
        }
    break;

    case THTTPEvent::EGotResponseBodyData:
      MHTTPDataSupplier* body = aTransaction.Response().Body();
      TPtrC8 dataChunk;
      body->GetNextDataPart(dataChunk);

      if (iReceiveBuffer)
        {
        HBufC8* temp = HBufC8::NewL(iReceiveBuffer->Length() +
            dataChunk.Length());
        TPtr8 tempPtr(temp->Des());
        tempPtr.Copy(*iReceiveBuffer);
        tempPtr.Append(dataChunk);

        delete iReceiveBuffer;
        iReceiveBuffer = temp;
        }
      else
        iReceiveBuffer = dataChunk.AllocL();
```

```
        body->ReleaseData();
    break;

    case THTTPEvent::ESucceeded:
      iResult = ESucceeded;

      CSTBencode* bencodedResponse =
      CSTBencode::ParseL
          (*iReceiveBuffer);

      if (bencodedResponse)
        {
        CleanupStack::PushL(bencodedResponse);
        iTorrent.ProcessTrackerResponseL(bencodedResponse);
        CleanupStack::PopAndDestroy(bencodedResponse);
        }

      aTransaction.Close();
      iRunning = EFalse;
    break;

    case THTTPEvent::EFailed:
      SetFailed();
      aTransaction.Close();
      iRunning = EFalse;
    break;

    default:
      if (aEvent.iStatus < 0)
        {
        SetFailed();
        aTransaction.Close();
        iRunning = EFalse;
        }
    break;
    }
}
```

7.4.9 The Torrent

The torrent class (CSTTorrent) is one of the more complex classes of SymTorrent, and thus it cannot be discussed in full detail here. The torrent establishes connections to the peers, and it is also responsible for periodically issuing tracker announces via a CSTTrackerConnection instance. The main part of the application logic is implemented in the OnTimerL() method which is triggered by a timer every second. The seconds passed since opening the torrent is counted by `iEllapsedTime`. The first part is responsible for maintaining the tracker connection: if there is an active connection, then its result is checked. If the tracker connection fails, then a new request is issued until the retry limit is reached (in our case, 10). In the second part of the method, two main tasks are carried out. Firstly, the tracker is announced if the specified timeout limit is reached. Secondly, the peers are updated and new peer connections are established if needed. `CSTPeer` is a class that stores the address and some general properties of a peer. When the peer is connected, a `CSTPeerConnection` instance is created:

```
void CSTTorrent::OnTimerL()
  {
  iEllapsedTime++;

  if (iTrackerConnection)
    {
    iTrackerConnection->OnTimerL();

    switch (iTrackerConnection->Result())
      {
      case CSTTrackerConnection::ESucceeded:
        iTrackerFailures = 0;

        iLastTrackerConnectionTime.HomeTime();
        delete iTrackerConnection;
        iTrackerConnection = NULL;
      break;

     case CSTTrackerConnection::EFailed:
        iTrackerFailures++;

        delete iTrackerConnection;
        iTrackerConnection = NULL;

        if (iActive && (iTrackerFailures < 10))
          AnnounceL();
       break;
      }
    }

  if (iActive)
    {
    if ((iEllapsedTime % iTrackerRequestInterval) == 0)
      AnnounceL();

    for (TInt i=0; i<iPeers.Count(); i++)
      {
```

```
        CSTPeer* peer = iPeers[i];
        peer->OnTimerL();

        // The peer is connected
        if (peer->State() != EPeerNotConnected)
          activeConnectionCount++;
        else  // The peer is not connected
          if (!iComplete) && (activeLocalConnectionCount <
              KMaxPeerConnectionCount))
            {
            peer->ConnectL(*this, iTorrentMgr);
            activeConnectionCount++;
            }
      }
    }
  }
```

7.4.10   The Torrent Manager

The torrent manager (CSTTorrentManager) is the central singleton class of SymTorrent's engine. It is responsible for creating the torrents and other system-level tasks. Here, we show the method that loads a new torrent file and adds it to the engine. Torrent files are loaded by the LoadL() method of CSTTorrent. If loading the file has been successful, then the newly created CSTTorrent instance is added to the array of torrents, and it immediately starts downloading:

```
TInt CSTTorrentManager::OpenTorrentL(const TDesC& aFileName)
  {
  CSTTorrent* torrent = new(ELeave) CSTTorrent(this);
  CleanupStack::PushL(torrent);
  torrent->ConstructL();
  TInt loadResult = torrent->LoadL(aFileName);

  if (loadResult == KErrNone)
    {
    iTorrents.AppendL(torrent);
    CleanupStack::Pop(); // torrent

    torrent->Start(); // Start downloading the torrent
    }
  else
    {
    CleanupStack::PopAndDestroy(); // torrent
```

```
    return loadResult;
    }
}
```

7.4.11   Differences in GridTorrent

As stated before, GridTorrent is built on top of the same engine as SymTorrent. Actually, we extended SymTorrent's engine with the features needed by GridTorrent. The most notable differences are in network connection handling and in the application logic of the peer connections. On the network connection level, SymTorrent requires only one type of active connection (e.g. 3G). In contrast to this, GridTorrent communicates with the local peers over a different network connection to that used for the standard peers acquired from the tracker. This means that the network manager needs to be able to handle several network connections, and these must be made available for the different networking objects, such as sockets. Another problem was that we had to add support for Bluetooth connections, which are handled somewhat differently to WLAN/3G/GPRS. Although Bluetooth also uses sockets, it is not supported by the access point framework and must be initialized in a completely different way. In GridTorrent, Bluetooth connections are used just like the other connections; most of the differences are handled in the network manager. However, there is one key difference: the nature of how Bluetooth networks work. Currently, devices based on Symbian OS support only the Bluetooth piconet scheme. Piconets have one master peer and up to seven slave peers. Connections can only be established by the master. GridTorrent supports both this point-to-multipoint scheme and the standard IP-based WLAN/GPRS networks. If the local connection is Bluetooth, the peer must choose between slave and master modes. If WLAN is used, connection can be established between the peers in both directions.

In addition to the network connection layer, peer connections and the piece selection strategy also work differently in GridTorrent. We introduced a couple of new messages that enable the peers in the local cluster to inform each other about their progress. Since peers know which pieces are available in the local cluster, they can focus on downloading the rarer pieces from the Internet. The piece selection strategy needs further work, but current results show that even this simple algorithm considerably increases the performance of the swarm.

7.5   Conclusion

In this chapter we have shown how a complex peer-to-peer application handles network connections and sockets. We have discussed the basics of the BitTorrent protocol and analysed a small part of the source code of a client written in Symbian C++. We have also outlined the concepts behind GridTorrent, the world's first BitTorrent client that utilizes local cooperation to save energy and increase transfer speed. Although we have not been able to discuss every part in detail, the source code of SymTorrent is freely available for anyone who is looking for a deeper insight into programming mobile peer-to-peer clients.

References

[1] Cohen, B., 'Incentives Build Robustness in BitTorrent'. In Proceedings of the 1st Workshop on Economics of Peer-to-Peer Systems, Berkeley, CA, June 2003.

[2] Cohen, B., 'The BitTorrent Protocol Specification'. Available at: http://www.bittorrent.org/beps/bep_0003.html [accessed 6 September 2008].

[3] Loewenstern, A., 'DHT Protocol'. Available at: http://www.bittorrent.org/beps/bep_0005.html [accessed 6 September 2008].

[4] Kelényi, I., 'SymTorrent webpage'. Available at: http://symtorrent.aut.bme.hu [accessed 25 February 2009].

[5] Willee, H., 'Symbian OS Support for Writeable Static Data in DLLs v2.3'. The Symbian Developer Network. Available at: http://developer.symbian.com/main/downloads/papers/static_data/SupportForWriteableStaticDataInDLLs.pdf [accessed 25 February 2009].

[6] Morris, B., 'CActive and Friends'. The Symbian Developer Network. Available at: http://developer.symbian.com/main/downloads/papers/CActiveAndFriends/CActiveAndFriends.pdf [accessed 25 February 2009].

8

Introduction to Network Coding for Mobile Peer to Peer (P2P)

Janus Heide
Aalborg University, speje@es.aau.dk

Leonardo Militano
University Mediterranea of Reggio Calabria, leonardo.militano@unirc.it

8.1 Introduction to Network Coding

This chapter provides an introduction to network coding and gives examples that demonstrate its advantages and motivate its deployment. It also includes a code example, in Symbian C++, that demonstrates how network coding can be incorporated in a chat application.

Network coding is a method of attaining maximum information flow in a network. It was introduced in 2000 by Ahlswede *et al.* [1], where it was demonstrated how, in some cases, network coding can increase the throughput of a network. It was shown that, if network coding is used, the capacity defined by the *Min-cut max-flow* theorem can be achieved in a point-to-point network. An informal interpretation of the *Min-cut max-flow* theorem is that the maximum flow of information between a sender and a receiver is dictated by the bottleneck of the network that connects them. We refer the interested reader to graph theory, where this theorem is thoroughly described [2].

The main claim of network coding is that it breaks with the traditional approach of moving data from a source to a sink. Traditionally, in *routing* (also called *store-and-forward*), data or packets cannot be modified in the network between the source and the sink. In network coding this is allowed, which in some cases can increase throughput but which also results in a more complex representation of the data. Basically, several packets can be combined (encoded) to form a new representation of the original data. These new representations can then be used by the sink to reconstruct (decode) the original data.

Mobile Peer to Peer (P2P) Edited by Frank H. P. Fitzek and Hassan Charaf
© 2009 John Wiley & Sons, Ltd

How this is done and why, and where this can be beneficial, will be explained throughout this chapter.

Network coding was first suggested for use in satellite communication [3], but has subsequently been suggested for a vast number of applications and in most levels of the OSI network stack. The interested reader can find a large collection of references related to network coding here [4]. In order to show that network coding can be used in more earthbound applications than satellite communication, at the end of this chapter we present a code example that demonstrates how network coding can be incorporated into a chat application.

The next sections will explain network coding in a network context. Such explanations often take a very theoretical and mathematical approach, which is not surprising, as network coding is rooted in information theory. This chapter, however, presents network coding with an informal approach, and thus the reader should only need a basic understanding of networks and computers. As a consequence, we will only consider a simple form of network coding that is based on XOR operation. Other more practical forms exist, but they are generally based on more advanced mathematics and will therefore only be briefly introduced at the end of this chapter.

8.2   The Butterfly Example

This section will provide a very simple example, the butterfly, that illustrates a network in which network coding is able to increase the throughput. The coding operations used in this chapter are based on XOR operation, which will be explained in this section. Readers with previous knowledge of network coding may be familiar with these concepts and may wish to skip this section.

The butterfly example network illustrates how throughput can be increased in a network by the use of network coding. The network consists of one source, node s, two sinks t1 and t2, and four relaying nodes, nodes 1, 2, 3, and 4. The source s wishes to transmit two units of information b1 and b2 to the two sinks t1 and t2. The term 'packet' will be used to denote information units, but all the examples presented also hold if information streams are considered instead. The butterfly example is illustrated in Figure 8.1.

All links have unit capacity and can therefore transfer one unit of information for each time unit. In this example we disregard the processing time at the relaying nodes and assume that packets are transferred instantaneously over the links. As an example, the source s can transfer packet b1 to nodes 1 and 2, which can then forward the packet to node 3 in one time unit. If we attempt to identify a solution that distributes both b1 and b2 to both t1 and t2 within a single time unit using *routing*, we find that this is not possible.

To verify this, we can attempt to find such a solution. The sink t1 needs both b1 and b2. It can receive b1 via node 1, and hence s->1->t1. The only remaining available capacity to t1 is via 4, and thus b2 must be distributed via the path s->2->3->4->t1. Now consider t2. Both 2 and 4 have unused capacity to t2, but they both hold the same packet, namely b2. As there is no remaining capacity into either 2 or 4, they cannot receive packet b1 from anywhere, and thus the distribution problem cannot be solved. Obviously there exist several other similar solutions that distribute three packets within one time unit, but none that distributes both packets to both sinks within one time unit.

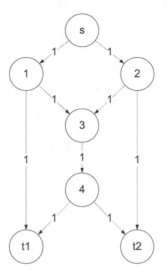

Figure 8.1 The butterfly example network, with the source s, sinks t1 and t2, and relaying nodes 1, 2, 3, and 4. All links have a capacity of 1

We now introduce the concept of network coding into the network. When network coding is applied to a network, the nodes between the sender and the receiver of a packet are enabled to operate on the packets that pass through them. This is the opposite to a *routing* network, where nodes can only store the received packet and forward it to nodes to which they are connected. These operations are denoted 'coding operations', and in this case encoding and decoding of packets are performed. In encoding, two or more packets are combined to form a new packet of the same size as one of the original packets. This new packet holds information about all the original packets, but none of the original packets can be immediately found in this form. The encoded packet must first be decoded to obtain the original packets. How this is done will be described in detail at the end of this section.

If network coding is applied, it is possible to solve the butterfly problem and thus distribute both packets to both sinks within one time unit. How this is accomplished is illustrated in Figure 8.2.

Receiver t1 receives b1 via node 1, and t2 receives b2 via node 2. Both 1 and 2 forward their packet to node 3 which holds both b1 and b2. Node 3 encodes b1 and b2 and transmits this encoded packet to 4, which in turn forwards it to t1 and t2. Receiver t1 thus holds b1 and b1+b2, and receiver t2 holds b2 and b1+b2. Both receivers can now decode the packet they are missing. For t1 this is done by removing b1 from b1+b2, which results in b2, and thus both packets have been received. The next section will outline how this is achieved and provides a calculation example.

8.3   Network Coding by XORing

Network coding can be implemented by using XOR, here denoted by ⊕, which is a simple logical operation that is completely specified by its truth table (see Table 8.1).

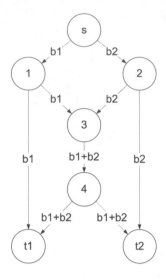

Figure 8.2 A solution to the distribution problem with the use of network coding

Table 8.1 The truth table
of the XOR operation

⊕	0	1
0	0	1
1	1	0

The XOR operation is easy to calculate for bits and can be performed by a computer very rapidly. Again, we consider the butterfly example network, which also serves the purpose of demonstrating that the solution found in the previous section is valid.

Firstly, we define the value of the packets b1 and b2, which are randomly chosen to be b1 = 1011 and b2 = 1101. Receiver t1 receives b1 via node 1, and receiver t2 receives b2 via node 2. Node 3 receives both b1 and b2 and encodes the two packets which produce the following:

$$b1 \oplus b2 = 1011 \oplus 1101 = 0110$$

The encoded packet is forwarded to node 4 which forwards it to t1 and t2. Thus, t1 possesses b1 and b1 ⊕ b2 and t2 possesses b2 and b1 ⊕ b2. Thereby both t1 and t2 can reconstruct the packet that they have not received, b2 and b1 respectively, as given below. In this way, both the receivers have received both the packets:

$$b1 \oplus (b1 \oplus b2) = 1011 \oplus 0110 = 1101 \ (= b2)$$
$$b2 \oplus (b1 \oplus b2) = 1101 \oplus 0110 = 1011 \ (= b1)$$

With this coding approach, encoding and decoding becomes relatively straightforward. However, to encode efficiently, the encoding node must have knowledge of which packets the other nodes in the network possess. Furthermore, decoding requires that the decoding node possess all but one of the packets that have been combined.

8.4 Network Coding in a Cooperative Context

Cooperative distribution neatly illustrates how network coding can be used to utilize bandwidth more efficiently. We therefore consider such a case and demonstrate the advantages of network coding over traditional routing.

Consider a small network where a source s wishes to transmit two packets b1 and b2 to three sinks t1, t2, and t3. All sinks are connected to the source via a cellular connection. Receiver t2 is connected to t1 and t3 via a local connection, but t1 and t3 are not connected. In Figure 8.3, three different ways to receive data are introduced, namely no cooperation, cooperation, and cooperation with network coding.

8.4.1 No Cooperation

If the nodes do not cooperate, they will all have to receive both packets from the source. In this case this would mean that all nodes would have to receive the packets via the cellular connection.

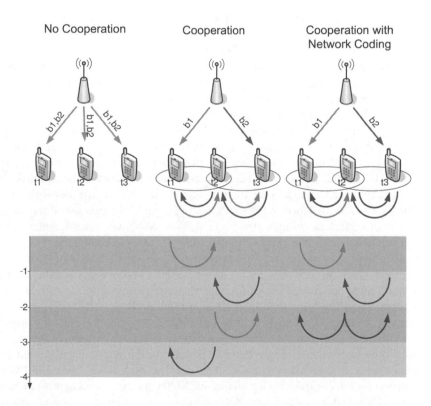

Figure 8.3 Data distribution from one source to multiple sinks with three different approaches

8.4.2 Cooperation

If the nodes cooperate, they can decrease the use of their cellular connection, which can decrease the cost and the delay of receiving the data. Receivers t1 and t3 transmit the packet they have received to t2, and t2 then forwards b1 to t3 and b2 to t1. With this approach, the distribution takes four time units.

8.4.3 Cooperation with Network Coding

When cooperation is combined with network coding, the usage of the local network can be decreased by comparison with traditional cooperation. Receiver t1 transmits b1 to t2, and receiver t3 transmits b2 to t2. Receiver t2 now holds both packets, and, because both t1 and t3 have one of these packets, t2 can encode these two packets and broadcast the combined packet b1 $\oplus$ b2. Receiver t1 can decode b1 $\oplus$ b2 with b1 and reconstruct b2. Receiver t2 can decode b1 $\oplus$ b2 with b2 and reconstruct b1. In this way, all receivers have received both packets after three time units. Thus, the time transmitting is reduced by 25% compared with the traditional cooperative scenario, which conserves bandwidth and energy.

8.5 Proof of Concept Implementation

As previously described in this chapter, the technique of network coding has a wide potential and applicability in wireless networks. In the remainder of this chapter we will introduce a simple but illustrative implementation of network coding on mobile phones. This not only has a demonstrative purpose but also shows how the very simple concept of XORing different data packets can bring important benefits in wireless communications. It is indeed the simplicity of the coding that makes the concept compelling, as it makes the deployment relatively straightforward.

The scenario for the demo application is a chat service based on network coding. This is a very different chat to that commonly used on the Internet today. The chat application is based on a WLAN ad hoc network, since most modern commercial mobile phones are equipped with IEEE 802.11b or 802.11g network interface cards. The main difference between a WLAN-based chat and an Internet-based chat is that the network has some practical limitations, for instance in the range of coverage. Thus, two users may be unable to start a chat conversation owing to the physical distance between them. Relay solutions, in which an intermediate node relays the data packets, are an established way to solve this problem.

As part of the relaying, network coding can be used to reduce the number of packets a relaying node must transmit. This will reduce the energy consumption of that node and maybe increase its willingness to collaborate as a relay node.

The scenario we have in mind is depicted in Figure 8.4, and we call this application *XORChat*. Alice and Bob want to communicate over a WLAN-based chat, but they are outside each other's coverage range. Peter is in the middle and can help them in their intent because he is able to listen to the packets coming both from Alice and from Bob. When he receives a packet from both of them, he XORs the two messages and broadcasts the obtained XORed packet. Alice and Bob will now both receive a message from Peter that is a XORed packet. This packet contains the information of their own message and

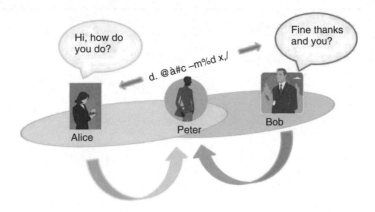

Figure 8.4   XORChat scenario

of the message from their friend. To extract the desired information from the received packet, they perform a XOR operation on the received packet and their own previously sent message. The message from the friend is now readable and the communication is successful.

8.6   The XORChat Implementation

In this section we will describe the implementation issues and the software that has been used to build the demo. The application has been implemented for Nokia S60 mobile phones and tested on Nokia N95 devices. These phones are based on Symbian OS v9.2, and the application was implemented using Symbian C++. We took the basic chat example, which is part of the Nokia SDK, and modified the code to implement the scenario of interest.

In this chapter we will highlight only the two main implementation features of the application. We will report and comment on the details of the implemented code.

The first important code we present establishes connectionless communication on a WLAN ad hoc network, which is based on UDP sockets and broadcast messages. In our reference scenario, depicted in Figure 8.4, Peter will receive packets from Alice and Bob and broadcast XORed packets. Similarly, Alice and Bob will send their messages to Peter and receive broadcast packets from Peter. The implementation of such a socket requires the use of the RSocket Symbian class from the es_sock.h library.

In the following code we show how the socket is initialized for datagram communications. When the application is started, the socket will be set to a receiving state, listening to any broadcast message. This is also the case when receiving all subsequent packets. From the code below we note that the KInetAddrAny parameter corresponds to IP address 0.0.0.0:

```
User::LeaveIfError(iSocket.Open(iSocketServer,KAfInet,
    KSockDatagram,KProtocolInetUdp));

iAddress.SetAddress(KInetAddrAny);
```

```
iAddress.SetPort(iPort);

iRemoteAddress.SetPort(iPort);

iRemoteAddress.SetAddress(KInetAddrBroadcast);

User::LeaveIfError(iSocket.Bind(iAddress));

SetState(EConnected);

iSocket.RecvFrom(iBuffer,iRemoteAddress,0,iStatus);

SetActive();
```

Similarly, when a message is to be sent, a socket transmission must be performed using datagram broadcast messages. Therefore, when a write operation is called on the socket, the remote address is set to KInetAddrBroadcast, which corresponds to the IP address 255.255.255.255, as shown below:

```
void CChatInet::SendMessageL(const TDesC& aText)

{

...

iSocket.CancelRecv();

TBufC<KChatTextBufLength> message(aText);

SetState(ESendingMessage);

HBufC* tempString=HBufC::NewLC(KChatTextBufLength+1);

if(iXoring)

  {

  tempString->Des().AppendNum(0);

  tempString->Des().AppendJustify(message,KChatTextBufLength,
      ELeft,' ');

  iMessage = HBufC8::NewL(tempString->Length());
```

```
      iMessage->Des().Copy(*tempString);

   }

 else

   {

   tempString->Des().AppendNum(1);

   tempString->Des().AppendJustify(message,KChatTextBufLength,
       ELeft,' ');

   iMessage = HBufC8::NewL(tempString->Length());

   iMessage->Des().Copy(*tempString);

   iMymessage.Copy(iMessage->Des().RightTPtr(KChatTextBufLength));

   iMymessagesent=ETrue;

   }

 iRemoteAddress.SetPort(iPort);

 iRemoteAddress.SetAddress(KInetAddrBroadcast);

 iSocket.SendTo(*iMessage,iRemoteAddress,0,iStatus);

 CleanupStack::PopAndDestroy(tempString);

 delete iMessage;

 iMessage=NULL;

 SetActive();

 }
```

From the code listed above we see that an additional byte is appended to the message. This is needed so the receiver knows whether the received message is a XORed message or a normal text message. Obviously, these two message types need to be handled in different ways. In this example, a '1' character is added to the packet for normal messages, and a

'0' character is added for XORed messages. When a packet is received, the application will check the content of the first byte and consequently handle it appropriately.

In the XORChat scenario from Figure 8.4, the messages that are not XORed will only be handled by Peter, while the XORed messages will be handled both by Alice and by Bob. Therefore, the packets in which a '1' is the first byte are of interest for the relaying node, and packets in which a '0' is the first byte are of interest to the nodes involved in the chat service. In the following code we show the first of the two cases:

```
_LIT8(one,"1");

TBufC8<1> One(one);

if(One.Compare(iBuffer.Left(1))==0)

  {

  cntpckrecv++;

  TInt ilength=iBuffer.Length()-1;

  if(cntpckrecv==2)

    {

    if(!iMymessagesent)

      {

      iMessage2length=ilength;

      iMessage2.AppendJustify(iBuffer.Right(ilength),
          KChatTextBufLength,ELeft,' ');

      iXORed.Append(_L("xxxxxxxxxxxxxxxxxxxx"));

      if(iMessage1length>=iMessage2length)

       maxlength=iMessage1length;

      else

       maxlength=iMessage2length;

      for(TInt k=0;k<maxlength;k++)
```

```
      {

         iXORed[k]=iMessage1[k]^iMessage2[k];

      }

      cntpckrecv=0;

      TBuf<KChatTextBufLength+1> text;

      text.Copy(iXORed.Left(maxlength));

      iXoring=ETrue;

      SendMessageL(text);

      }

    }

  else if(cntpckrecv==1)

  {

    iMessage1length=ilength;

    iMessage1.AppendJustify(iBuffer.Right(ilength),
        KChatTextBufLength,ELeft,' ');

  }

  }
```

Note from the code that the relaying node just stores the first received packet, and, when the second packet is also received, it XORs the two packets in order to construct the packet to be broadcasted.

From this example, the potential of network coding becomes clear; only one packet is now sent, containing the information for two different messages received from two different devices. Obviously, a limitation of this scenario is that the relay node needs to wait for the second message before it can send the XORed packet. This introduces a delay into this chat application, but the scenario still demonstrates a practical use for network coding.

In the following code we show the message-handling code for the devices involved in the chat service, which is called when a XORed packet is received:

```
_LIT8(zero,"0");

TBufC8<1> Zero(zero);

if(Zero.Compare(iBuffer.Left(1))==0)

  {
  _LIT8(Str,"XORed Message:");

  TBufC8<20> iMessageNews1(Str);

  textResource=HBufC::NewLC(20);

  textResource->Des().Copy(iMessageNews1);

  iLog.LogL(*textResource);

  CleanupStack::PopAndDestroy(textResource);

  textResource2=HBufC::NewLC(iBuffer.Length());

  textResource2->Des().Copy(iBuffer);

  iLog.LogL(textResource2->Right(iBuffer.Length()-1),mark);

  CleanupStack::PopAndDestroy(textResource2);

  iDeXORed.Append(_L("yyyyyyyyyyyyyyyyyyyyy"));

  for(TInt k=0;k<KChatTextBufLength;k++)

   {

   iDeXORed[k]=iMymessage[k]^iBuffer[k+1];

   }

  iDeXORed=ETrue;

 }

  if(iDeXORed)

   {
```

```
_LIT8(Str,"DeXORed Message:");

TBufC8<20> iMessageNews(Str);

textResource3=HBufC::NewLC(20);

textResource3->Des().Copy(iMessageNews);

iLog.LogL(*textResource3);

CleanupStack::PopAndDestroy(textResource3);

textResourceDeXORed=HBufC::NewLC(20);

textResourceDeXORed->Des().Copy(iDeXORed.
    Left(KChatTextBufLength));

iLog.LogL(*textResourceDeXORed,mark);

CleanupStack::PopAndDestroy(textResourceDeXORed);

... }
```

In the code listing above, note that a node receiving a XORed packet will perform a XOR operation with the previously sent message (which has been stored as a local copy). By doing this, the message from the other device can be extracted from the message. This message can then be stored locally and shown to the end-user.

Further details on the implementation of the XORChat application are beyond the scope of this chapter, but it is relevant to mention that *Symbian active objects* have been used for socket transactions, and that an S60 GUI has been implemented to support the chat service. In Figure 8.5 we show some screenshots of the application.

The screenshots in Figure 8.5 show the main features of the application. In the upper left screenshot we see how, by pressing the *Start XorChat* button, the application is started. As XORChat starts up, a socket is initialized for UDP datagram communications and the device starts listening for incoming broadcast messages. The user can now select to write a text message to another user on the network, for example 'Hi, how do you do?' (see the upper right screenshot in Figure 8.5). Before sending the message, an access point must be chosen (see the lower left screenshot). In our tests we used an Adhoc 802.11g link, but the application was also successfully tested on an infrastructure WLAN network.

The lower right screenshot depicts what the user can see on the phone screen. The first line shows the message the user sent to his friend, and the third line shows the XORed message that was received from the relaying node. After performing a XOR operation with his own previously sent message, the message from his friend appears and can be displayed on the screen, in this case 'Fine thanks, you?'.

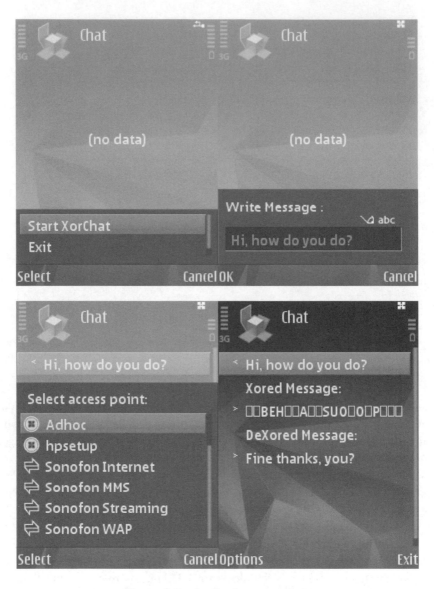

Figure 8.5 Application screenshots

This simple implementation could be extended to a more complex scenario where more device pairs are chatting together, or a single chat in which more than two users are chatting together. In both cases the idea would be to have one single relay node in the middle. The relay node could collect all the messages and XOR them together in one single packet to be sent in broadcast. The difference in these cases is that all the nodes need to have knowledge about $N - 1$ packets received from the N nodes in the chat to obtain the information of the missing packet. The benefits of network coding will obviously increase with the number of entities involved.

This implementation has demonstrated that network coding using XORing can function on modern commercially available mobile phones. It also shows that the number of packets to be transmitted in the scenario presented can be reduced. This property is important in wireless networks, because it can increase throughput and decrease energy consumption compared with the simple relay technique, which is important for communication systems and especially for battery-driven devices such as mobile phones.

8.7 Outlook

A wide range of applications can benefit from the use of network coding. To demonstrate this, we will present such scenarios in this section and explain how they can benefit from network coding. Furthermore, network coding can be implemented with alternatives to XORing, which opens the way for even more applications. The properties of one such alternative method and its applicability will briefly be presented and discussed.

Consider a wireless broadcast network with several nodes that are dispersed randomly geographically. Each node can receive and transmit packets to and from the nearby nodes. As all nodes are not directly connected, some form of routing is obviously necessary to enable all nodes to communicate with all other nodes. In this network there exist pairs where one node is the source and the other is the sink (see Figure 8.6). Such a network can be made up of laptops, smartphones, or similar devices typically found in offices, airports, and public areas. The flows could be, but are not restricted to, file transfers, audio/video streaming sessions, IM chats, or voice over IP.

As can be seen in Figure 8.6, several of the packet flows intersect each other, and each intersection represents a potential coding possibility. Let us assume that the pairs s3, t3 and s4, t4 cannot communicate directly, and that node 2 therefore forwards packets to enable communication. Firstly, s3 and s4 each broadcast a packet, and both packets are received by 2. Because t4 is close to s3, it will also be able to receive this packet, and the same holds for t3 and s4. Hence, if 2 encodes the packets received from s3 and

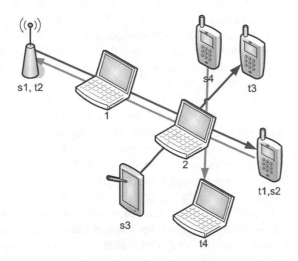

Figure 8.6 A wireless network containing pairs of devices that exchange packets

s4 and broadcasts the resulting packet, both t3 and t4 will receive this packet and be able to decode the packet they need. More intersecting flows can increase the number of packets that can be coded together, which may lead to an increased throughput.

In a real network, such flows will stop and start, and the nodes might move around within the network or be completely removed from the network. Thus, there are a number of practical problems that must be solved before network coding can be deployed in this type of network. Such a solution is presented in [5], where a test bed is implemented and benchmarked in a large wireless network. The authors propose approaches to performing and optimizing coding in a real network and demonstrate that network coding can achieve impressive performance gains in such a scenario.

Network coding can also be used to optimize error correction in reliable wireless broadcast networks. Consider a small broadcast network where a source s1 broadcasts 10 packets to three receivers t1, t2, and t3. In this case we assume a conservative packet error probability of 10% for all three receivers, and thus the most likely event will be that all receivers will receive nine out of the 10 packets. Packet losses are typically assumed to be uncorrelated, and the receivers will therefore most likely lose different packets. With the traditional approach, s1 would have to retransmit each of the three lost packets; with the use of network coding instead, this can be reduced to one packet transmission only. The source encodes all 10 packets and transmits the resulting packet, and thus each of the receivers can decode the encoded packet with its nine received packets and will reconstruct the packet it did not receive. In this example, the benefit of network coding will increase as the number of receiving nodes increases.

Another related application is the self-repairing cluster. Consider the aforementioned example, but now the source cannot retransmit packets – maybe the delay from the source to the receivers is too long, or maybe the receivers do not have any feedback channel to the source. In this case the receivers cannot rely on error correction from the source; instead, the receivers in the cluster must repair any errors themselves. In the traditional case the receivers must transmit three packets to correct all three errors. With network coding, two of the receivers can encode all nine of their received packets and broadcast the resulting packet. This will enable all three receivers to decode the packet they have lost. In fact, if one of the receivers has lost two packets, it will be able to recover both missing packets. This approach can also reduce the complexity of the necessary error correction system, which is beneficial, as cooperative systems tend to be very complex.

A more advanced alternative to XORing, for implementation of network coding, is linear network coding. We will not explain linear network coding in detail here, but instead provide a short introduction that hopefully will induce the reader to seek more knowledge on this topic. Essentially, linear network coding is performed by adding linear combinations of the packets, which means that each packet is first multiplied by a unique constant. Thus, all packets available at the encoding node are coded together, which is contrary to XORing where generally only a subset of packets are encoded together. The reason for this is that with XORing there is only one way in which all packets can be coded together, while in linear network coding there are many such combinations. Galois field (GF) arithmetic is typically suggested for implementation of linear network coding. This mathematical construct is also frequently used for cryptography. In fact, network coding by XORing can be thought of as a special case of linear network coding where the GF(2) is used. Random linear network coding is a form of linear network coding that is often proposed for implementation of file transfers or streaming in real-life networks [6]. The main benefit of this approach is that, from a set of N original packets, any N packets encoded with random linear network coding can be used to reconstruct the original file or stream. Furthermore, packets can easily be recoded within the network, which guarantees maximal data dispersion throughout the network. The main disadvantage is that an overhead is added to all packets, which in some cases can be significant. Another important property is that random linear network coding is not well suited for mixing of streams, such as the example in Figure 8.6. Instead, it is best suited for correction of errors in reliable wireless sessions.

This chapter has introduced network coding with the use of XORing and provided examples that illustrate how network coding is performed and how it can be beneficial. A proof of concept implementation has been presented that should make the reader able to implement network coding in his/her application of choice. Finally, examples for deployment are given, and alternative forms of network coding are briefly discussed.

References

[1] Ahlswede, R., Cai, N., Li, S.Y.R., and Yeung, R.W., 'Network Information Flow', *IEEE Transactions on Information Theory*, **46**(4), 2000, 1204–1216.

[2] Wallis, W.D., *'A Beginner's Guide to Graph Theory'*, Springer, New York, NY, 2007.

[3] Yeung, R.W. and Zhang, Z., 'Distributed Source Coding for Satellite Communications', *IEEE Transactions on Information Theory*, **45**(4), 1999, 1111–1120.

[4] *'The Network Coding Home Page'*. Available at: https://hermes.lnt.e-technik.tu-muenchen.de/DokuWiki/doku.php?id=networ/%k_coding:bibliography_for_network_coding. Extensive (250+) but incomplete list of publications related to network coding.

[5] Katti, S., Rahul, H., Hu, W., Katabi, D., Medard, M., and Crowcroft, J., 'Xors in the Air: Practical Wireless Network Coding', in *Proceedings of the 2006 Conference on Applications, Technologies, Architectures, and Protocols for Computer Communications (SIGCOMM'06)*, Pisa, Italy, 11–15 September 2006, ACM Press, New York, NY, 2006, pp. 243–254.

[6] Ho, T., Koetter, R., Medard, M., Karger, D., and Ros, M., 'The Benefits of Coding over Routing in a Randomized Setting', in *Proceedings of the IEEE International Symposium on Information Theory (ISIT'03)*, Pacifico Yokohama, Kanagawa, Japan, 29 June–4 July 2003.

9

Mobile Social Networking – Beyond the Hype

Bertalan Forstner
Budapest University of Technology and Economics, bertalan.forstner@aut.bme.hu
Imre Kelényi
Budapest University of Technology and Economics, imre.kelenyi@aut.bme.hu

9.1 Introduction

With the web 2.0 revolution, applications that declared themselves as harnessing the power of individuals' social networks moved to the Internet. These networks represent people connected to each other by specific types of relationship, such as friendship, common school or profession, or even similarity in hobby, taste, etc. According to Wikipedia,[1] mobile social networking is social networking where one or more individuals of similar interests or commonalities converse and connect with one another using the mobile phone.

The evolution of smartphone technology, combined with the fact that the smartphone is regarded as being a more personal and intimate device than the desktop computer, means that social networking applications transition well to a mobile environment. A phone typically accompanies the user throughout the day – it may remain switched on during the night and is present when the user interacts with other people during the day.

As well as increased connection with the user, the developments in smartphone hardware offer all kinds of possibility for novel applications to integrate social networking, with 3G, WLAN, high-quality camera, larger colour display, or GPS services now fairly commonplace on mobile.

Therefore, we believe that *social networking on mobile phones* is not only a buzz term for today's technology enthusiasts but also provides real possibilities to users.

---

[1] http://en.wikipedia.org/wiki/Mobile_social_network

Mobile Peer to Peer (P2P)   Edited by Frank H. P. Fitzek and Hassan Charaf
© 2009 John Wiley & Sons, Ltd

In this chapter we will firstly present the background to a couple of projects from our institute (the Department of Automation and Applied Informatics, Budapest University of Technology and Economics), to give some idea of how this power can be harnessed by useful, innovative, or just entertaining applications. We will then discuss an example social networking application to investigate the idioms from the programmer's point of view. Most of the institute's projects can be accessed from the research area of our web page [1].

The first project is called Myth (MeetYouThere) and is a meeting organizer that helps in finding the optimal place and time for meeting participants. People usually take the same routes to travel to work, school, the shops, etc. They usually pass the same way at around the same time, each day or each week periodically. On a GPS-enabled phone, these routes can be recorded. Sofware that records location can start to make decisions based on the probability of the user taking a particular route. When a meeting is to be scheduled by people who do not mind sharing the necessary information, the MeetYouThere application can calculate and propose the time and location for the meeting that are optimal for the participants, based on their calendars and recorded route data. This is a social application that can hardly be implemented on desktop computers because they are tied to the desk. MeetYouThere is written in C++ for Symbian OS.

The next idea is a typical who-is-who for mobile phones, with a slight twist. The rules of *Smiwle* (Figure 9.1) specify that a relationship between two participants can be confirmed when a common photograph of them is uploaded and the parties declare that they are both visible on that photo. What is more, the photos can contain more than just two people, allowing users to upload this 'evidence of relationship' from social happenings such as at parties, on excursions, in the classroom, etc. All these pictures result in a useful photo album that helps to verify identity and to establish contact with people who are genuinely connected through some event or meeting. Since the majority of smartphones come equipped with a camera, it makes sense to develop our application on a Symbian OS phone. The run time chosen to host our application is Nokia's *WidSets*

Figure 9.1   Smiwle! in action

technology,[2] which provides a good match for our requirements. The completed widget can be deployed most easily from the WidSets library.

Being a University, we have the opportunity to design a social mobile application where the participants are all programmers. This gave us the idea to define a common, social homework to a group of students of our mobile programming course. Sometimes students try to cheat by cooperating in the completion of homework assignments. However, in this study, cooperation was encouraged. The desired application was a role-playing game (RPG) written in Python for the S60 platform (PyS60), and therefore we called it HomeWoRPG. Each student implemented a 'framework' program according to the specifications to manage the movement and activity of the hero, the main character, on the map. The tiles of the map contain 'challenges', each of them developed by a different student as a dynamic PyS60 module downloaded and executed on-the-fly by the framework when the player accepts the specific challenge. The challenges include creative and classic microgames ranging from the classic hangman, bomberman, or scorched earth to the creative 'mixer shaking' or tomato-bowling ones.

In this chapter we will introduce a distributed file-sharing network client implementing the Gnutella protocol. We have called this *Symella*. However, the connections in an unstructured protocol such as Gnutella are often selected randomly, which means that these links do not represent any similarity in the fields of interests of the users, so a query for any data must be passed from node to node several times before the content is found. Therefore, we will investigate a simple way of utilizing metadata to connect people who share common interests. On this occasion we want to find others who share the same musical taste as our user. For this reason we will design and implement a higher-level network layer as a generic Gnutella protocol extension. We will concentrate on communication programming; readers interested in the whole application can visit the Symella project home page to follow the latest developments.

9.2   Gnutella and GGEP

From the communication programming point of view, this chapter is mainly about implementing an advanced protocol and its extensions over sockets. Therefore, it is essential to understand the Gnutella protocol. Do not be put off by the thought of learning a new protocol, since the basic protocol consists only of a couple of message types without significant payload.

The first Gnutella client was released in 2000 by Nullsoft. This piece of software made it possible to query for and retrieve files shared at any computer employing the client application. The latest Gnutella protocol version is 0.6 [2]. However, a couple of protocol extensions exist owing to the flexible general Gnutella extension protocol (GGEP). The basic Gnutella network consists of a large set of users running Gnutella clients. A client has to bootstrap at start-up and find at least one other client to connect to. Then it obtains addresses of other active clients and tries to connect to them until a specific maximum number of connections is reached. When connected, the user can send out search messages to each node to which it is connected. The message contains keywords, for example, words from the title of the searched file. Each node forwards the requests to the other nodes to

---

[2] http://www.widsets.com/

which it is connected, until the message reaches a predefined hop distance from the query issuer; the distance is called the time-to-live (TTL) parameter.

If a node finds a match to the search keywords, then it sends back the details of the hit to the query issuer. The replies are sent back through the same route of nodes on which the original message arrived. Once received, the issuer and the content owner can negotiate over the file download method. Clients sitting behind a firewall can request the target node to push the content to the requester; otherwise, the file download can begin directly. Advanced Gnutella clients may also support swarming, which means that, if a file is found at multiple nodes, then the query issuer can start downloading different parts of the given file in parallel in order to load balance and increase the download speed.

On account of problems with scaling the service, the ultrapeer system was introduced. This divides the peers into two categories:

- Ultrapeers are the backbone of the network: they are stable clients with ample resources.
- The leaf nodes, which have sparse resources or short uptime, connect to them. An ultrapeer only forwards a query to a leaf if, according to the result of a negotiation with the query routing protocol, it believes the leaf can answer it.

A disconnecting node may save all the addresses of the nodes that it came to know during connection in order to ease the connecting method next time.

The original Gnutella protocol employs five different packet types:

- *Ping*: to discover hosts on the network and ensure heartbeat of connected hosts.
- *Pong*: a reply to the Ping message.
- *Query*: to search files that match keywords.
- *QueryHit*: a reply to the Query message.
- *Push*: to request the download of a file found by a firewalled node.

These messages can be extended with one or more GGEP blocks. The Gnutella clients must recognize the existence of the extensions, even if they cannot process them. This ensures that clients supporting special features can cooperate smoothly with standard clients supporting other extensions or no extension at all. When the nodes connect, they can negotiate over the extensions they support in the headers of the handshaking messages.

The Gnutella messages consist of a message header and a payload. The payload for each message type has a standard structure, which can be optionally completed with the GGEP block. The header contains a message identifier (16 bytes), the type of the message, the TTL and hop number values of the message, and then the length of the contained payload in 4 bytes. The values are given in Table 9.1.

9.3 Finding Peers

Since Gnutella is a distributed system, there is an obvious question: how can we find the nodes participating in the network if there is no coordinating central server? When first connecting to the network, the client needs some help from the user. There are so-called web caches with well-known addresses. These contain IP addresses of probably

Table 9.1   Header structure

Bytes	Description
0–15	Globally unique ID (GUID)
16	Type of the message
17	TTL value
18	Hop number
19–22	Payload length

active nodes. However, this solution goes against the concept of a fully distributed network. When making subsequent connections, the client should use the *host cache*, a local database with a couple of hundred addresses of peers. This list is populated with the address information obtained from the web caches and Pong or QueryHit messages while the user was connected the first time. By storing as many potential addresses as possible, it is likely that one of these will still be active during the next connection.

During the handshaking process, nodes may send special headers that contain addresses of other peers or ultrapeers that they found active in the network. There are also other concepts such as that of the UDP host cache, but these are not dealt with in this book.

9.3.1   Host Cache

The host cache in the Symella application is implemented by the CSAHostCache class. (All Symella engine classes have the prefix 'SA'.) The classes of the project[3] are located mostly in a file that uses the class name. It differentiates between four kinds of host cache. Peers that are declared as ultrapeers or leaves (for example, by the handshaking headers) are inserted in the iUltrapeers and iLeaves pointer arrays; otherwise, the address goes to the iUnindentifiedNodes array. If the client can successfully connect to an ultrapeer or unidentified node, the host cache promotes it by placing it in the iWorkingNodes array.

The constructor of the CSAHostCache class calls the LoadHostCachesL() function, which loads all of the four types of host cache address from a file. The control class of Symella (CSAControl) has a timer that from time to time checks whether there are enough active connections (the desired number can be set by the user). If not, it initiates a connection to a node in the working nodes array in the host cache. If there are no such nodes available, then firstly it tries the ultrapeers array and then the unidentified nodes.

9.3.2   Web Caches

The web caches help the bootstrapping process by providing addresses of previously active hosts. Web caches have well-known addresses and therefore can be found easily by the clients. They can provide both host addresses if the http request is sent with the 'hostfile = 1' GET parameter, and addresses of other web caches if the parameter is 'urlfile = 1'. The response from the host cache should contain 10–20 lines of address and port information, each in a separated line, in the usual format.

---

[3] http://symella.aut.bme.hu

In the Symella software package, the class CSAGWebCache is responsible for dealing with web caches. It implements both the MHTTPSessionOpenObserver and the MHTTP-TransactionCallback interfaces. The constructor parameters declare whether the class should initiate a hostfile or an urlfile request. The address of the web cache is also set. The available web caches are provided by the preferences class.

After construction, the CSAControl class starts the HTTP transaction on the CSAGWebCache by calling StartTransactionL(), which in turn opens the HTTP session via the network manager class. If successful, the request is initiated in the callback function as follows:

```
void CSAGWebCache::HTTPSessionOpenedL(TBool aResult,
    RHTTPSession& aHTTPSession)
  {
  //in case of success
  if (aResult)
    {
    // Parse string to URI (as defined in RFC2396)
    TUriParser8 uri;
    uri.Parse(*iUri);

    // Get request method string for HTTP GET
    RStringF method = iSession.StringPool().StringF(HTTP::EGET,
      RHTTPSession::GetTable());

    // Open transaction with previous method and parsed uri.
    // This class will receive transaction events in MHFRunL
    // and MHFRunError.
    iTransaction = iSession.OpenTransactionL(uri, *this,
        method);

    // Set headers for request; user agent and accepted
          //content type
    RHTTPHeaders hdr =
          iTransaction.Request(). GetHeaderCollection();
    SetHeaderL(hdr, HTTP::EUserAgent, KUserAgent);
    SetHeaderL(hdr, HTTP::EAccept, KAccept);

    iConnecting = ETrue;
    iTimeoutCounter = KConnectTimeout;
    // Submit the transaction. After this the framework will
    // give transaction events via MHFRunL and MHFRunError.
    iTransaction.SubmitL();
    }
  else
```

```
        //opening failed
        {
        iRunning = EFalse;
        SetFailed();
        iControl.ConnectionObserver()->ModifyWebCacheL(
        MSAConnectionObserver::EError);
        }
    }
```

The iUri member variable is set according to the web cache address obtained by the constructor. After submitting the transaction as an asynchronous request, the transaction can succeed or fail, and the appropriate callback function is called. However, the server may also produce errors as it fails, which will be indicated in the response status code. According to the standards, the 200 status code means that everything has gone OK. Only in this case are we interested in the response body. The appropriate part of MHFRunL() is shown next:

```
void CSAGWebCache::MHFRunL(RHTTPTransaction aTransaction,
    const THTTPEvent& aEvent)
  {
  switch (aEvent.iStatus)
    {
    case THTTPEvent::EGotResponseHeaders:
      {
      iConnecting = EFalse;
      // HTTP response headers have been received. Use
      // aTransaction.Response() to get the response.

      // Get HTTP status code from header (e.g. 200)
      RHTTPResponse resp = aTransaction.Response();
      TInt status = resp.StatusCode();

     if  (status != 200)
        {
        SetFailed();
        Cancel();
        break;
        }
      }
      break;

    case THTTPEvent::EGotResponseBodyData:
      {
      [...]
```

In case of errors, we should implement some other functionality according to the status code. If the error seems permanent, for example '404 Not found', then we had better fire the web cache address from our list. The `SetFailed()` function notifies the user interface about the error situation, and the `CSAControl` class initiates another request to a new web cache.

When we get a part of the response body data, we copy the content to a buffer (`iReceiveBuffer`). The return value of the `GetNextBodyPart()` method of the `MHTTP-DataSupplier` class indicates whether this is the last chunk of the body, but it is more appropriate to rely on the `ESucceeded` event as an indicator that the whole amount of data was received. The return value of `GetNextBodyPart()` can miscount that the received chunk is not the last one when a multipart response arrives without a content length field:

```
case THTTPEvent::EGotResponseBodyData:
  {
  iConnecting = EFalse;
  // Part (or all) of response's body data received.

  // Get the body data supplier
  MHTTPDataSupplier* body = aTransaction.Response().Body();
  TPtrC8 dataChunk;

  // GetNextDataPart() returns ETrue, if the received part
  //is the last one.
  const TBool isLast = body->GetNextDataPart(dataChunk);

  if (iReceiveBuffer)
    {
    iReceiveBuffer = iReceiveBuffer->ReallocL(
        iReceiveBuffer-> Length() + dataChunk.Length());
    iReceiveBuffer->Des().Append(dataChunk);
    }
  else
    iReceiveBuffer = dataChunk.AllocL();

  // Always remember to release the body data.
  body->ReleaseData();
  }
  break;
```

At this point we have the response of the server in `iReceiveBuffer` as host addresses separated by new-line characters. We receive the `ESucceeded` event, which means that we can start analysing the results. In the function body, we look for the new-line separators with the help of the `TLex` class. When found, we expect that there is a host cache address in the given line, and give it to `ParseHostFileL()` in order to extract the IP address and port from it. At the end, we save the modified host cache to the disk:

```
case THTTPEvent::ESucceeded:
  {
  iConnecting = EFalse;
  iResult = ESucceeded;

  iControl.ConnectionObserver()->ModifyWebCacheL(
    MSAConnectionObserver::EConnected);

  _LIT8(KEndOfLine,"\n");
  TInt offset = 0;
  TInt index = 0;
  TPtr8 buf(iReceiveBuffer->Des());
  TLex8 lex(iReceiveBuffer->Des());

  // number of hosts returned by the webcache
  TInt hostCount = 0;

  //check if there is a finished row in the buffer
  while ( lex.Peek() )
    {
    lex.Mark();
    TChar c = lex.Peek();

    while (c && (c != '\n'))
      {
      lex.Inc();
      c = lex.Peek();
      }

    if (c == '\n')
      {
      if (ParseHostFileL(lex.MarkedToken()))
        hostCount++;
      lex.Inc();
      }
    else
      break;
    }

    if (iRequestType == EHostFileRequest)
    iControl.HostCache().SaveHostCacheL();
```

```
        aTransaction.Close();
        iRunning = EFalse;

        if (hostCount > 0)
        PREFERENCES->MoveWebCacheToTopL(*iFullWebcacheAddress);
        }
      break;
```

In `ParseHostFileL()` we exploit the host or web cache address from the descriptor. In the case of a hostfile request, we search for the semi-colon that separates the IP address and the port number. `TInetAddr` helps in deciding whether the IP address has a valid format, and with a `TLex` we can also check whether the port is an integer. If these are both all right, we add the host as unidentified to the host cache.

In the case of web cache addresses, we regard each row as a web cache address and add it directly to our web cache list on the disk:

```
TBool CSAGWebCache::ParseHostFileL(const TPtrC8 aBuf)
  {
  TBool correctIP;
  TInetAddr addr;
  TBuf8<30> ip;
  //helper
  TBuf<30> ip2;
  TBuf8<8> port;
  //port2 is integer
  TUint port2;
  TLex8 lex2;
  //semicolon position
  TInt separ;
  TInt portlength;

  if (iRequestType == EHostFileRequest)
    {
    if ((separ=aBuf.Find(_L8(":")))!=KErrNotFound)
      {
      correctIP = ETrue;
      //split the string to ip and port
      ip = aBuf.Left(separ);
      ip2.Copy(ip);
      //Because buf can be e.g. "&ERROR: Client returned
      //too early".
      //We cannot assume the right part to be max 8 bytes.
      portlength = aBuf.Length() - separ - 1;
      if(portlength>8) portlength = 8;

      port = aBuf.Right(portlength);
```

```
     lex2.Assign(port);
     if (lex2.Val(port2) != KErrNone) correctIP = EFalse;
     if (addr.Input(ip2) != KErrNone) correctIP = EFalse;
     if (correctIP != EFalse)
       {
       addr.SetPort(port2);
       //add the ip to the hostcache
       iHostCache->AddUnidentifiedL(addr);

       //modify got address count
       iReceivedAddresses++;
       iControl.ConnectionObserver()->SetWebCacheAddressCountL(
         iReceivedAddresses);

       return ETrue;
       }
     }
   }
 else
   //webcache addresses
   {
   TLex8 lex(aBuf);
   lex.Mark();

   while ((lex.Peek() != 0) && (lex.Peek() != '\r'))
     lex.Inc();

   if (lex.MarkedToken().Length() > 0)
   PREFERENCES->AddWebCacheL(lex.MarkedToken(),
     PREFERENCES->WebCacheCount());
   return ETrue;
   }

 return EFalse;
}
```

One missing point is to deal with the cases where the HTTP transaction fails. In this case we simply notify the user interface observer in order to let it display the error to the user. We also set the web cache as failed in order to let the control class know that another transaction to a different web cache should be initiated:

```
case THTTPEvent::EFailed:
  {
  iConnecting = EFalse;
  SetFailed();
```

```
    iControl.ConnectionObserver()->ModifyWebCacheL(
    MSAConnectionObserver::EError);

    aTransaction.Close();
    iRunning = EFalse;
    }
    break;
```

9.4   Connecting to Random Peers

Now that we have addresses of candidate peers, it is time to connect to them. In Gnutella, this is done by a handshaking process. We have a CSANode class that represents such a connection. A part of its definition is as follows:

```
class CSANode : public CSocketBase
   {
   public:
   enum TNodeState
      {
      ENotConnected = 0,
      EResolving,
      EConnecting,
      EHandshaking,
      EGnutellaConnected,
      EClosing
      };

   CSANode(CSAControl& aControl, CNetworkManager* aNetMgr);
   ~CSANode();
   void ConnectL(const TInetAddr& aAddr);
   void CloseL(const TDesC8& aReason, TBool aSendBye = EFalse);
   inline TBool IsUltrapeer();
   inline const TInetAddr& RemoteAddress();
   inline TNodeState State();

   private: // from CSocketBase

   void OnReceiveL();
   void HandleReadErrorL();
   void HandleWriteErrorL();

   // from MSocketOpenObserver
   void SocketOpenedL(TBool aResult, RSocket& aSocket);
```

```
void OnTimerL();
void ParseHandshakeL(const TDesC8& aBuf);
static TInt ReadHeaderFieldName(TLex8& aLex, TPtrC8&
    aHeaderName);
TInt ParseHeaderXUltrapeer(TLex8& aLex);
TInt ParseHeaderXTryUltrapeersL(TLex8& aLex);
TInt ParseHeaderRemoteIP(TLex8& aLex);
void ChangeState(TNodeState aState);

private:

CSAControl& iControl;
RHostResolver iResolver;
TNameEntry* iNameEntry;
TNodeState iState;
TInetAddr    iRemoteAddress;
//... some parts not shown here
};
```

When the callback of the timer in the CSAControl class finds that the number of out-bound connections is less than a predefined number, it instantiates new CSANodes and calls their Connect() function with an address from the host cache. CSANode derives from CSocketBase, a class wrapping the methods of sockets such as connecting, sending data, calling a callback with the data received, etc. The status of the connection of the node is stored in a variable of type TNodeState. When starting the connection, it is set to EConnecting, followed by the EHandshaking status. This latter is again a connection phase, but at a higher network level. From this point, it is our application's duty to handle the handshaking process of the Gnutella protocol, parsing the incoming messages and sending the appropriate answers. The handshake starts with the line 'GNUTELLA CONNECT/0.6', followed by non-vendor-specific capability headers (for example, the version of GGEP supported) in '<Field name>: <Value>' form. The other party replies with a status code: 'GNUTELLA/0.6 200 OK' if everything is fine. It also sends its capabilities in the reply headers. The initiating node can then accept the negotiated parameters again with a 'GNUTELLA/0.6 200 OK'. In each case, the end of the block of headers is marked with a double <cr><lf>.

In Symella, this handshaking process is started in the RunL() function when the connecting request is returned without errors. At the same time, the CSANode class starts listening on the socket. When the reply is sent by the other peer, the OnReceiveL() function is called back and the incoming headers are parsed as follows:

```
void CSANode::OnReceiveL()
  {
  switch (iState)
    {
    case EHandshaking:
      {
```

```
        // checking for buffer owerflow (handshake failed)
        if ( (iRecvBuffer->Size() < KMaxHandshakeBufferSize))
          {
          _LIT8(KHandshakeHeadersEnd, "\r\n\r\n");
          //double <cr><lf>
          TInt offset;
          TPtr8 buf(iRecvBuffer->Ptr());

          //check if the remote side has finished transfering
          if ( (offset = buf.Find(KHandshakeHeadersEnd) )
               != KErrNotFound )
            {
            offset += 4;
            //Here we should check the real answer of the
            //other party
            ParseHandshakeL(buf.Left(offset));
            iRecvBuffer->Delete(0, offset);
            }
          }
        else
          // handshake failed
          {
          //node is not a good choice as ultrapeer neither
          //is working
          iHostCache->DegradeUltrapeerL(iRemoteAddress);
          iHostCache->DegradeWorkingNodeL(iRemoteAddress);
          CloseL(KHandshakeBufferOwerflow);
          }
        }
        break;

    case EGnutellaConnected:
        {
        //some code goes here later to parse the incoming
        //messages
        }
        break;

  default:
    break;
  }
 }
```

If we are in the handshaking state, and the reply fits our buffer, we should parse the
headers from line to line to find if the connection is OK (200), and to work with the

other pieces of information the peer has sent us. If the handshake fails, we store this information in the host cache. The descriptor containing the header lines is passed to the function `ParseHandshakeL()`. In the following snippet, we concentrate only on a few headers (the rest can be found on the project home page). From the field values, we set up the properties of the CSANode class. We can see that the answer is sent by the `SendL()` function, which is inherited from the RSocketBase. It requires the data to be sent as an 8-bit descriptor:

```
void CSANode::ParseHandshakeL(const TDesC8& aBuf)
  {
  _LIT8(KGnutella, "GNUTELLA/");
  _LIT8(KGet, "GET ");
  _LIT8(KHandshakeGnutella200Ok, "GNUTELLA/0.6 200 OK\r\n");
  _LIT8(KHandshakeInvalid, "Invalid handshake");
  _LIT8(KHandshakeEnd, "\r\n");
  _LIT8(KHandshakeFieldXTryUltrapeers, "X-Try-Ultrapeers");
  _LIT8(KHandshakeInvalidProtocolVersion,
      "Handshake failed, invalid protocol version");
  _LIT8(KHandshakeHeaderParsingFailed,
      "Handshake failed, invalid headers");
  _LIT8(KHandshakeErrorLeafMode,
      "GNUTELLA/0.6 503 In leaf mode\r\n");

  //If not a gnutella handshake
  if (aBuf.Left(9).Compare(KGnutella) != 0)
    {
    CloseL(KHandshakeInvalid);
    return;
    }

  TLex8 lex(aBuf);

  // Extracting protocol version, we only accept 0.x where
  // x is higher then our version (currently 6)
  lex.Inc(11); // GNUTELLA/0.~6~
  lex.Mark();
  TInt version;
  if ((lex.Val(version) != KErrNone) ||
    (version < KGnutellaProtocolVersion))
    {
    CloseL(KHandshakeInvalidProtocolVersion);
    return;
    }

  TBool connectAccepted = EFalse;
  lex.Inc();
```

```
lex.Mark();
//Looking for the answer code, we expect 200
while (lex.Peek().IsDigit()) lex.Inc();
_LIT8(K200, "200");
if (lex.MarkedToken().Compare(K200) == 0)
  {
  connectAccepted = ETrue;
  }
else
  {
  lex.Mark();
  while (lex.Peek() !='\r') lex.Inc();
  iLog->WriteLineL(lex.MarkedToken());
  }
TChar tempchar;
//Proceeding to the first header
while (tempchar = lex.Get() != '\n' && tempchar != 0)
  {
  }
if(tempchar==0)
//invalid input stream
return;

lex.Mark();
TPtrC8 fieldName;
TBool parsingFailed = EFalse;
//Parsing all the headers
while(lex.RemainderFromMark().Compare(KHandshakeEnd) != 0)
  {
  //Trying to get the next header name
  if (ReadHeaderFieldName(lex, fieldName) != KErrNone)
    {
    parsingFailed = ETrue;
    break;
    }

  // Header X-Try-Ultrapeers:
  if (fieldName.CompareF(KHandshakeFieldXTryUltrapeers) == 0)
    {
    //This function tries to exploit the IP adress values
    if (ParseHeaderXTryUltrapeersL(lex) != KErrNone)
      {
      parsingFailed = EFalse;
      break;
      }
```

```
    //... LEAVING OUT SOME OTHER HEADERS, SEE PROJECT WEBPAGE


   //proceeding to the next header
   while (tempchar = lex.Get() != '\n' && tempchar != 0);

 lex.Mark();
  } // while

if (parsingFailed)
  {
  CloseL(KHandshakeHeaderParsingFailed);
  iHostCache->RemoveUltrapeer(iRemoteAddress);
  }
else
  {
  if (connectAccepted)
    {
    //We're leaf so we should only connect to an
    //ultrapeer
    if (iUltrapeer)
      {
      SendL(KHandshakeGnutella200Ok);
      SendL(KHandshakeEnd);

    // We are connected to the node!
    ChangeState(EGnutellaConnected);
    CTR->ConnectionObserver()->SetStateL(

   iRemoteAddress,MSAConnectionObserver::EConnected);
    //The first ping packet
    PACKETPARSER->SendPingPacketL(*this);
    }
  else
    // disconnect, sorry, we are in leaf mode
    {
    SendL(KHandshakeErrorLeafMode);
    SendL(KHandshakeEnd);
    CloseL(_L8("In leaf mode"));
    iHostCache->SetLeafL(iRemoteAddress);
    }
  }
else
  {
  CloseL(_L8("Connection rejected"));
  iHostCache->DegradeUltrapeerL(iRemoteAddress);
```

```
          iHostCache->DegradeWorkingNodeL(iRemoteAddress);
        }
    }
}
```

The implementations of the functions that do the processing of the value fields of the individual headers (such as `ParseHeaderXTryUltrapeersL()` in our example) are straightforward. It is also worth mentioning that, in the case of protocols that often employ strings in communication, the use of string pools is widespread.

9.5   Protocol Messages

Once connected, the peers start to send and receive the protocol messages as described in the introduction of Gnutella. We have already seen that the nodes have a callback function called `OnReceiveL()`, which is called every time data through the socket of the given node is received, and that they also employ a `SendL()` function (through `RSocketBase`) that sends the raw 8-bit descriptor data to the address of the node. However, parsing the descriptors that contain the incoming messages and composing the others to send out are not the responsibility of the node. Instead, we have a class called `CSAPacketParser` that implements the protocol-dependent message handling.

Let us start with the hardest part: receiving and parsing the messages. The `CSANode::OnReceiveL()` in method checks whether the whole message has arrived, and then passes the raw descriptor to the packet parser class. The layout of the message helps, in that the header contains the size of the message. Now we can complete the `OnReceiveL()` function with the missing part:

```
[...]
case EGnutellaConnected:
 {
 // reseting timeout counter - this is needed to check
 //whether the
 //  connection is still alive
 iEllapsedTime = 0;

 // checking if a message header has been received
 //(23 bytes)
 if (iRecvBuffer->Size() >= KMessageHeaderLength)
   {
   TPtr8 buf = iRecvBuffer->Ptr();

   // getting the payload length from the header
   TUint32 payloadLength = (buf[22] << 24) | (buf[21] << 16)
    | (buf[20] << 8) | (buf[19]);

   // if we have a full message then parse it
```

```
    if ((TUint)iRecvBuffer->Size() >= KMessageHeaderLength +
        payloadLength)
    {

    //try to parse the packet
    if (payloadLength == 0)
      PACKETPARSER->ParsePacketL(*this,
          buf.Left(KMessageHeaderLength), TPtrC8());
    else
      PACKETPARSER->ParsePacketL(*this,
        buf.Left(KMessageHeaderLength),
        buf.Mid(KMessageHeaderLength, payloadLength));

    // the message has been processed, we can delete it
    iRecvBuffer->Delete(0, KMessageHeaderLength +
        payloadLength);
    }
  }
 }
 break;
[...]
```

In the snippet, PACKETPARSER is a macro that provides the instance of the packet parser class. The ParsePacketL() function is responsible for deciding which type of the message is present and to extract the data from the header of the message. If the message has a known message type, it passes its parameters and payload to the appropriate message-dependent function. We show only a part of the ParsePacketL() function because the rest looks fairly similar:

```
TInt CSAPacketParser::ParsePacketL(CSANode& aNode,
  const TDesC8& aHeader, const TDesC8& aPayLoad)
  {
  //variables
  TInt result = KErrNone;

  //header variables
  TGuid guid;
  TUint8 payloadType;
  TUint8 ttl;
  TUint8 hops;
  TUint32 payloadSize;

  if(aHeader.Length()<25)
    return KErrInvalidFormat;
```

```
//get the message guid
for (TInt i=0;i<16;i++)
  guid.iGuid[i] = aHeader[i];
//get the payloadType (offset=16)
payloadType = aHeader[KPayloadtypeOffset];
//get the ttl (offset=17)
ttl = aHeader[KTTLOffset];
//get the hops (offset=18)
hops = aHeader[KHopsOffset];
//get the payloadSize (offset=19..22)
payloadSize = (aHeader[KPayloadSizeOffset+3] << 24) |
   (aHeader[KPayloadSizeOffset+2] << 16) |
   (aHeader[KPayloadSizeOffset+1] << 8) |
        (aHeader[KPayloadSizeOffset]);

if ((payloadType!=PACKET_PING) && (payloadType!=PACKET_PONG) &&
      (payloadType!=PACKET_PUSH) && (payloadType!=
            PACKET_BYE) &&
      (payloadType!=PACKET_QUERY) && (payloadType!=
            PACKET_QUERY_HIT))
  result = KWrongPayLoadType;

//continue only if there was no error parsing the header
if (result == KErrNone)
  {
  //continue with the correct parsing based on the payloadType
  switch (payloadType)
    {
    case PACKET_PING:
      {
      //handle the ping request
      HandleIncomingPing(aNode,guid,ttl,hops, aPayLoad);
      }
      break;
    case PACKET_PONG:
      {
      //Pong payload variables
      TUint16 port;
      TUint32 ipn;
      TUint32 sharedFiles;
      TUint32 sharedAmount;
      //parse the pong payload
      //port
      port = TUint16((aPayLoad[0]) |  (aPayLoad[1] << 8));
      //ip
```

```
        ipn = (aPayLoad[2] << 24) | (aPayLoad[3] << 16) |
        (aPayLoad[4] << 8) | (aPayLoad[5]);
        TInetAddr ip;
        ip.SetAddress(ipn);
        ip.SetPort(port);
        //shared files
        sharedFiles = (aPayLoad[6]) | (aPayLoad[7] << 8) |
            (aPayLoad[8] << 16) | (aPayLoad[9] << 24);
        //shared amount
        sharedAmount = (aPayLoad[10]) | (aPayLoad[11] << 8) |
          (aPayLoad[12] << 16) | (aPayLoad[13] << 24);

      //handle the incoming pong
      HandleIncomingPong(aNode, ip, port, sharedFiles,
          sharedAmount, aPayLoad);
      }
      break;

  [...]

    default:
      {
      //Not Gnutella supported header, or out of sync
      result = KWrongPayLoadType;
      }
      break;
    }
  }

//return with the result
return result;
}
```

It can be seen that `ParsePacketL()` prepares the message for the message-dependent functions, having the naming form `HandleTYPEPacket()`. These functions should modify the internal state of our client, for example, marking a connection as being alive, or checking the query hits for one of our queries.

Let us examine the two message-handling methods that are also shown in the previous code part. The first one is very easy: it creates a simple reply message to an incoming Ping, and sends it out. This means that, besides the functions that interpret the incoming messages, we need separate ones to compose and send out other, new or reply messages. Therefore, in the next example we will also show the implementation of one of the Send*TYPE*Packets(): the `SendPongPacket()`, for Pong messages. As each outbound message should have the message headers, it is straightforward to create a common function called `CreatePacketHeader()`:

```
void CSAPacketParser::HandleIncomingPing(CSANode& aNode,
    const TGuid&
    aGuid, const TUint8 aTTL, const TUint8 aHops,
        const TDesC8& aPayLoad)
{
//send replies with the same guid, and larger TTL than
//the source ping and with 0 hops
TInetAddr ip(0, PREFERENCES->GetPort());
CTR->NetMgr()->Address(ip);
SendPongPacket(aNode,aGuid,ip,PREFERENCES->GetPort(),0,0);
}
```

Firstly, we get our IP address and port, as the Pong message should contain them. The IP is queried from the network manager and the port from the preferences class. The method `SendPongPacket()` has six parameters: the node to which the message should be sent, the identifier of the message (which should be the same as that of the Ping), the IP address and the port number of our client, and the number and size of shared files. As we are working in leaf mode, let us examine the two message-handling methods (`HandleIncomingPing` and `HandleIncomingPong`), which are set to 0.

The method to create the packet header is dealt with next. It copies the header to the first descriptor parameter. Note that the size of the message payload should already be known at this point:

```
void CSAPacketParser::CreatePacketHeader(TDes8& aBuffer,
    const TGuid&
            aGuid, const TUint8 aFunction, const TUint8 aTTL,
    const TUint8
            aHops, const TUint32 aPayLoad)
{
//initialize
aBuffer.Zero();
//put the Guid in it
for (TInt i=0;i<16;i++)
aBuffer.Append(aGuid.iGuid[i]);

//put the message type in it
aBuffer.Append(aFunction);

//write TTL
aBuffer.Append(aTTL);

//write Hops
```

```
aBuffer.Append(aHops);

//write Payload size
aBuffer.Append((aPayLoad & 0x000000FF));
aBuffer.Append((aPayLoad & 0x0000FF00) >> 8);
aBuffer.Append((aPayLoad & 0x00FF0000) >> 16);
aBuffer.Append((aPayLoad & 0xFF000000) >> 24);
}
```

The payload of the Pong message is given in Table 9.2.

The IP address is in big-endian format. The size of the message header is constant at 26 bytes, and therefore, without GGEP extension, the size of a Pong message is 36 bytes. Having this information, the implementation of `SendPongPacket()` is straightforward:

```
void CSAPacketParser::SendPongPacketL(CSANode& aNode,
    const TGuid& aGuid,const TInetAddr& aInetAddr,const
        TUint16 aPort,
    const TUint32 aSharedFiles,const TUint32 aSharedAmount)
{
//count the packet length = 36 + 1 (0x00 closing char)
TInt length = 37;
HBufC8 * msg = HBufC8::NewL(length);
CleanupStack::PushL(msg);
TPtr8 pong = msg->Des();

CreatePacketHeader(pong,aGuid,PACKET_PONG,KMaxTTL,0,
        14+ggep->Length());

//copy the port to the descriptor
pong.Append(aPort & 0x00FF);
pong.Append((aPort & 0xFF00) >> 8);

//copy the address to the descriptor
TUint32 address = aInetAddr.Address();
pong.Append((address & 0xFF000000) >> 24);
pong.Append((address & 0x00FF0000) >> 16);
pong.Append((address & 0x0000FF00) >> 8);
pong.Append((address & 0x000000FF));

//copy the shared files counter to the descriptor
pong.Append((aSharedFiles & 0x000000FF));
pong.Append((aSharedFiles & 0x0000FF00) >> 8);
pong.Append((aSharedFiles & 0x00FF0000) >> 16);
pong.Append((aSharedFiles & 0xFF000000) >> 24);
```

```
//copy the shared kb-s counter to the packet
pong.Append((aSharedAmount & 0x000000FF));
pong.Append((aSharedAmount & 0x0000FF00) >> 8);
pong.Append((aSharedAmount & 0x00FF0000) >> 16);
pong.Append((aSharedAmount & 0xFF000000) >> 24);

//send
aNode.SendL(pong);

CleanupStack::PopAndDestroy(msg);
}
```

These three functions were used to answer an incoming Ping message. The interpretation of the answer-type messages (Pong or QueryHit) is slightly different. Firstly, we have to make sure that the message is for us by checking the identifier of the message. For this reason, we should take care to store the GUIDs of messages initiated by us. This is very important in the case of QueryHit messages. Secondly, we do not need to send out a message in reply to these packets. Thirdly, we should utilize the content part of the message, for example, updating the heartbeat variables for the connection or parsing the query hits and showing them to the user in order to enable downloads.

Here, we are going to deal with the easiest reply message, the Pong. In the following code part, we give the address information to the host cache as an unidentified node. It is the host cache's duty to check whether this address is already known. Later in this chapter, we will complete this function to extract and interpret the protocol extensions:

```
void CSAPacketParser::HandleIncomingPong(CSANode& aNode,
    TInetAddr& aInetAddr, const TUint16 aPort,
        const TUint32 aSharedFiles,
    const TUint32 aSharedAmount, const TDesC8& aPayLoad)
{
//put the ip to the unidentifiedList
aInetAddr.SetPort(aPort);
CTR->HostCache().AddUnidentifiedL(aInetAddr);
}
```

Table 9.2 Message structure of the Pong message

Bytes	Field	Description
0–1	Port number	The host accepts messages on this port
2–5	IP address	The address of the host
6–9	Number of shared files	How many files are shared by the host
10–13	Amount of shared files	The total amount of shared files in kbytes
14–	Optional GGEP block	Extension block, see later

9.6 Putting Intelligence into the Peer Selection

9.6.1 The Simplest Way: Fetching the Musical Genre

At this point we know how to find and connect to random peers. However, with a little effort we can introduce a little intelligence into the process. Our idea is well known from everyday life. In real life, people's human relations are not random as in a standard, decentralized P2P network. Relations are organized along common interests such as similar job, hobby, taste, and other characteristics. We use the term 'fields of interest' to describe these kinds of category. From these fields of interests it follows that these people form certain groups. Communication on the organizing topic is more frequent within these groups than with other people. Therefore, the search for files in a Gnutella network can be more efficient if we connect to those people who share similar fields of interest and therefore are more likely to have relevant documents.

Without going into detail, let us just imagine that we can find out the musical taste of the user. This is not very complicated in the case of sharing MP3 files, since they usually have metadata in the form of an ID3 tag. One byte in the ID3 tag represents the musical genre. Based on the tags of the MP3 files stored on the phone, we can gather statistics that may provide an indicator of the user's musical preference. If we supplement the Gnutella protocol with a component that returns the musical taste of a node, then we can decide whether that particular node is similar to us, that is, the two users have the same musical taste. Thinking a bit further, we can also exploit keywords from text documents with a suitable algorithm (the best known of them is the term frequency–inverse document frequency method), and use these keywords in concept hierarchies (taxonomies) to construct a description of the interests of the user. In order to make some sense of the data, there are databases of established hierarchies that can be used to categorize words (such as WordNet for the English language).

In order to use semantic information, we will need a structure to store and deliver information about the fields of interest. These are semantic profiles. In the case of Symella, we designed semantic profiles that can hold any type of concept hierarchy as metadata. However, in our example we will only use them to store the musical genre tags. Therefore, we will not go into the details of programming the profiles; we will just regard them as a descriptor containing serialized data. It is enough to know that there is a class called `CSRLocalProfilesManager` that provides an interface to the semantics-related functions.

9.6.2 Now I Know Who to Connect to!

Concluding all our ideas, we have the following tasks to complete in order to connect to nodes with similar musical taste:

- Collect information on the stored and downloaded MP3 files and build up the profile of the user. We are not going to investigate this subtask here.
- Be able to send our semantic profile as an extension with Pong or QueryHit messages to the other party.
- Be able to recognize and interpret this extension.

- Based on this information, decide whether to connect to the node. The CSRLocalPro-
  filesManager helps to decide this, and the connection is made in the same way as
  described earlier in this chapter.

The change in the communication between peers will be investigated here. More precisely,
we will append the extension to the messages and, on the other side, recognize and
interpret them. Of course, there is no need to attach the profile to all of the messages; for
example, once we are connected to a node, it is no longer interested in our profile.

Let us start with the reply messages. As the extension is the same for both Pong and
QueryHit messages, we will show the modifications in the case of a Pong message. We
should note here that, in order to enable connections to our node, we should run in
ultrapeer mode:

```
void CSAPacketParser::SendPongPacketL(CSANode& aNode,
    const TGuid& aGuid, const TInetAddr& aInetAddr,
        const TUint16 aPort,
    const TUint32 aSharedFiles, const TUint32 aSharedAmount,
    const TInt32 aLevel)
{
HBufC8 * ggep = HBufC8::NewL(0);
//Call the function that composes the extension block
CTR->LocalProfilesManager()->GetReplyGGEPL(ggep);
CleanupStack::PushL(ggep);

//count the packet length = + 1 (0x00 closing char)
const TInt length = 37+ggep->Length();
HBufC8 * msg = HBufC8::NewL(length);
CleanupStack::PushL(msg);
TPtr8 pong = msg->Des();

CreatePacketHeader(pong, aGuid, PACKET_PONG, KMaxTTL, 0,
        14+ggep->Length());
```

From this point, the code that composes the Pong message's body is the same as shown
earlier. The code is structured enough to have a separate function to compose the extension
block. As described earlier, the LocalProfilesManager is responsible for storing the
semantic profiles. Therefore, it is also responsible for serializing the taxonomy into a
descriptor.

At the end of the SendPongPacketL() function, we should append the GGEP extension
obtained from the LocalProfilesManager to the message, and take care of the clean-up
stack. If we would like to add some other extensions, the code can be modified very easily,
with only a slight change to the body of the function:

```
pong.Append(*ggep);

//send
aNode.SendL(pong);

CleanupStack::PopAndDestroy(msg);
CleanupStack::PopAndDestroy(ggep);
}
```

In the next snippet, we will examine the `GetReplyGGEPL(HBufC8 * &aBuffer)` function. From the source of `SendPongPacketL()` we can see that, at the point of calling the function, we do not know about the size of the extension block. Therefore, the caller should provide a buffer that will surely be reallocated. When calling `ReAllocL()` to an `HBufC`, the buffer may move around in memory. Therefore, the function should take a reference to the pointer. In our example, we do not call leaving functions, which makes things somewhat easier.

The implementation for serializing the semantic profile is left out because it is not important from the communication programming point of view. The existence of GGEP extensions is marked with a magic byte `0xC3`. This is followed by any number of extension headers and extension data. The structure of the GGEP extension header is given in Table 9.3.

The flags contain information about the encoding, compression, or size of the extension name and are listed in Table 9.4.

It is important to note that, for protocol implementation reasons, the extension block must not contain `0x0` bytes. Therefore, a special encoding is required, as detailed in

Table 9.3 GGEP extension

Max bytes	Field	Description
1	Flags	Describes the extension, see later
1–15	Extension ID	Unique name of the extension (e.g. "SemPeer")
1–3	Data length	The size of the raw extension data

Table 9.4 Extension of the GGEP

Bit pos.	Field	Description
7	Last extension?	Bit is set if this is the last extension
6	Encoding	Marks if the data is encoded
5	Compression	Marks if the data is compressed
4	Reserved	Reserved for future use
3–0	ID length	Extension ID size (1–15)

the GGEP specification. The functions `Int32ToGGEP()` and `GGEPToInt32()` make the appropriate encoding and decoding. The encoding also ensures that the exact size of the integer is also known:

```
void CSRLocalProfilesManager::GetReplyGGEPL(TInt aLevel,
    HBufC8 * &aBuffer)
  {
  TBuf8<8> temp;
  aBuffer = aBuffer->ReAllocL(12+KProfileRawData);
  TPtr8 ptr = aBuffer->Des();

  //Here we left out the part that fills out the raw data
  //of the extension.
  //In order to get the size of the raw data, we append it
  //first to the buffer by calling lots of ptr.Append(temp);

[...]

  //And now the header of the extension

  TInt rawlength = ptr.Length();
  temp.SetLength(2);
  temp[0]=195;  //magic byte
  //GGEP Flag. Do not add +128 if more extensions would follow.
  temp[1]=7+128;
  ptr.Insert(0,temp);
  //Extension name
  ptr.Insert(2, _L8("SemPeer"));
  //GGEP-encoded the raw size of the extension
  Int32ToGGEP(temp, rawlength);
  ptr.Insert(9,temp);
  }
```

The composition of the extensions and completing the messages are very similar to the other messages. On the other hand, we have to be able to interpret the incoming extensions. We complete the `HandleIncomingTYPE()` functions with the appropriate parts. Considering `HandleIncomingPong()`, we should extend it in order to extract the semantic profile from the extension, if it exists:

```
void CSAPacketParser::HandleIncomingPong(CSANode& aNode,
    TInetAddr&
    aInetAddr, const TUint16 aPort, const TUint32 aSharedFiles,
    const TUint32 aSharedAmount, const TDesC8& aPayLoad)
  {
  //put the ip to the unidentifiedList
```

```
    aInetAddr.SetPort(aPort);
    CTR->HostCache().AddUnidentifiedL(aInetAddr);

    const TInt length = aPayLoad.Length();
    //We will get the semantic profile into this variable
    //if exists.
    CSRReplyProfile* semanticProfile = NULL;
    //The function dealing with reply payloads
    HandlePongPayloadL(aPayLoad.Mid(14), semanticProfile);
    if(semanticProfile != NULL)
      {
      //Check whether we like that connection
      CSRLocalProfilesManager* manager =
          CTR->LocalProfilesManager();
      manager->CheckProfile(semanticProfile, aInetAddr, aPort);
      }
    delete semanticProfile;
    }
```

The function seems fairly simple. However, it holds the most important part of the extension: the one that gets the semantic profile of an unknown node and gives that profile to the `LocalProfilesManager` in order to decide whether it deserves to initiate a connection to that node.

`HandlePongPayloadL()` gets the raw payload from the message and constructs the profile from the serialized data (if it exists). The function `CheckProfile()` compares the profile with the fields of interest of the user, and then initiates the connection in a similar way to the method of getting random addresses from the host cache.

The last task of the implementation of the extension is to write the `HandlePongPay-loadL()` function:

```
TInt CSAPacketParser::HandlePongPayloadL(const TDesC8& aPayLoad,
    CSRReplyProfile* &aSemanticProfile)
  {
  TInt offset=1;
  TInt size=0;
  TInt error=0;
  const TInt length = aPayLoad.Length();

  TInt esize=0; //extension name size
  //Big enough to contain GGEP extension && magic byte 0xC3 is OK
  if(length>10 && aPayLoad[0] == 195)
    //while not the last extension
    do
    {
    //extension name size
```

```
      esize=aPayLoad[1]&15;
      //Checking the ID for our semantic "SemPeer" extension
      if(aPayLoad.Mid(offset+1,esize).Compare(KSemPeer)==0)
        {
        //OK, it is a SemPeer extension
        //extension size
        size = CTR->LocalProfilesManager()->GGEPToInt32L(
          aPayLoad.Mid(offset+1+esize));
        TRAP(error, HandleSemanticProfileGGEPL( aPayLoad.Mid(
          offset+1+esize+size/64+1, size), aSemanticProfile));
        }
      else
        {
          //proceed to the next extension
          offset += 1+esize+size/64+1 +size;
        }
      }
      // do while last extension (the header flag shows it)
      while(length <= offset && aPayLoad[offset]&128 != 128);

   return error;
     }
```

Similarly to the `SendPongPacket()` function, it is simple to complete the function with other extensions. The `HandleSemanticProfileGGEPL()` function gets the serialized profile and constructs the taxonomy structure from it.

9.7 Conclusion

This chapter has investigated social mobile networks. Special attention has been paid to distributed systems. Some idea of how to implement a peer-to-peer protocol, Gnutella, from the handshaking process to communication on the application level has been given. Moreover, with an idea from everyday life, the protocol has been extended: our goal was to reach people who shared similar fields of interest. Thus, we have seen a protocol extension, and, what is more, a standard one, since we have used the means provided by the generic Gnutella protocol extension.

From this chapter, the reader should have learned how communication programming works on the application level, and hopefully will also have gained some idea of how to develop a P2P application using Symbian sockets or HTTP APIs.

References

[1] http://amorg.aut.bme.hu/
[2] http://wiki.limewire.org/index.php?title=GDF

10

Using Location-based Services on Mobile Phones

Péter Ekler
Budapest University of Technology and Economics, peter.ekler@aut.bme.hu
Gábor Zavarkó
Budapest University of Technology and Economics, gabor.zavarko@aut.bme.hu

10.1 Introduction

Location-based services (LBS) are information and entertainment services that make use of the geographical position of the mobile device. Since LBS appeared on mobile phones, they have become more and more popular. The first big success of LBS was navigating turn-by-turn to any address (e.g. iGo [1]), a service that was available in specialized navigation SatNav devices, personal navigation devices (PNDs), and personal digital assistants (PDAs). These navigation-based applications were designed to guide drivers from their current position to a target address by calculating an optimal route and then relaying turn-by-turn instructions both visually and by voice.

Most of these devices are based on global positioning system (GPS) technology, which is a fully functional global navigation satellite system (GNSS). The GPS uses at least 24 medium Earth orbit satellites which transmit precise microwave signals that enable receivers to determine their location, direction, speed, and time.

The great success of GPS-based navigation applications has motivated mobile phone manufacturers to add location awareness to mobile handsets. The two main ways to determine location with mobile phones are as follows:

- *GPS-based location service*: the mobile phone contains a GPS receiver.
- *Cellular-network-based location service*: the mobile device gets the location based on the radio signal delay of the closest cell-phone towers.

Mobile Peer to Peer (P2P) Edited by Frank H. P. Fitzek and Hassan Charaf
© 2009 John Wiley & Sons, Ltd

An additional technique is A-GPS, which make use of cell ID. With the help of these technologies, mobile phones are able to determine their position and expose this to applications and services running on the phone or on the Internet. Examples of services are finding the closest ATM or pharmacy, locating where people are on a map, etc.

This chapter introduces how LBS and mobile peer-to-peer networks can be combined. For mobile peer-to-peer networks, knowledge of where partner entities (other phones that can be involved in a cooperative network) are is very relevant to preparing for upcoming events to build mobile peer-to-peer networks. In this chapter we discuss the technological background of location-based services and we show an implementation of a complete location-based application, called *FindFriends*. FindFriends allows us to search for people on the basis of how far they are from us. Based on this example and the source codes provided in this chapter, we can adapt easier location-based services in peer-to-peer networks.

Section 10.2 will discuss GPS technology and the general concept of location-based services. Section 10.3 will describe API implementation of Nokia S60 [2], and will also give an insight into the location API provided by Java ME on Symbian OS. Section 10.4 will describe the architecture, database structure, and network-handling engine of the FindFriends application. Finally, Section 10.5 will conclude the chapter and propose possible future functionalities to FindFriends.

10.2 Background

In this section we will briefly describe GPS technology and location-based services. GPS helps us to determine our location very accurately: after the receiver has found four satellites, the system works very smoothly. Mobile phones are ideal for location-based services because they are small, portable computers that can perform complex operations based on location information.

10.2.1 GPS-based Positioning

The GPS design originally called for 24 satellites, eight in three circular orbital planes, but this was modified to six planes with four satellites each [3]. Orbital planes are centred on the Earth, not rotating with respect to the distant stars. The orbits are arranged so that at least six satellites are always within line of sight from almost anywhere on the surface of the Earth. Orbiting at an altitude of approximately 20,200 km, each satellite makes two complete orbits each sidereal day. As of March 2008, there are 32 actively broadcasting satellites in the GPS constellation. The additional satellites improve the precision of GPS receiver calculations by providing redundant measurements. They also increase the reliability and availability of the system, even when multiple satellites fail.

After GPS receivers had become small enough, it was possible to build GPS chips in mobile phones, which allow them to determine their current location (Figure 10.1). Mobile phones have several multimedia and networking capabilities that make these devices ideal for location-based services – we just have to think of a simple image upload function from the mobile phone that contains the location where the image was taken.

A GPS receiver uses four or more satellites to calculate its position. Each of them transmits messages that contain the current time and additional parameters to determine the location of the satellite, the general system health, and the predicted location. The

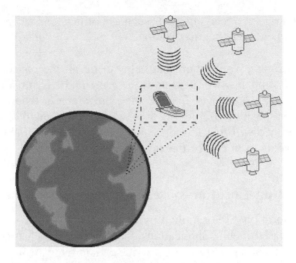

Figure 10.1 GPS receiver in mobile phones

signals travel at the speed of light through outer space (they slightly slow down through the atmosphere). The receivers use the arrival time of the messages to measure the distance to the satellite and determine the position of the receiver with the help of geometry and trigonometry. The results of the calculations are converted into more user-friendly formats such as the combination of latitude and longitude or the position on a map that can be presented to the user.

It is possible to determine position with only three satellites, given that space has three dimensions, but this solution requires the time to be known to a precision of 1 ns, which is far more precise than any non-laboratory clock can provide. Using four or more satellites allows the receiver to solve an overdetermined system of equations to get time as well as geographical position, eliminating the need for a superaccurate clock. In this way, the receiver uses four measurements to compute four variables: x, y, z, and t.

10.2.2 Location-based Services

Location-based services make use of the current position of the specific device. They include services to identify the location of a person or object, such as discovering the nearest ATMs or the whereabouts of a friend or employee. LBS services also include vehicle-tracking systems or even location-based games.

LBS present a completely new business opportunity for application developers, operators, and also content producers. Location information in mobile phones differentiates these types of mobile application from traditional PCs, because several location-based services exploit the fact that they run on a portable device.

Location-based services have several different types, for example:

- *Turn-by-turn navigation*: the goal is to calculate the optimal route to a specific address.
- *Finding someone or something*: locating people on a map displayed on the mobile phone screen or finding people of a certain profession on the basis of current location.

- *Proximity-based services*: receiving alerts such as notifications when one of our friends is close to us or when we pass a gas station.

FindFriends is the example application that helps to tie all the concepts of this chapter together. FindFriends contains two main units, a server and a Symbian C++ client. With the application, we will be able to find people who are less than a specific distance away from our current position. Before Section 10.4 goes into the details of the complete FindFriends solution, we will first introduce the location API available on the Symbian OS, and we will give an example for the Java ME location API.

10.3   Implementing Location-based Services on Mobile Phones

The purpose of the location APIs supplied by Symbian OS v9 is to let developers easily implement location-based mobile applications. Considering the characteristics of mobile devices, the aim of location APIs is to provide a natural way to use location-based information. Basically, the location API is a compact package of classes and interfaces that is easy to use. The three main features that the location API brings to mobile phones are:

- the ability to determine the location of the device;
- the possibility of creating, editing, storing, and retrieving landmarks;
- the possibility of obtaining the orientation of a device.

In this section we will first introduce the location API provided by Symbian OS, after which we will give a brief overview of the location API of Java ME (JSR.179 [4]).

10.3.1   Location API of Symbian OS

Symbian OS provides two different ways to determine the current location of the mobile phone. The '*Quick Recipes Taster*' booklet from Symbian Press [5] gives an example of how to obtain a list of the available positioning technology modules. '*Quick Recipes on Symbian OS*' [6] provides more recipes related to location-based services. In this section we will first explain how to utilize GSM cell-based position via the `CTelephony` class. We will then introduce GPS-based location functions via `RPositionServer` and `RPositioner` classes.

10.3.1.1   Cell-ID-based Location

`CTelephony` is a general class that is able to provide information about the mobile network. This information contains the mobile country code, the mobile network code, the location area code, and the cell ID (unique identification of the cell where the phone is). Unfortunately, we can determine the estimated geographic coordinates from this information only by using a database. As the GSM cells are larger in sparsely populated areas, this method can provide relatively reliable information on the current position only in cities.

In order to obtain cell-based location information, we first have to create a `CTelephony` object, and with the help of the method

```
void GetCurrentNetworkInfo(TRequestStatus &aReqStatus,
  TDes8 &aNetworkInfo
```

we can obtain the network information.

In order to use this class, we need the `etel3rdparty` library, and we also have to use an active object, which is familiar to every Symbian developer. Next, we will give a simple example of using the `CTelephony` class.

The header file should contain the following:

```
#include <Etel3rdParty.h>

// typedef TPckg<TNetworkInfoV1>
//      CTelephony::TNetworkInfoV2Pckg; - package pointer
//      descriptor
CTelephony::TNetworkInfoV1Pckg& iNetworkInfoPkg
CTelephony::TNetworkInfoV1& iNetworkInfo
```

The package pointer descriptor refers to an already existing object (`iNetworkInfo`). It is otherwise used in a similar way to the package buffer descriptor.

Note that we have to include `Etel3rdParty.h` to use `CTelephony`. The following source code demonstrates how we can retrieve the network information with an active object implementation:

```
CMyClass::CMyClass() : iNetworkInfoPkg(iNetworkInfo)
  {
  }


CMyClass::GetCurrentNetworkInfo()
  {
  // iTelephoni is a pointer member instance of CTelephony
  iTelephony->GetCurrentNetworkInfo(iStatus,
    iNetworkInfoPkg);
  SetActive();
  }


CMyClass::RunL()
  {
  // iNetworkInfo contains the information about the network
  // iNetworkInfo.iCountryCode
  // iNetworkInfo.iNetworkId
  // iNetworkInfo.iLocationAreaCode
  // iNetworkInfo.iCellId
  }
```

10.3.1.2   GPS-based Location

Mobile phones with a built-in GPS receiver are able to determine their current position more accurately. Symbian provides the `RPositionServer` and `RPositioner` classes to access the GPS device. These classes also work with active objects.

`RPositionServer` is used to establish the primary connection to the location server. After the primary connection has been established, its handle is passed as a parameter to `RPositioner` in order to create a subsession. The `RPositionServer` class can also be used to discover what position technology modules are available. In mobile phones there are typically one or two modules:

- a network protocol module that the location server uses to obtain location information from the network;
- an A-GPS module that the location server uses to obtain location information from a GPS or A-GPS chipset.

However, this is only required if a client application actually needs to use a particular module. Table 10.1 summarizes the main functions related to position technology modules.

The `RPositioner` class is used to create a subsession with the server in order to obtain the current position. In addition to actually obtaining position information, this class also provides mechanisms for determining the last known position and the general status of

Table 10.1   Functions related to position technology modules

Function	Description

`TInt GetDefaultModuleId(`
`   TPositionModuleId`
`     &aModuleId) const`
	The method obtains the identifier of the default system positioning module.

`TInt GetNumModules(` `   TUint &aNumModules) const`	The method gets the current number of available positioning modules.

`TInt GetModuleInfoByIndex(`
`   TInt aModuleIndex,`
`   TPositionModuleInfoBase`
`     &aModuleInfo) const`
	Return value contains module details specified by the index.

`TInt GetModuleInfoById(`
`   TPositionModuleId aModuleId,`
`   TPositionModuleInfoBase`
`     &aModuleInfo) const`
	Return value contains module details specified by ID.

`TInt GetModuleStatus(`
`   TPositionModuleStatusBase`
`     &aPosModuleStatus,`
`   TPositionModuleId aModuleId)`
`   const`
	This method obtains information about the specified positioning module.

the positioning module, changing how often it wants to receive position updates, as well as identifying itself to the location framework.

To use these functions, the application of course needs the Symbian location PLATSEC capability. Table 10.2 describes the functions of the RPositioner class.

Since getting the position from the GPS takes some time, the methods are asynchronous. We first need to pass an iPosInfo object to NotifyPositionUpdate(). When the position has been acquired, the system calls the RunL() method of the active object, and we can get the position by calling the iPosInfo.GetPosition() function. The current position is stored in a TPosition object which carries other useful information besides the coordinates (Table 10.3).

In order to set special details, we can use the TPositionUpdateOptions class. These details, for instance, can be: refresh interval, timeout (if information does not arrive from a position), maximum permitted age of the desired information (default value is 0), and whether partial updates are accepted (default value is false). The following code snippets demonstrate how we can use the previously introduced classes and methods.

Firstly, we need to declare some variables in the header file:

```
RPositionServer iPositionServer;
RPositioner iPositioner;
TPositionInfo iPositionInfo;
```

Table 10.2 Main functions of the RPositioner class

Function	Description
TInt Open(RPositionServer &aPosServer)	This function creates a subsession with the positioning server.
TInt SetRequestor(CRequestor::TRequestorType aType CRequestor::TRequestorFormat aFormat, const TDesC &aData)	This function sets the requestor of the location information that will be obtained through this subsession.
TInt SetUpdateOptions(const TPositionUpdateOptionsBase &aPosOption)	This method can be used to modify the behaviour of NotifyPositionUpdate() requests.
void NotifyPositionUpdate(TPositionInfoBase &aPosInfo, TRequestStatus &aStat) const	This asynchronous method can be used to obtain position updates.
void GetPosition(TPosition &aPosition) const	This function is used to get the position.

Table 10.3 Functions of the `TPosition` class

Function	Description
`TTime Time() const`	This function retrieves the time information related to the position data.

`TInt Speed(const TPosition`
`    &aPosition,`
`  Treal32 &aSpeed) const`
	This method calculates the horizontal speed between the current position and the `aPosition` parameter, since both contain time information as well.

`TReal32 HorizontalAccuracy()` `  const`	This method retrieves the horizontal accuracy of the coordinate for which it is called.
`TReal32 VerticalAccuracy()` `  const`	This method retrieves the vertical accuracy of the coordinate for which it is called.

`TInt Distance(`
`  const TCoordinate`
`    aCoordinate,`
`  Treal32 &aDistance) const`
	This method calculates the distance between this coordinate and the supplied coordinate.

`TInt BearingTo(`
`  const TCoordinate`
`    &aTargetCoordinate,`
`  Treal32 &aBearing) const`
	This method calculates the bearing from the coordinate to the supplied coordinate.

`TReal64 Latitude() const`	Accessor for latitude.
`TReal64 Longitude() const`	Accessor for longitude.
`TReal32 Altitude() const`	Accessor for altitude.

We can use `RPositionServer` and `RPositioner` objects to determine the location in an active object:

```
iPositionServer = new (ELeave) RPositionServer;
User::LeaveIfError(iPositionServer.Connect());

User::LeaveIfError(iPositioner.Open(iPositionServer));
User::LeaveIfError(iPositioner.SetRequestor(
  CRequestorBase::ERequestorService,
  CRequestorBase::EFormatApplication,
  KRequestorData));

void CMyClass::GetPosition()
  {
  TPositionUpdateOptions updateOptions;
  updateOptions.SetUpdateInterval(KInterval);
```

```
    iPositioner.SetUpdateOptions(updateOptions);
    iPositioner.NotifyPositionUpdate(iPositionInfo, iStatus);
    SetActive();
    }

void CMyClass::RunL()
    {
    // we got the network information in iPositionInfo
    TPosition position;
    iPositionInfo.GetPosition(position);
    //position.Latitude()
    //position.Longitude()

    //Get the next position information
    iPositioner.NotifyPositionUpdate(iPositionInfo, iStatus);
    SetActive();
    }

    // To stop call:
    iPositioner.CancelRequest(EPositionerNotifyPositionUpdate);
```

We can see from the example that determining the position is relatively easy, and the retrieved TPosition contains other useful information about the location.

In this section we have described the main classes of the Symbian OS related to determining location. Next, we will show, with a simple example, how we can use the Location API of Java ME for retrieving the position of the mobile phone.

10.3.2 Location API of Java ME

The location API is defined in JSR 179 [4]. This optional package enables developers to write location-based mobile applications. The API works with the J2ME CLDC v1.1 and CDC configurations. In this section we will introduce the API through an example that demonstrates how we can get the current location of the phone.

Firstly, we need to create a class (MyLocationReader) that helps to retrieve the location from a LocationProvider object. In order to execute this type of request, we have to separate it into a different thread because determining the coordinates takes some time and this task should not hang the whole application:

```
public class MyLocationReader extends Thread {
    private LocationMidlet midlet;

    public MyLocationReader(LocationMidlet aMidlet) {
        midlet = aMidlet;
    }
```

```
  public void run() {
    try {
      midlet.getStringItemLocation().setText(
        "please wait...");
        displayCoordinates();
      } catch (Exception ex) {
        // handle exception
        midlet.getStringItemLocation().setText(
          ex.getMessage());
      }
  }

  private void displayCoordinates() throws Exception {
    // set criteria
    Criteria cr= new Criteria();
    cr.setHorizontalAccuracy(500);
    // get location provider
    LocationProvider lp =
      LocationProvider.getInstance(cr);
    // get location (60 sec timeout)
    Location l = lp.getLocation(60);
    // get coordinates
    Coordinates coord = l.getQualifiedCoordinates();
    if (coord != null ) {
      midlet.getStringItemLocation().setText(
        "\nlatitude: " + coord.getLatitude() +
        "\nlongitude: " + coord.getLongitude());
    } else {
      midlet.getStringItemLocation().setText(
        "Failed to determine location");
    }
  }
}
```

Note that the MyLocationReader class extends the Thread class. In this way it can execute asynchronous location detection without halting the entire application. The displayCoordinates() function is basically the core of the MyLocationReader class. Firstly, we have to create a Criteria object, which is used to indicate criteria for choosing the location provider in the LocationProvider.getInstance() method call. The implementation considers the different criteria fields to choose the location provider that best fits the defined criteria. The main criteria fields are: horizontal accuracy, vertical accuracy, preferred response time, power consumption, allowed cost, requirements for speed and course, altitude, and address info.

After creating the Criteria object, we can ask for a LocationProvider instance, which represents a location-providing module for generating Locations. The current location can be queried from the `LocationProvider` object by calling the `getLoca-tion(int timeout)` method. The result of this method is a `Location` object, which represents the standard set of basic location information.

By calling the `isValid()` method, we can determine whether `LocationProvider` was able to determine the current location correctly. A `Location` object may be either 'valid' or 'invalid'. A valid `Location` object represents a location with valid coordinates, which is the return value of the `getQualifiedCoordinates()` method. An invalid `Location` object does not have valid coordinates, but we can determine why it was not possible to provide a valid `Location` with the `getExtraInfo()` method.

The return value of `getQualifiedCoordinates()` is a `Coordinates` object, which basically represents latitude–longitude–altitude values; they are expressed in degrees using floating-point values.

The following MIDlet implementation demonstrates how we can use the previously introduced `MyLocationReader` class:

```
public class LocationMidlet extends MIDlet
  implements CommandListener {

  private Form locationForm;
  private StringItem stringWelcome;
  private StringItem stringItemLocation;
  private Command getLocationCommand;
  private Command exitCommand;

  private void initialize()
  {
    // create ui
    locationForm = new Form("My location reader");
    stringWelcome = new StringItem(
      "Welcome!","\nThis midlet "+
      "detrmines the coordinates of the device.");
    stringItemLocation = new StringItem(
      "Location:","-");
    locationForm.append(stringWelcome);
    locationForm.append(stringItemLocation);
    // set commands
    getLocationCommand =
      new Command("Get location",Command.SCREEN,0);
    exitCommand = new Command("Exit",Command.EXIT,0);
    locationForm.addCommand(getLocationCommand);
    locationForm.addCommand(exitCommand);
    locationForm.setCommandListener(this);
    // display the form
    getDisplay().setCurrent(locationForm);
  }
```

```
  public Display getDisplay() {
    return Display.getDisplay(this);
  }

  public void startApp() {
    initialize();
  }

  public void pauseApp() {
  }

  public void destroyApp(boolean unconditional) {
  }

  public StringItem getStringItemLocation() {
    return stringItemLocation;
  }

  public void commandAction(Command command,
    Displayable displayable) {
  if (displayable == locationForm) {
    if (command == getLocationCommand) {
      // show location
      stringItemLocation.setText("");
      new MyLocationReader(this).start();
    } else if (command == exitCommand) {
      exitMIDlet();
    }
  }
}

  public void exitMIDlet() {
    getDisplay().setCurrent(null);
    destroyApp(true);
     notifyDestroyed();
  }
}
```

The MIDlet basically displays a form (`locationForm`) that shows the coordinates in a `StringItem` after selecting the 'Get location' menu item. Figure 10.2 shows some screenshots of the `LocationMIDlet`.

By examining the proposed simple examples, we can realize that implementing location-based functions does not require special programming techniques. In subsequent sections we will introduce the FindFriends application, which demonstrates a complete location-based service implementation.

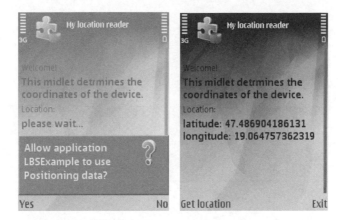

Figure 10.2   User interface of the proposed LocationMIDlet

10.4   FindFriends Example Application

This section will give an example of how to implement a location-aware application. We will describe a complete application, which will help us to understand how to create mobile applications that use the GPS coordinates supplied by the mobile phone.

The proposed application is entitled *FindFriends*. As the name suggests, the application realizes a small location-based social network in which people are connected if they are within a specific distance from each other. The basic idea is to create a relatively simple application that makes it possible to find other people near to us. As a second step, we can send short messages or make phone calls to people whom the application has found within its specified search range.

The architecture of the FindFriends solution comprises three main parts: a website (server), a background database, and a mobile client. The clients send their location information and profile to the website, which in turn exposes this information to the other users. In this section we will follow a top-down approach to describing the example application. Firstly, we will describe individual use cases of FindFriends. Secondly, we will discuss the overall architecture of FindFriends, after which we will give an insight into the client and the server applications. Finally, the network communication with the website will be described.

10.4.1   Use Cases

The server application is central to the network and is responsible for storing the information provided by the mobile clients. It stores information in a database and sends the current list of the users to other clients in the network.

Apart from providing this simple service, the FindFriends server has a fully fledged web user interface where we can see the list of the users and their profile, as well as their current location on a map. The server also stores the location history of each user (if the user permits it) so that we can follow their path. Figure 10.3 summarizes the main functions of the server.

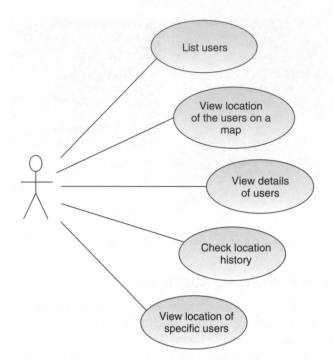

Figure 10.3   Functions of the FindFriends server

Each of the functions is elaborated below:

- *User list.* On the user list, we can see the current list of those who are exposing their profile and current location to the server. Each user is represented by a box where we can check their location on a map and the complete location history related to them.
- *Location of the users.* The server also allows us to check the current location of the users on an easy-to-use map.
- *Details of users.* We can see the user profile in the user detail view, including their current location with a timestamp, which shows the last update time.
- *Location history.* The server stores the location history (current location and timestamp) of each user, and thus it is possible to check where the user was at a specific time.
- *Location of specific users.* The user detail view also contains an embedded map that shows the last location of the user.

The main objective of the Symbian-based mobile client is to determine the current position of the device (as described in the previous sections) and send this information to the server. Other functions allow downloading and listing of user profiles, and it also makes it possible to search for others, based on a range value parameter. This value filters users whose distance from us is larger than the specified range. Figure 10.4 summarizes the functions of the mobile client.

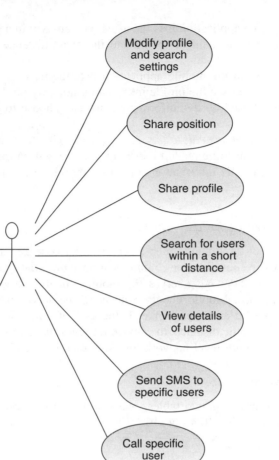

Figure 10.4   Functions of the FindFriends mobile client

The details of the functions are as follows:

- *Profile and search settings.* The settings view on the mobile device makes it possible to set personal information such as first name, last name, nickname, phone number, gender and personal notes. If necessary, the application uploads these together with the location information. The settings view also allows the upload frequency (in seconds) and the maximum distance to look for other people (in metres) to be specified.
- *Send current position to the server.* The client calculates its current GPS position in the previously described manner and uploads the coordinates to the server.
- *Send profile.* When the client sends its location to the server, the message also contains the current profile of the user, and thus the profile information on the server is always up-to-date.

- *Search for users.* The application lists the users who are within a specific distance from us. The list items also contain the name and the exact distance of the other users in metres.
- *Details of users.* When the mobile application lists the users, it also downloads their profile, and thus we can see the profile information not only on the website but also on the mobile phone. Based on this information, we can choose to call a specific nearby user.
- *Send SMS, or make a phone call to the selected user.* This function enables an SMS to be sent or a phone call to be made to specific users, based on data sent by the server, provided that their profile information contains a mobile phone number.

10.4.2   The Design of FindFriends

FindFriends consists of three main units: a server, a database and any number of mobile clients. The server is responsible for communicating with a database where the relevant information is stored, and it also serves the mobile clients. Besides this, it also has a web-based user interface. Mobile clients connect to the server periodically to transmit their location information and user profile. If the user of a mobile device wants to look for persons within a specific distance, the device retrieves the list of users from the server. Figure 10.5 shows the high-level network topology of FindFriends.

10.4.2.1   Database Structure

The background database has two tables, one storing the user profile and the other the location information. Tables 10.4 and 10.5 show the structure of these database tables.

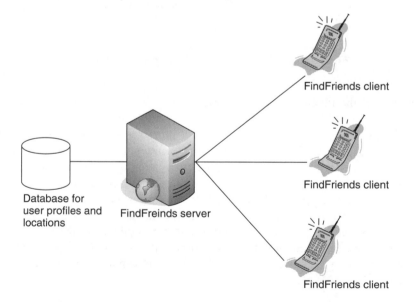

Figure 10.5   The high-level network topology of FindFriends

Table 10.4 Persons table

Column name	Type
imei	varchar(30)
fullname	varchar(45)
nickname	varchar(45)
phonenumber	varchar(45)
birthday	varchar(45)
sex	int(10)
note	varchar(200)

Table 10.5 Location table

Column name	Type
lid	int(10)
imei	varchar(30)
longitude	double
latitude	double
timestamp	timestamp

The *persons* table stores the user profiles, where the primary key of the table is the IMEI number of the mobile device, which is unique for each mobile phone. (However, testing the application in an emulator can prove to be difficult because the IMEI number is often set to 0 in this environment, so multiple emulated devices share the same number.)

The *location* table stores the location information supplied by the mobile phones. The key is a unique but otherwise arbitrarily chosen value, which we call *lid*. Recall that FindFriends has a location history function so that in this case the IMEI is not a good choice for a primary key, because multiple location data can belong to a single mobile phone.

The location table also has a timestamp column, which shows when the specific location was uploaded so that the latest coordinate of the device can easily be determined.

10.4.2.2 The FindFriends Server

The FindFriends server is a PHP-based web application that communicates with a database and handles requests from the mobile clients. There are two types of request (in terms of HTTP): one occurs when the mobile client sends its profile and current location, and the other when it asks for the list of the users.

In this section we will introduce the user interface of the web application, and the network communication will be described later. As the source code of the website would demand a fair amount of paper, we will not discuss it in detail.[1] However, in order to understand the concept of FindFriends, it is important to show its user interface. Figure 10.6 shows the start page of the website.

---

[1] The FindFriends website is available at http://www.freeweb.hu/findfriends/

Figure 10.6   FindFriends start page

The left side of the website contains the main menu, where we can reach the individual functions:

- *Start page*. Navigates to the start page of the website.
- *Persons*. Lists the persons including their personal details, current location and location history.
- *Instructions*. Describes what the main functions of FindFriends are and how we can use them.
- *Download*. Here we can download the mobile client directly to our mobile phone.
- *About*. This site contains basic information about the application and the authors.

If we select the *Persons* menu, we can see the list of those users who have uploaded their profile and location information (Figure 10.7). In this view we can see basic information about a person, such as their name, phone number and the last time their position was updated. A small box (so-called person card) belongs to each person and contains links to the current position, profile details and location history related to the specific person.

If we select the globe icon, a map appears on which we can see the last known location of the person. By selecting the person details icon, we can see the profile and the location of the selected person (Figure 10.8). Since the person card shows a timestamp, we can see when this position was uploaded.

Figure 10.7 List of users

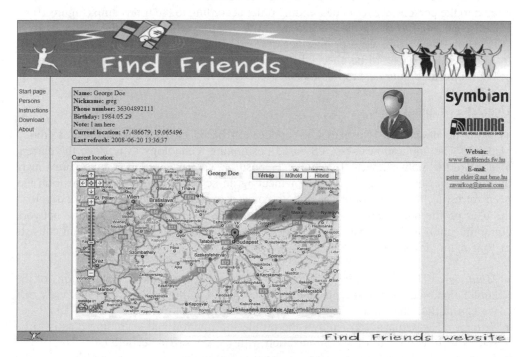

Figure 10.8 Person detail view

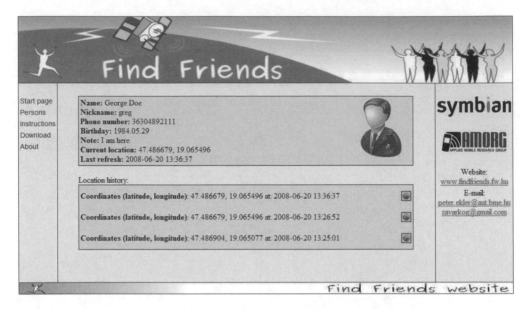

Figure 10.9   Location history of the selected user

The person detail icon shows the detail profile of the selected person as received from his/her mobile device. If we select the location history icon, a list of known locations related to the person appears in descending order according to the timestamp (Figure 10.9). It is also possible to check these locations on the map by clicking on the globe icon.

Basically, the web-based user interface of FindFriends allows the information uploaded from the mobile phone to be checked in a simple browser interface. In this way, we can provide information to desktop computer users as well.

10.4.2.3   Mobile Client

The mobile client is a Symbian C++ application based on the Nokia S60 3rd edition platform. The application uses GPS-based positioning technology to retrieve the current location of the mobile device. To retrieve the position, we have used the method previously introduced in Section 10.3.1.2, by implementing an active object. Once the position has been retrieved, the active object is able to connect to the FindFriends server and upload the user profile and location information. The source code that implements the network communication will form part of the next section. The FindFriends mobile client consists of four main views, which are as follows:

- *Main view*. This is an initial view from where we can reach the main functions of the application, such as the settings and the user list. In addition, it is from this view that we can initiate the communication with the FindFriends website.
- *Settings*. The settings view allows the profile information and searching details to be set, as well as the rate of synchronization with the server (in seconds).
- *User list*. On the user list we can see the list of those users who are within a specific distance from us. The list shows their name and their exact distance calculated from

the GPS coordinates. This view also allows an SMS to be sent to the selected user, or we can even call this user if the profile contains a phone number.

- *User detail view.* In this view, we can see the detailed profile of the selected user, and this view also contains the location of the user in GPS coordinates.

If we start the application, the main view appears (Figure 10.10) where a label shows the connection status. After we have selected the 'Connect' menu, the application starts the GPS routine and tries to determine its location. If the application succeeds, it uploads the profile and the coordinates to the server. After a successful data exchange with the server, a 'Users' menu appears where we can ask for the list of users.

If we select the 'Settings' menu, the settings view appears (Figure 10.11).

Figure 10.12 shows the user list. We can see how each list item contains the full name of the user and the exact distance from our device.

Figure 10.10   Main view

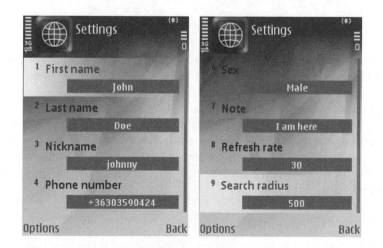

Figure 10.11   Settings view

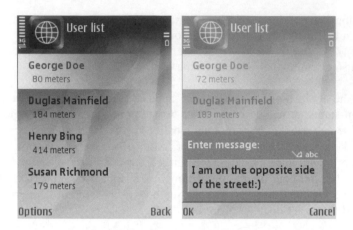

Figure 10.12 User list

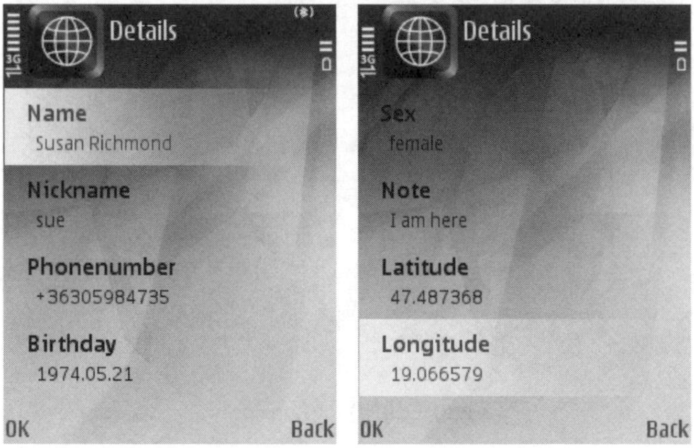

Figure 10.13 User detail view

If we select a user on the list, we can initiate a phone call or send a new SMS message by selecting the appropriate command from the 'Options' menu. The 'Options' menu also contains a 'Details' command from where we can reach the details view which shows the profile of the selected user and this user's last known coordinates (Figure 10.13).

Even though the mobile client is a simple application, the proposed functions are likely to become very popular. Nowadays, people are using their mobile devices more frequently, and the capabilities of the devices are improving rapidly as well. In the next section we will discuss the part of the source code of the FindFriends mobile client that implements the communication with the server.

10.4.3 Network Communication

The communication between the mobile client and the FindFriends server is marshalled via simple HTTP requests. The *upload.php* web page on the server side is responsible for receiving the user profile and user coordinates. This data is expected in the following URI format:

```
http://www.freeweb.hu/findfriends/upload.php?imei=123&fullname=
NAME&nickname=NICK&phonenumber=PHONE&birthday=BIRTHDAY&sex=
1&note=NOTE&lat=47.4866&long=19.0654
```

The mobile client builds the URL with the proper parameters and connects to the server, which parses the parameters and stores them in the database.

In order to fetch the list of users, the mobile client has to connect to the following address:

```
http://www.freeweb.hu/findfriends/getpersons.php
```

After successful connection, the list of users is downloaded in the following format:

```
IMEI&NAME&NICK&PHONE&BIRTHDAY&SEX&NOTE&LONG&LAT#NEXT_USER#...#
```

As can be seen above, ampersands (&) delimit data items, and number signs (#) separate data records.

A real-world protocol would not send data in clear text, since names, phone numbers and location are very sensitive data. The format used above is for illustrative purposes for understanding the concepts; in a real application, security and privacy would have to be considered very carefully.

The HTTP Client API of the Symbian OS provides a client interface for applications to use the HTTP protocol for communicating with HTTP servers over the Internet. By using the API correctly, the application can operate as an HTTP 1.1 compliant client. There are five key concepts used in the API: sessions, transactions, headers, data suppliers (with a signalling mechanism) and filters.

A *session* encapsulates the HTTP activity of the client over the duration of the client's execution. The corresponding class is provided by the `RHTTPSession` resource class. `RHTTPTransaction` exposes a *transaction* object, which basically represents an interaction between the HTTP client and an HTTP server. The *header* portion of the requests and responses is provided by the `RHTTPHeaders` class; the header values can contain zero or more fields, which are used to transmit information using standard HTTP headers between the HTTP client and server. The main bulk of data is in the body portion of the requests and responses. Data is read and written by the HTTP stack using the `MHTTPDataSupplier` mix-in, which developers must supply. The HTTP stack request data to be sent in small chunks and the mix-in abstraction allow the data to be sent over the HTTP to originate from a descriptor in memory or be generated on the fly by the HTTP client application. Signalling between the client and the transport layer ensures that body data is only consumed or emitted at a rate that the client can support. This means that clients can assemble the body of their requests piece by piece, have each piece transmitted only when it is ready, and be signalled when the transmission is complete. *Filters* (not shown on the example) are add-on modules that provide additional behaviour to a session beyond the simple request–response transaction described above.

Next, we will show how the FindFriends mobile client communicates with the website. The `CHttpTransport` class is responsible for connecting to the server and sending/retrieving relevant data. The source code of the header is as follows:

```
#ifndef HTTPTRANSPORT_H_
#define HTTPTRANSPORT_H_

// Include files
#include <http\mhttpdatasupplier.h>
#include <http\mhttpsessioneventcallback.h>
#include <http\mhttptransactioncallback.h>
#include <http\rhttpsession.h>
#include <http\rhttptransaction.h>
#include <http\thttpevent.h>

class CHttpTransport:
  public CBase,
  public MHTTPSessionEventCallback,
  public MHTTPTransactionCallback,
  public MHTTPDataSupplier
  {

public:
  static CHttpTransport* NewL(const TInt aSocketServer,
    const TInt aSocketConnection);
  ~CHttpTransport();

protected:
  CHttpTransport();
  void ConstructL(const TInt aSocketServer,
    const TInt aSocketConnection);

public:
  void SendRequestL(const TDesC8& aUrl,
    const TDesC8& aData);

public: // from MHTTPSessionEventCallback
  virtual void MHFSessionRunL(
    const THTTPSessionEvent& aEvent);
  virtual TInt MHFSessionRunError(TInt aError,
    const THTTPSessionEvent& aEvent);

public: // from MHTTPTransactionCallback
  virtual void MHFRunL(RHTTPTransaction aTransaction,
    const THTTPEvent& aEvent);
```

```
   virtual TInt MHFRunError(TInt aError,
     RHTTPTransaction aTransaction,
     const THTTPEvent& aEvent);

public: // from MHTTPDataSupplier
   virtual TBool GetNextDataPart(TPtrC8& aDataPart);
   virtual void ReleaseData();
   virtual TInt OverallDataSize();
   virtual TInt Reset();

private: // data members
   RHTTPSession iHttpSession;

   HBufC8* iData;
   HBufC8* iReceivedData;
   };

#endif /*HTTPTRANSPORT_H_*/
```

The CHttpTransport class contains several methods because it implements three interfaces (we have indicated with comments which function is from which interface). The SendRequestL() method is responsible for connecting to a remote party, based on a URL, and sending the relevant parameters. The received data is available via the MHFRunL() method when it is ready for processing. The CHttpTransport class is implemented as follows:

```
#include <Uri8.h>
#include <HttpStringConstants.h>
#include <http\mhttpdatasupplier.h>
#include <http\rhttpheaders.h>
#include <http\rhttpresponse.h>

#include "HttpTransport.h"

// Two-phased constructor
CHttpTransport* CHttpTransport::NewL(const TInt aSocketServer,
   const TInt aSocketConnection)
   {
   CHttpTransport* self = new (ELeave) CHttpTransport();
   CleanupStack::PushL(self);
   self->ConstructL(aSocketServer, aSocketConnection);
   CleanupStack::Pop(self);
   return self;
   }
```

```
// Destructor
CHttpTransport::~CHttpTransport()
  {
  iHttpSession.Close();  // close the HTTP session object
  delete iData;          // delete sent and received datas
  delete iReceivedData;
  }

// Constructor
CHttpTransport::CHttpTransport()
  {
  }

// Perform second phase construction of this object
void CHttpTransport::ConstructL(const TInt aSocketServer,
  const TInt aSocketConnection)
  {
  iHttpSession.OpenL(); // opens the HTTP session object
  RHTTPConnectionInfo connctionInfo =
    iHttpSession.ConnectionInfo();
  connctionInfo.SetPropertyL(iHttpSession.StringPool().
    StringF(HTTP::EHttpSocketServ,
    RHTTPSession::GetTable()), aSocketServer);
  connctionInfo.SetPropertyL(iHttpSession.StringPool().
    StringF(HTTP::EHttpSocketConnection,
    RHTTPSession::GetTable()), aSocketConnection);
  }

// Example functionof how to send an HTTP request
void CHttpTransport::SendRequestL(const TDesC8& aUrl, const
    TDesC8& aData)
  {
  RStringF aMethod;
  TUriParser8 url;
  url.Parse(aUrl);
  RHTTPTransaction trans = iHttpSession.OpenTransactionL(
    url, *this, iHttpSession.StringPool().StringF(
    HTTP::EPOST, RHTTPSession::GetTable())));

  iData = aData.AllocL();
  trans.Request().SetBody(*this);

  trans.SubmitL();
  }
```

```
void CHttpTransport::MHFSessionRunL(
        const THTTPSessionEvent& /*aEvent*/)
  {
  }

TInt CHttpTransport::MHFSessionRunError(TInt /*aError*/,
        const THTTPSessionEvent& /*aEvent*/)
  {
  return KErrNone;
  }

void CHttpTransport::MHFRunL(RHTTPTransaction aTransaction,
    const THTTPEvent& aEvent)
  {
  switch (aEvent.iStatus)
    {
    case THTTPEvent::EGotResponseBodyData:
      MHTTPDataSupplier* body =
        aTransaction.Response().Body();
        TPtrC8 dataChunk;
        if (iReceivedData == NULL)
          iReceivedData = HBufC8::NewL(0);

        // get the next received data. return value is
        // true when this is the last part
        body->GetNextDataPart(dataChunk);
        // alloc new descriptor
        iReceivedData = iReceivedData->ReAllocL(
          iReceivedData->Des().Length() +
          dataChunk.Length());
        iReceivedData->Des().Append(dataChunk);
        body->ReleaseData();
        break;
      case THTTPEvent::EResponseComplete:
        break;
      case THTTPEvent::ESucceeded:
        aTransaction.Close();

        // we can process here the received data
        if (iReceivedData)
          {
          delete iReceivedData;
          iReceivedData = NULL;
          }
        break;
```

```
      case THTTPEvent::EFailed:
        aTransaction.Close();
        break;
      default:
        break;
    }
  }

// Called when the MHFRunL leaves
TInt CHttpTransport::MHFRunError(TInt /*aError*/,
       RHTTPTransaction /*aTransaction*/,
       const THTTPEvent& /*aEvent*/)
  {
  return KErrNone;
  }

// The HTTP engine calls this method to
// fetch the next data part,
// which will be sent to the server
TBool CHttpTransport::GetNextDataPart(TPtrC8& aDataPart)
  {
  if (iData)
    aDataPart.Set(iData->Des());
  else
    aDataPart.Set(KNullDesC8);
  return ETrue;
  }

// The HTTP engine calls this method, when we can release
// the data we passed to the
// GetNextDataPart method before
void CHttpTransport::ReleaseData()
  {
  if (iData)
    {
    delete iData;
    iData = NULL;
    }
  }

// we should return here the size of the data,
// which will be sent
TInt CHttpTransport::OverallDataSize()
  {
  if (iData)
```

```
     return iData->Des().Length();
  else
     return KErrNotFound;
  }

// Resets the state of the HTTP transport layer
TInt CHttpTransport::Reset()
  {
  if (iData)
     return KErrNone;
  else
     return KErrNotFound;
  }
```

Note a comment in the MHFRunL() method that indicates where we can process the data retrieved from the server. In order to use the class, we first have to instantiate it:

```
iTransport = CHttpTransport::NewL(iSocketServer.Handle(),
       reinterpret_cast <TInt> (&iIapConnection->Connection())));
```

In subsequent code, we can use this class to connect to the server and send or retrieve data.

In our last example, we will describe the implementation of the DownloadPositionsL() method which connects to the FindFriends server and downloads the list of all users:

```
void CFindFriendsContainer::DownloadPositionsL()
  {
  // allocate buffer to URL
  // URL length is 69 bytes with IMEI (15 characters)

  HBufC8* url = HBufC8::NewLC(69);
  url->Des().Append(_L8(
    "http://www.freeweb.hu/findfriends/getpersons.php?imei="));

  url->Des().Append(*iImei);
  iTransport->SendRequestL(*url, KNullDesC8);
  iTransportState = EDownloadPositions;
  CleanupStack::PopAndDestroy(url);
  }
```

Note that the implementation of the DownloadPositionsL() method also shows how we can add a parameter to the connection request. The server provides the list of users only to those mobile phones that have previously uploaded their profile at least once. Consequently, the IMEI parameter is required to make a decision on the server side as to whether the phone has a right to download the list of the users.

Although the CHTTPTransport class has been used as part of the FindFriends mobile client, its generality allows it to be reused in other applications that require HTTP communication.

In the following example we will show how location is fetched from LBS and attached to the request:

```
void CFindFriendsContainer::PositionCompleteL(TPositionInfo&
   aPositionInfo, TRequestStatus& aStatus)
   {
   TPosition position;
   aPositionInfo.GetPosition(position);
   TRealFormat realFormat;
   realFormat.iPoint = '.';

   // for advanced URI manipulation we should use the CUri8
   // class, which is under InetProtUtils library
   // you can find an example in Chapter06
   HBufC8* url = HBufC8::NewLC(1024); // enough for all data
   url->Des().Append(_L8(
      "http://www.freeweb.hu/findfriends/upload.php?imei="));
   url->Des().Append(*iImei);
   url->Des().Append(_L8("&fullname="));
   url->Des().Append(*iFullName);
   url->Des().Append(_L8("&nickname="));
   url->Des().Append(*iNickName);
   url->Des().Append(_L8("&phonenumber="));
   url->Des().Append(*iPhoneNumber);
   url->Des().Append(_L8("&birthday="));
   // we use the birthday here only as a simple string
   url->Des().Append(*iBirthday);
   url->Des().Append(_L8("&sex="));
   url->Des().AppendNum(iSex);
   url->Des().Append(_L8("&note="));
   url->Des().Append(*iNote);
   url->Des().Append(_L8("&lat="));
   url->Des().AppendNum(position.Latitude(), realFormat);
   url->Des().Append(_L8("&long="));
   url->Des().AppendNum(position.Longitude(), realFormat);
   iTransport->SendRequestL(*url, KNullDesC8);
   CleanupStack::PopAndDestroy(url);
   }
```

In the example above we have not considered UTF and URL encoding in order to make the structure of the function shorter and clearer.

10.5   Summary

With the increasing popularity of GPS technology, the proliferation of location-based services, and the integration of GPS receivers into the newest smartphones, location-sensitive mobile applications are likely to play an ever increasing role in our everyday life. Obviously, mastering the necessary interfaces in order to create applications that harness the benefits of GPS and other location-based technologies is a must for mobile software developers.

In this chapter we have given a short overview of GPS technology and location-based services. Section 10.3 has given an insight into the location API provided by the Symbian OS, illustrated with simple examples for retrieving the current position of the device. We have also briefly discussed the location API of Java ME through a simple example demonstrating that the implementation of the location-based application does not require any special programming skills.

Finally, we have discussed the FindFriends example application, which is a complete implementation of a location-based service. The application allows a search for other users within a specific distance from us. The application consists of three main parts: a web server, a background database and a mobile client. Section 10.4 has described the constituents of FindFriends, as well as the communication protocol between the mobile client and the website and the implementation of network communication interfaces. The FindFriends application can be extended, with several interesting features such as alert functionality if a specific user comes within a specific range, or showing the complete location history path of the users on a map.

With FindFriends, we would like to encourage the reader either to implement other location-based applications or extend FindFriends with additional features. We sincerely hope that this chapter will help the reader to understand the basics of location-based services and the concepts of developing applications based on this technology.

References

[1] *'iGO GPS Navigation Software'*. Available at: http://navngo.com/pages/global/eng/startpage/ [accessed 4 October 2008].
[2] *'S60 3rd Edition SDK for Symbian OS'*, Maintenance Release, Nokia. Available at: http:// www.forum.nokia.com/Resources_and_Information/Tools/Platforms/S60_Platform_SDKs/ [accessed 27 February 2009].
[3] Dana, P. H., 'Global Positioning System (GPS) Time Dissemination for Real-Time Applications. Real-Time Systems', *The International Journal of Time Critical Computing Systems*, **12**(1), 1997.
[4] *'Java Specification Request 179'*. Available at: http://jcp.org/en/jsr/detail?id = 179 [accessed 5 July 2008].
[5] Godwin, A. and Stichbury, J., *'Quick Recipes Taster'*, Symbian Press (2008). Available at: http:// developer.symbian.com/main/documentation/booklets/booklets_using.jsp [accessed 10 August 2008].
[6] Aubert, M., *et al.*, *'Quick Recipes on Symbian OS'*, ISBN-10: 0470997834, John Wiley & Sons, Inc., Hoboken, NJ, 2008.

11

Developing Java Games on Symbian OS-based Mobile Devices

Péter Ekler
Budapest University of Technology and Economics, peter.ekler@aut.bme.hu

11.1 Introduction

Developing games for mobiles provides unique challenges. The amount of time and the attention span of a mobile user are different from those of a user of a desktop/dedicated games console, and this makes it difficult to see which game concepts transfer well to mobile. In addition, the controllers of mobile phones are limited, which we have to take into consideration. For instance, it is hard to handle the keyboard, there is no mouse-like pointing device, and the screen size of the mobile phone is small, which makes it difficult to display the game area effectively. This shows that developing games for mobile phones requires creativity from developers.

The mobile peer-to-peer architecture is an essential tool when implementing networked games. In this chapter we will demonstrate how multiple mobile phones can be involved in an interactive game application. We have to realize that mobile devices have some special capabilities that make them unique from the gaming point of view. In this way, we also have the possibility of creating games for mobile phones that would not be possible to implement on desktop computers. Table 11.1 summarizes the advantages and disadvantages of mobile phones from the game development perspective.

Before we start developing games for mobile phones, our first task is to decide what kind of mobile platform we want to support. Most of the games for mobile phones are written in Java so that they can run on several types of mobile phone because of the platform independency Java provides. The capabilities of the phone running the JVM are

Mobile Peer to Peer (P2P) Edited by Frank H. P. Fitzek and Hassan Charaf
© 2009 John Wiley & Sons, Ltd

Table 11.1 Comparing the advantages and disadvantages of mobile phones in terms of game development

Advantages	Disadvantages
Mobility.	Small screen size.
Integrated multimedia devices: camera, microphone, accelerometer, etc.	Limitation of input methods.
Different types of networking capability: Bluetooth, WLAN, etc.	Slower processor.
Good battery life.	Limited available memory.
Personal identity (IMEI) – a phone is often more personal than a PC.	Frame rate is limited not just by polygons but also by pixels to be drawn.
Mobile games are increasingly more suited to our stop/start lifestyles.	

quite limited, whereas the requirements of a game can be especially demanding. In fact, games can be very complex; 3D games, in particular, require extreme processing power.

The characteristic of the Java virtual machine are especially apparent on low-end devices, which is due to hardware constraints. The hardware capabilities of smartphones provide a good fit for Java games, as more resource-intensive Java applications can be run on them.

Symbian is the most widespread mobile operating system for smartphones and hosts a rich and powerful Java ME platform. It treats Java applications, called MIDlets, as first-class citizens on Symbian OS, and therefore there is no explicit limit on either the size of the application or on the heap size available to the process in which the MIDlet is executing. Basically, to the user, MIDlets are indistinguishable from native applications. Figure 11.1 introduces the high-level architecture of how MIDlets run on Java-enabled Symbian OS devices.

There are several existing books and publications about game development on mobile phones. In her book *Games on Symbian OS*, Jo Stichbury [1] shows the potential for creating mobile games for Symbian smartphones such as S60 3rd edition, UIQ 3, or FOMA devices. It covers various aspects of mobile games on Symbian OS, with contributions from a number of experts in the mobile games industry. In this chapter we will focus on

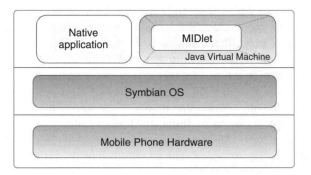

Figure 11.1 MIDlets on Symbian OS

a less extensively covered area. Generally speaking, we can classify mobile games into two main categories. The first category contains the established games genres such as arcade games, strategy games, card games, multiplayer games, etc. The second category, which will be investigated in this chapter, contains interactive games where we use mobile phones as a key accessory rather than a platform for the game.

What makes these games really unique is that they exploit the special capabilities of mobile phones, such as the camera, microphone, GPS, etc. However, using these sensors in a game needs a great deal of processing power as well as available memory. In particular, reading images from the camera or recording sounds from the microphone are especially computationally and energy intensive. In most cases, the hardware capabilities of low-end mobile phones are insufficient for these functionalities, or they process multimedia content more slowly. For this reason, in this chapter we will introduce interactive games on the Symbian OS platform, an open platform that allows creative use of mobile APIs within games as well. As a programming language we have chosen Java because of its popularity in the field of mobile games.

Firstly, we will introduce the basics of interactive game development for mobile phones. The following section will describes the characteristics of Java ME on Symbian OS and demonstrate the processing power of MIDlets. The third section will introduce some technologies related to game development on mobile phones. Section 11.4 will then describe an interactive example application, called MobSensor, where we use the mobile phone as a motion and noise detector. This section will also demonstrate how we can build an ad hoc WLAN network that can sense from mobile devices using the MobSensor application. This application has several uses including actual game play, where the task of one player is to build up a sensor network from a specific number of mobile phones in a large area and the task of the other is to go through the area without being detected. Section 11.5 will conclude the chapter and highlight the key points.

11.2   The Java Virtual Machine Implementation of Symbian OS

Java ME is based on three main elements: configurations, profiles and optional packages. Configurations [2] describe the capabilities of the virtual machine and provide the basic set of libraries for a broad range of devices. The configuration targeting resource-constraint devices such as mobile phones is called the connected limited device configuration (CLDC).

For defining a higher-level API, the Java ME platform specifies profiles on top of the different configurations. The combination of mobile information device profile (MIDP) [3] with CLDC is widely used to provide a complete Java application environment for mobile phones and similar devices.

Furthermore, if we want to use other technology-specific APIs in our application, we can import different kinds of optional package that can be found in different Java specification requests (JSRs) [4].

As support for MIDP/CLDC becomes standard on mobile phones, Java is an increasingly attractive option for many wireless application development projects. By taking the Java approach, porting applications between phones is greatly simplified by leveraging cross-platform standards in the form of the Java programming language and the standard APIs offered by CLDC and MIDP specifications.

Any implementation of a JSR (for example CLDC 1.0 – JSR 30, MIDP 2.0 – JSR 118, etc.) must pass a technology compatibility kit (TCK) ensuring conformance to the specification defined by that particular JSR. Conformance does not mean that JSR implementations are identical, since JSRs have optional features that are not mandatory requirements for a conformance, and also differences in the underlying platform and handset may yield slightly different results.

For example, it is possible that we can play an mp3 file on one phone but not on another, even if both phones support the mobile media API (JSR 135).

In this section we will introduce the key points of the Java virtual machine running on Symbian OS. We will then demonstrate the processing power of MIDlets on several Symbian OS-based mobile phones with a simple application. Finally, we will describe important factors to consider when implementing networking functions.

11.2.1 Programming Java on Symbian OS

In his papers on SDN, Martin de Jode [5, 6] has investigated what developers need to know about Java ME on Symbian OS. One reason why Java development is attractive is that it hides the developer from the complexity of dealing directly with the OS and OS-specific issues. Sometimes, however, it is inevitable that we become familiar with the platforms on which we plan to develop our MIDlet, especially when we encounter problems, because different platforms usually handle APIs in a different way. Since Java uses Symbian OS services and APIs, it is useful to understand some of the paradigms used within the Symbian OS.

11.2.1.1   Multitasking

Java applications, and games in particular, may use several threads. Occasionally, it is good to know how the host platform handles them to gain a better understanding of possible errors. Symbian OS is a fully multitasking OS supporting multiple processes and multiple threads within each process. As a result, Java MIDlets continue to run in the background when another task (e.g. an incoming phone call) comes into the foreground. A game running in a multitasking environment should consider if pausing the game is appropriate while the screen is not visible.

Symbian OS makes extensive use of the client/server framework, whereby a server runs in one thread and does work on behalf of multiple clients in other threads. A server will typically deal with each request from its many clients sequentially on a first come first serve basis (although in some cases a server may spawn threads for dealing with multiple requests).

In order to handle the queue of requests, a Symbian OS server typically has just one (event-handling) thread running an active scheduler that schedules requests from one or more active objects. A simple server has one active object waiting to complete when a client connects or sends a command [7]. In other words, Symbian OS servers use an event-handling framework rather than multiple threads to serve multiple clients.

JVM is run as a (native) thread in its own process space on Symbian OS. In addition to the JVM thread, Java components need to receive callbacks from native code; this is achieved via a native Java event server. These Java components (or, more correctly, their native peers) are clients of an instance of the Java event server. The Java event server runs in a native thread external to the JVM process and makes use of the Symbian OS client–server framework to handle multiple client requests.

Java threads may be mapped to underlying OS threads or may be implemented by the VM (lightweight threads). The advantage of lightweight threads is that they lead to greater platform independence, since native threading models vary with the OS (for instance, in terms of scheduling schemes and thread priority levels). The basic Symbian implementation uses a lightweight threading model to support Java threads, so they are not mapped directly to native Symbian OS threads.

11.2.1.2 Fewer Limitations

The resource limitations and narrow access to services of the Java platform mainly depend on the hardware and software capabilities of the specific mobile phone, and it is not uncommon on mainstream phones for the capabilities of the Java platform to be further limited by the operating system on which the device is running. Additionally, we can read other constraints on phone specifications such as the maximum JAR size, maximum heap size, etc.

Symbian OS imposes no restrictions on MIDlets, other than the finite limitations of available memory and disk space. For example, there are no constraints related to the size of the MIDlet JAR file that can be installed. This is a very important feature from the gaming point of view, because games with special graphical effects may contain several resource files like images that can lead to large JAR files. Table 11.2 summarizes where Symbian OS does not pose any hard limits and thereby provides more capabilities compared with featured phones, and how these are important from the gaming perspective.

Instead of specifying a fixed heap size for Java ME applications, Symbian OS enables dynamic heap usage for MIDlets. In other words, MIDlet memory usage is only limited by the available memory on the device, and a MIDlet heap can grow or shrink according to the demands of an executing MIDlet suite.

Previously, we implemented a Java ME-based BitTorrent peer-to-peer (P2P) client, called MobTorrent, and examined its behaviour on low-end devices as well as on Symbian OS. Figure 11.2 shows how Symbian OS allocated more and more memory to MobTorrent as it was downloading more and more torrents at the same time.

Table 11.2 Java platform capabilities on Symbian OS

Provided capability	Description
No limits on the number and size of record management system (RMS) records.	MIDlets can store a large amount of data in the RMS, and they can use it even for caching.
No limit on the size of the MIDlet JAR.	Games can contain larger amounts of images, sounds, and other resources.
No restriction on the number of Java threads that can be created.	Complex games with more threads can be executed.
No limit on the number of socket connections that can be created.	Multiplayer games can contain several socket connections, which is important, for instance, in peer-to-peer-like games.

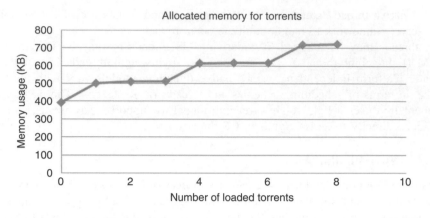

Figure 11.2   Memory usage of MobTorrent

The results returned by the Java ME `Runtime.getFreeMemory()` method call cannot be relied upon to be accurate, since another thread can allocate/deallocate memory at any time. The `getFreeMemory()` method only returns a snapshot of the free heap memory currently available, and becomes invalid after a subsequent allocation to the heap. The initial heap size for MIDlets on Symbian OS is around 400 kB.

11.2.1.3   Java ME Application Life Cycle

The life cycle model for MIDlets is specified by MIDP; correct understanding of the MIDP life cycle is essential for Java ME developers. It is also worth mentioning some interesting points related to the Symbian OS implementation:

- The three states of the MIDlets are: active, paused, destroyed. However, on some platforms (such as Series 40) the pause state is never entered into.
- The application management system (AMS) is responsible for transferring the MIDlet between states and notifying the MIDlet of the state change by calling one of the MIDlet class methods as appropriate: `startApp()`, `pauseApp()`, `destroyApp()`. However, the MIDlet may itself request a state change by invoking one of the `notifyPaused()`, `resumeRequest()`, `notifyDestroyed()` methods.
- On Symbian OS, the behaviour of the AMS is customizable by the license. In particular, the circumstances under which `pauseApp()` is called vary between UI reference designs. On Series 60, `pauseApp()` is not called when a MIDlet is sent to the background, whereas on UIQ phones the AMS calls `pauseApp()` when the MIDlet moves to the background.
- If the developers wish to ensure that the MIDlet moves into the paused state in response to being sent to the background, then they should use the `Displayable isShown()` method and the `Canvas showNotify()` and `hideNotify()` methods to monitor the state of the display and take the appropriate actions when the MIDlet is sent to the background.

11.2.2   Processing Power of MIDlets

In order to give an estimate of the processing power of MIDlets on Symbian OS, we implemented a MIDlet based on a simple formula (Figure 11.3) that calculated the value of the mathematical constant PI through a specific number of iterations, and we measured how long this calculation took on different mobile phones running Symbian OS.

We also implemented the native Symbian version of the PI-computing application so that we could compare the processing power of MIDlets and native applications on Symbian OS. Figure 11.4 shows the user interface of the Symbian C++ (left) and the Java (right) applications.

The results (Table 11.3) show that, in this particular example, the native Symbian C++ application is twice as fast as the corresponding Java version.

$$\pi = \frac{4}{1} - \frac{4}{3} + \frac{4}{5} - \frac{4}{7} + \frac{4}{9} - \frac{4}{11} \cdots$$

Figure 11.3   Calculating the value of the mathematical constant PI

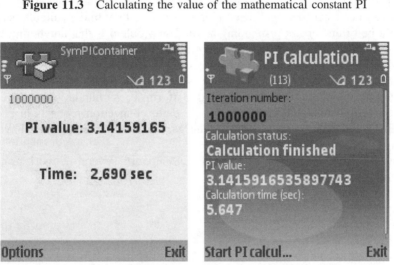

Figure 11.4   Java ME and native Symbian PI calculating applications

Table 11.3   Processing power of MIDlets and native applications on Symbian OS

Device type	Nokia N93	Nokia N91	Nokia 6630	Sony Ericcson W960i
CPU	ARM11	ARM9	ARM9	ARM9
	332 MHz	220 MHz	220 MHz	208 MHz
Java application	3.702 s	5.647 s	5.703 s	6.269 s
Symbian C++ application	1.695 s	2.690 s	2.882 s	3.221 s

This benchmark is not based on scientific measurements; it just shows a common behaviour of the same Symbian C++ and Java application.

The difference between the Java implementation and the native Symbian C++ version is probably because of the limited support for floating-point operation handling and the overhead of the JVM. In general we can say that fixed-point operations are still faster and are used extensively in mobile games.

These results should be considered during game development because complex games can use several real-time calculations and it is important that they do not slow down the entire game; thus, we have to optimize our algorithms.

11.2.3 Network Handling

The networking implementation of Java ME on different platforms is important to consider when developing mobile applications making extensive use of communication services. We have previously seen, in relation to MobTorrent [8], that there are limitations in connection with the network-handling implementation of Java ME. Since MobTorrent is a peer-to-peer application, it is ideal for testing network-handling issues. P2P applications usually have to connect to several peer addresses before they find a suitable peer. Several peers might be offline or not responding at all. The problem is that an attempt to connect to a peer – over WLAN or 3G – that is not online causes a long delay. The timeout when the system realizes that the address is not responding is 244 s on Series 40 (mainstream phone platform of Nokia) devices and 163 s on S60 devices. The situation is further complicated by a limitation of the Series 40 platform: it can handle only one connection request at a time, while S60 is able to handle eight connection requests in parallel. We have to take these issues into account during game development, and we have to avoid connecting to offline addresses.

The Java ME implementation of Symbian OS supports several network protocols and connection types including:

- HTTP, HTTPS;
- sockets;
- secure sockets;
- server sockets;
- UDP datagrams.

The powerful networking support provided by the Java ME on Symbian OS offers exciting possibilities. Not only does it open up a myriad of opportunities to communicate with remote hosts, it also allows MIDlets to communicate with local native applications using the localhost loopback address (127.0.0.1). For example, support for client sockets combined with the full multitasking support offered by Symbian OS allows a MIDlet to open a two-way communication channel with a C++ application running on the same phone. We can use this feature during game development if we need some low-level functionality, because in this case our MIDlet can connect to a native application that executes the specific low-level functionality and sends back the results.

11.3   Writing Games for Mobile Phones

Most of the applications developed on mobile phones are games, and most of them are based on Java ME because of its platform independency. There are several different game genres, many of which rely on different application architectures and technologies:

- *Arcade-style game.* These types of game require fast interaction processing; if the player hits a button on the phone, the application must react immediately. The Java ME `GameCanvas` class, which will be introduced later in this section, is ideal for arcade-style game implementation.
- *First-person shooter (FPS).* FPS games usually require 3D graphics, which tend to involve a lot of calculations and hence processing. On Java ME there are two existing APIs for displaying 3D graphics. JSR 184 [9] is an object-oriented API, and JSR 239[1] (OpenGL ES API) [10] is based on the OpenGL ES specification. The OpenGL ES API for Java ME caters for the needs of those developers who are already familiar with OpenGL ES and do not require any of the high-level functionality provided by JSR 184. With the abundance of OpenGL ES applications on the market, having an API based on the OpenGL ES specification lessens the efforts of porting these applications to the J2ME platform.
- *Real-time strategy.* Implementing real-time strategy games for mobile phones is challenging because these games usually require large maps while the screen size of the phones is small. As a result, it is hard to present a suitable overview for players in real time. Creating maps for strategy games most commonly requires tile-based game design. A tile-based game is a game that builds up a large terrain by drawing tiles, usually of equal size, representing areas such as grass, mountain, and walls. Tiles have different meanings depending on how they are used. Typically, tiles are used as part of the graphic output and/or unit movement system. There is an existing game builder tool for NetBeans (Figure 11.5) that helps to design tile-based games [11].

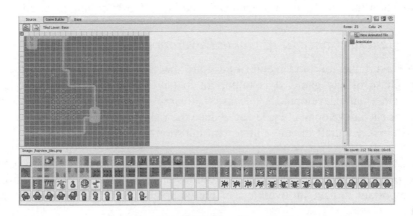

Figure 11.5   NetBeans game designer

---

[1] None of the current Symbian OS devices supports this JSR.

- *Turn-based games.* Turn-based games on mobile phones are a great success because players have time to look through the state of the game and consider the next move. These games are typically strategy game variants, and the aforementioned tile-based game design is also applicable to designing the game map.
- *Multiplayer games.* Multiplayer games on mobile phones are typically based on Bluetooth communication. Nowadays, almost all mobile devices support Bluetooth technology, making these games very popular. Java ME supports Bluetooth communication via JSR 82 [12]. However, WLAN technology is also becoming increasingly widespread on smartphones, so that games running over an ad hoc network by means of WLAN communication are an alternative to Bluetooth-based games. In this section we will introduce an example implementation for ad hoc WLAN-based communication.
- *Massively multiplayer online games.* These games typically connect to one or more Internet servers by means of which players can participate in usually role-playing games. In these types of game we should consider the previously mentioned socket-handling issues and avoid connecting to offline addresses. For example, a server should filter offline addresses for the mobile clients. Adapting massively multiplayer online games to mobile phones is a new field that became feasible through 3G and WLAN networks and the flat-rate pay system.

MIDP has been a winner in the mobile game world to date. With over 1 billion Java ME-enabled handsets sold [13], developing MIDP games is an exciting field to get into. MIDP game development continues to gain importance with each passing year. As technologies evolve, customer demand pushes game development studios to squeeze more and more out of mobile devices. Sam Mason [14] introduced the basics of game development via a game called 'Third Degree'. The paper examines a number of design decisions made, and discusses game frameworks, physics, AI and, in particular, the game's life cycle events. In this section we will introduce the general concept of game design and the Java ME `GameCanvas`, and finally we will show an example implementation for network communication that can be used in games for ad hoc WLAN communication as well.

11.3.1 General Concepts of Game Development

There are a number of fundamental questions that should be answered in the initial planning phase of any game. It is important to have clear answers to these questions before starting game development, because they simplify game design, decrease the time required for each development cycle and reduce the risks associated with the development process. Below, we draft the most important questions:

1. *What is meant by 'Victory' and 'Game Over'?* We should define 'Victory' conditions in the planning phase because these conditions are used to stop the game threads and it is important to have an overview of the complete game life cycle in the planning phase.
2. *How can the player control the game?* The controllers of the game have a great influence on the whole architecture. We should define an input-handling unit responsible for reading user input and execute the actions related to the specific types of input.
3. *How is system- and user-initiated pause handled?* It is important even in the planning phase to have an idea of how the game will react to a pause event. When the game

pauses it should suspend the necessary game threads, but it is also important not to lose any game-related data when the game returns from the suspended state.

4. *How is the game world represented and simulated?* The game world basically corresponds to a virtual world with virtual time, and the game world engine is responsible for controlling the rules of the game such as game physics, AI, etc.

5. *How does the game handle different display sizes?* Different types of mobile phone have different screen resolutions so that we should design and implement the UI of the game to be able to adapt to the screen size of the mobile phone on which the game runs. Resizing images on mobile phones can be slow, and thus we should avoid resizing images to the current screen resolution on demand. Instead, we should resize images only once and store them in the RMS² of the MIDlet for future use. In general, scaling images is fairly rapid, but sometimes it is not enough.

6. *How can the player continue the game?* In general, people often abruptly stop playing a mobile game, for example when their bus has arrived and they are to get off. On Java ME we can store the game state in the RMS until the player restarts the game. Consequently, it is important to make a choice as to what data should be saved and to design how we can restore the game state.

7. *What kinds of media effect are used?* Media effects, such as audio, vibration and video, are a very important part of the game because they can greatly increase user experience. We can use simple tone sequences with MIDP 2.0, but, if we want special sounds or even music, we should use the mobile media API defined by JSR 135 [15] or the advanced multimedia supplements defined by JSR 234 [16]. Vibration belongs to the media effects category as well, but we should use it sparingly because its overuse may quickly drain the battery.

11.3.2 GameCanvas

Since games are one of the most popular applications on mobile phones, it was no surprise when the Java Community Process group, which was responsible for defining MIDP 2.0, introduced basic game capabilities as well. In what follows, we introduce the `GameCanvas` class, which is the core of the gaming capabilities provided by MIDP 2.0.

The `javax.microedition.lcdui.game` package contains the `GameCanvas` class which extends the `Canvas` class. `Canvas` lets an application draw screens using low-level API, and also receive key and pointer events directly. The reason for introducing `GameCanvas` is that simple `Canvas` gives the application no control over when a canvas repaints itself or how quickly key and pointer events get delivered to the canvas (all an application can do is to request a repaint). This lack of control can cause speed-sensitive games to feel slow and unresponsive. `GameCanvas` was designed specifically to address these weak points.

There are some differences between `Canvas` and `GameCanvas`. Firstly, the constructor of `GameCanvas` takes a `boolean` to indicate whether certain key events are to be suppressed. Secondly, the `Canvas.paint()` method is overloaded by `GameCanvas` which supplies its own implementation that renders the off-screen buffer; it is double buffered,

---

² The Java ME record management system (RMS) provides a mechanism through which MIDlets can persistently store data and retrieve it later.

and a call to `flushGraphics()` will force an immediate repaint based on the current contents of the off-screen buffer. However, the most significant difference is that we can implement a game loop in `GameCanvas` much better.

In general, MIDP UI components are event driven, which means that the system invokes methods directly, in response to device events. These events are queued and delivered to the application one at a time, and there may be a delay between the time the event occurs and the time the application receives it, which particularly affects painting events. The `GameCanvas` class tries to solve this problem; it lets the application poll for key events quickly, and repaints the canvas in a timely fashion. This polling and repainting is normally done in a loop on a separate thread (game loop).

To poll for key events, we can use the `getKeyStates()` method. It returns a bit mask representing the change in the state of action keys since the last call to `getKeyStates()`. Each bit value of the key in the mask will be 1 if it is currently down, or has been pressed since the last call; otherwise it will be 0. The following source code represents how can we use the `getKeyStates()` method:

```
int keyState = getKeyStates();

if( (keyState & RIGHT_PRESSED) != 0 )
{
   // handle right key pressed event
}
```

This key-handling technique lets the application check the key state in a tight loop and respond quickly to any changes. Note that key events are still received by `GameCanvas` as usual, except that you can suppress events involving the action keys.

Next, we will introduce the implementation of a simple `GameCanvas` on which we are able to move a red rectangle in the game loop with the help of the `getKeyStates()` method:

```
public class MyFirstGameCanvas extends GameCanvas
     implements Runnable
{
   private static final int BOX_WIDTH = 40;
   private static final int BOX_HEIGHT = 40;

   private int boxX = 20;
   private int boxY = 20;
   private Graphics graphics;
   private volatile Thread thread;
   private boolean running = false;

   public MyFirstGameCanvas() {
      super(true);

      graphics = getGraphics();
```

```
      graphics.setColor(255, 255, 255);
      graphics.fillRect(0, 0, getWidth(), getHeight());
  }

  // The game loop.
  public void run() {
    while (running    {
      int state = getKeyStates();

      if ((state & DOWN_PRESSED) != 0) {
        boxY+=1;
      }
      else if ((state & UP_PRESSED) != 0) {
        boxY-=1;
      }
      else if ((state & RIGHT_PRESSED) != 0) {
        boxX+=1;
      }
      else if ((state & LEFT_PRESSED) != 0) {
        boxX-=1;
      }

      // Repaint the screen

      // Paint background
      graphics.setColor(255, 255, 255);
      graphics.fillRect(0, 0, getWidth(), getHeight());

      // Paint box
      graphics.setColor(255, 0, 0);
      graphics.fillRect(boxX, boxY, BOX_WIDTH, BOX_HEIGHT);

      // Refresh display
      flushGraphics();

      // Sleep..
      try {
        Thread.currentThread().sleep(10);
      }
      catch (InterruptedException e) {
        // handle exception
      }
    }
  }
```

```
// When the canvas is shown, start a thread to
// run the game loop.
protected void showNotify() {
  running = true;
  thread = new Thread(this);
  thread.start();
}

// When the game canvas is hidden, stop the thread.
protected void hideNotify() {
  running = false;
  thread = null;
}
}
```

We can see that the game loop can be implemented easily by implementing the `Runnable` interface. In this example, the game loop is responsible for checking the key state and executing the drawing method. The example also demonstrates that the `showNotify()` and `hideNotify()` methods are still called in `GameCanvas` when the canvas is shown and hidden.

11.3.3 Ad Hoc WLAN-based Multiplayer Games on Java ME

WLAN technology is becoming increasingly popular in mobile phones, and a number of Symbian-based smartphones already support this technology. In WLAN-capable mobile phones we are able to establish ad hoc networks. In order to do so, we have to define a new access point in the phone settings menu, after which the new access point will appear in the access point selection list.

In the following section we will introduce a simple network-handling engine that can even be used in games. By understanding the engine, we will be able to create MIDlets easily on top of it. Figure 11.6 shows the flow design from NetBeans IDE of a MIDlet that uses this engine and realizes a simple chat application.

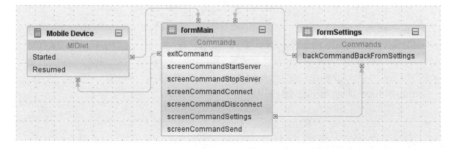

Figure 11.6 MIDlet flow design based on the proposed network-handling engine

Figure 11.6 shows the main functions of the MIDlet and the network-handling engine. The engine is able to start listening via a `ServerSocket`, and, if we start the application on another phone, the engine makes it possible to connect to this socket, after which we can send and receive messages on both phones.

The network-handling engine contains three classes: `ServerConnection`, `Client-Connection`, and `NetworkCommunication`.

The `ServerConnection` class is responsible for accepting incoming connections. It contains a `startServer()` method, which will start listening on a specific port in a separated thread in order not to block the main thread:

```java
public class ServerConnection {
  private ServerSocketConnection serverconn = null;
  private HttpConnection hc = null;
  private InputStream is = null;
  private NetworkExampleMIDlet midlet = null;
  private StartServerThread startServerThread = null;
  private NetworkCommunication networkCommunication = null;

 // Constructor
  public ServerConnection(NetworkExampleMIDlet aMidlet) {
      midlet = aMidlet;
  }

 // Start server thread
  private class StartServerThread extends Thread {
    public void run() {
      try {
        try {
          hc = (HttpConnection) Connector.open(
            "http://www.example.com");
          is = hc.openInputStream();
        } catch (IOException ex) {
          // handle exception
        } catch (Exception ex) {
          // handle exception
        }

        serverconn = (ServerSocketConnection)
          Connector.open(
          "socket://:10000", Connector.READ_WRITE);
        // notify midlet
        midlet.getFormMain().append("server started");
        SocketConnection sc =
          (SocketConnection)serverconn.acceptAndOpen();
        // notify midlet
        midlet.getFormMain().append(
```

```
            "connection accepted");
          networkCommunication =
            new NetworkCommunication(midlet, sc);

        try {
          if (is!=null)
            is.close();
          if (hc!=null)
            hc.close();
          is = null;
          hc = null;
        } catch (IOException ex) {
          // handle exception
        }

      } catch (IOException ex) {
        // handle exception
      }
    }
  }

// Start server
 public void startServer() {
    startServerThread = new StartServerThread();
    startServerThread.start();
 }

// Stop server
 public void stopServer() {
    if (serverconn!=null) {
      try {
        serverconn.close();
        serverconn = null;
      } catch (IOException ex) {
        // handle exception
      }
    }
  }
}
```

We can see a strange part in the StartServerThread: before it opens the ServerSocket, it opens a HttpConnections to a non-existing address. This is because, if we leave this part out, Java ME will not ask for the access point and it will create a ServerSocket automatically on the 127.0.0.1 (localhost) address.

The `ClientConnection` class contains a `startClient(String aAddress, int aPort)` method, which starts a thread that tries to open a `SocketConnection` on the specific address:

```
public class ClientConnection {
    private SocketConnection clientSocket = null;
    private NetworkExampleMIDlet midlet = null;
    private StartClientThread startClientThread = null;
    private NetworkCommunication networkCommunication = null;

  // Constructor
  public ClientConnection(NetworkExampleMIDlet aMidlet) {
    midlet = aMidlet;
  }

  // Start connection thread
  private class StartClientThread extends Thread {
    private String address;
    private int port;

    public StartClientThread(String aAddress, int aPort) {
      address = aAddress;
      port = aPort;
    }

    public void run() {
      try {
        clientSocket =
          (SocketConnection)Connector.open(
          "socket://"+address+":"+port);
        midlet.getFormMain().append("connected");
        networkCommunication =
          new NetworkCommunication(
            midlet, clientSocket);
          } catch (IOException ex) { // handle exception
          }
      }
  }

  // Start connection
  public void startClient(String aAddress, int aPort) {
    startClientThread = new StartClientThread(
      aAddress, aPort);
    startClientThread.start();
  }
}
```

Note that after the `SocketConnection` has been established, a `NetworkCommunica-`
`tion` object is created in both `ServerConnection` and `ClientConnection` classes. This
object is responsible for creating input and output streams. It is able to send messages
and it also listens for incoming messages in a separate thread:

```java
public class NetworkCommunication {

  private SocketConnection sc;
  private DataInputStream dataInputStream;
  private DataOutputStream dataOutputStream;
  private boolean readEnabled;
  private NetworkExampleMIDlet midlet = null;
  private ReaderThread myReaderThread;

  // This class is a Therad, which reads
   // the messages from the connection
   class ReaderThread extends Thread {
     public void run() {
       while(readEnabled) {
         // read data
         try {
           String incommingMessage =
             dataInputStream.readUTF();
           // append message to the midlet
           midlet.getFormMain().append(
             incommingMessage);
         }
         catch(InterruptedIOException e) {
           disconnect();
         }
         catch(IOException e) {
           disconnect();
         }
         catch(Exception e) {
           disconnect();
         }
       }
     }
   }

  // Constructor
  public NetworkCommunication(NetworkExampleMIDlet aMidlet,
    SocketConnection aSc) {
      midlet = aMidlet;
```

```
      sc = aSc;
      try {
        dataInputStream = sc.openDataInputStream();
        dataOutputStream = sc.openDataOutputStream();
        readEnabled = true;
        myReaderThread = new ReaderThread();
        myReaderThread.start();
      } catch (IOException ex) {
        // handle exception
      }
      // Set network communication for the midlet
      midlet.setNc(this);
  }

  // Send message
  public void sendMessage(String aMessage) {
    try {
      dataOutputStream.writeUTF(aMessage);
      dataOutputStream.flush();
    } catch (IOException ex) {
      disconnect();
    }
  }

  // Disconnect
  public void disconnect() {
    readEnabled = false;

   if (dataInputStream!=null) {
      try {
        dataInputStream.close();
      } catch (IOException ex) {
        // handle exception
      }
    }

    if (dataOutputStream!=null) {
      try {
        dataOutputStream.close();
      } catch (IOException ex) {
        // handle exception
      }
    }

    if (sc!=null) {
```

```
    try {
      sc.close();
    } catch (IOException ex) {
      // handle exception
    }
  }

  myReaderThread = null;
  // notify midlet
  midlet.setNc(null);
  midlet.handleDisconnect();
  midlet.getFormMain().append("disconnected");
  }
}
```

The constructor of the `NetworkCommunication` class opens the `DataInputStream` and the `DataOutputStream`, and it creates a `ReaderThread` object, which reads incoming messages. In some specific parts of the code we can find the 'notify midlet' comment, which shows where we can notify the MIDlet about special events, such as having success-fully opened the server socket, having established a connection, and having disconnected.

This network-handling engine can be easily modified for games; all we have to do is specify the format of outgoing messages and parse the incoming messages correctly.

11.4   MobSensor

In the previous sections we have described the main characteristics of Java ME applications running on Symbian OS. We have discussed the issues of memory usage, life cycle and processing power. We have then discussed the basics of game development on mobile phones, and we have outlined a network-handling engine that was able to handle ad hoc WLAN connections as well. In this section we introduce MobSensor, which is a Java ME-based application that was developed and tested on Symbian OS. The application turns the mobile phone into a motion and noise detector, and thus is an example of how interactive games could make use of the special capabilities of the mobile phone such as the camera and the microphone.

In this section, we introduce the functions of MobSensor, the main elements of its architecture and the motion and noise detection algorithm.

11.4.1   MobSensor Functions

The main idea behind creating the MobSensor application was that mobile phones are basi-cally small computers with different types of multimedia capability and network-handling technology. MobSensor is able to sense its environment; it listens for changes via a motion and noise detector and fires an alert if it detects a change.

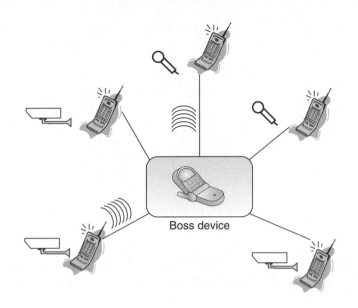

Figure 11.7 Ad hoc WLAN network established by cooperating MobSensor applications

The motion detector unit uses the camera of the phone and detects differences in the environment. If the difference measure calculated by the comparison algorithm is higher than a specific value, the application alerts by playing an mp3 file. The noise detector works in the same way; it uses the microphone of the mobile device and detects the noise difference. In both cases, users are able to set the sensitivity of the sensor algorithms to fit the current environment.

MobSensor also has networking functionality; users are able to establish a network of mobile devices with ad hoc WLAN technology or with the help of a WLAN router. In order to establish the sensor network in the current implementation of MobSensor, one device has to become a central 'boss' device that will behave as a server so that other phones can connect to it. The 'boss' device has a special ability: it can temporarily disable other sensors. In this way, we can walk with the 'boss' device in the network without triggering any alerts. Figure 11.7 shows how mobile phones can establish an ad hoc WLAN network with MobSensor.

11.4.2 MobSensor Architecture

After introducing MobSensor functions, we will discuss the main architectural elements (Figure 11.8) of MobSensor. The application has four main units, each of which is responsible for a different functionality. The motion and noise detector units implement the sensor functions, the user interface unit is responsible for showing the most important information on the phone screen, and the network manager implements the networking functions.

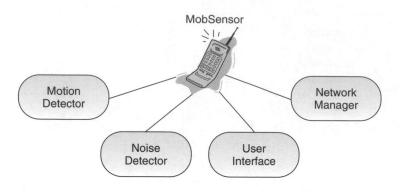

Figure 11.8   MobSensor units

The network manager unit is based on the previously introduced network-handling engine; therefore, we will not discuss it in any more detail. Instead, we will focus on the more interesting motion and noise detector algorithms in this section.

11.4.2.1   The Motion and Noise Detector Algorithm

The motion detector algorithm is based on continuous image recording and comparison. Figure 11.9 illustrates the algorithm on a flow diagram. We have not shown any exit points on the diagram because the user can stop the motion detector at any time.

MobSensor uses MMAPI [15] for capturing images and recording sounds. The core of the motion detector is basically the following thread:

```
class MotionDetecting extends Thread {
  public void run() {
    byte[] imageBinary; // image from the camera
    Image image;
    int diffValue;

    // while motiondetecting is enabled
    while (motionDetecting_Enabled) {
      try {
        //--- reading the snapshot
        imageBinary = null;
        try {
          imageBinary = videoControl.getSnapshot(
            "encoding=jpeg");
        }
        catch (MediaException ex) {
        // handle exception
        }
        //--- comparing images
```

```
        if (imageBinary!=null) {
          // create image from the binary data
          image = Image.createImage(
            imageBinary, 0, imageBinary.length);
          // if there was no previous image
          if (previousImage == null) {
            previousImage = image;
          }
          // else compare images
          else {
            diffValue =
              pixelDifference_BetweenImages(
                previousImage,image,sensibility);
            if (!alert_disabled &&
              diffValue>diff_limit) {
              alert();
              previousImage = null;
            }
            else {
              previousImage = image;
            }
          }
          imageBinary = null;
          System.gc();
        }
      } catch (Throwable t) {
        // handle exception
      }

      try {
        sleep(100);
      } catch (InterruptedException ex) {
        // handle exception
      }
    }
  }
}
```

The loop in the thread reads an image into the imageBinary byte array. After this, an Image object is created from the byte array, which will be compared with the previous image. If there is no previous image, then we store this new Image object and start the whole loop again. Otherwise, the comparison algorithm calculates a difference value (diffValue) from the current and the previous image with a specific sensitivity parameter (set by the user). If this value is higher than a specific number, then the sensor alerts.

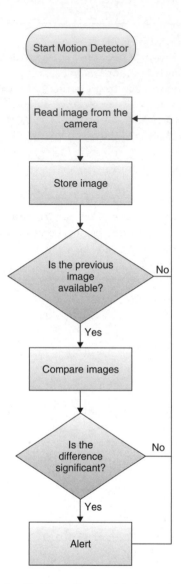

Figure 11.9   The flow diagram of the motion detector

The algorithm that calculates the difference value from the images is implemented in the following two functions:

```
public static int pixelDifferencesBetweenImages(Image a,
   Image b, int aSensitivity) {
   int[] aImagePixels = getPixels(a);
   int[] bImagePixels = getPixels(b);
   int pixelDifference = 0;
```

```
  for (int i=0; i<aImagePixels.length; i++) {
      if (getDifferenceFromARGB(
          aImagePixels[i],bImagePixels[i])> aSensitivity)
        pixelDifference ++;
  }
  return pixelDifference;
}

// a simple algorithm to calculate difference between
// two pixels
public static int getDifferenceFromARGB(int firstPixel,
  int secoundPixel) {
    int red1 = (firstPixel >> 16) & 0xff;
    int green1 = (firstPixel >> 8) & 0xff;
    int blue1 = firstPixel & 0xff;

    int red2 = (secoundPixel >> 16) & 0xff;
    int green2 = (secoundPixel >> 8) & 0xff;
    int blue2 = secoundPixel & 0xff;

    int result = 0;

    result+=Math.abs(red1-red2);
    result+=Math.abs(green1-green2);
    result+=Math.abs(blue1-blue2);

    return result;
}
```

This current initial implementation is rather simple as it checks every pixel of the image and calculates a pixelDifference value based on the colour of the pixels. Note that this comparison algorithm has a weak point: if we put the sensor in a dark room and just turn on the light, it will also alert. To avoid this false alert, we have to extend the algorithm with an extra condition: if the colour change for all pixels is rather large, then the motion detector should not alert.

The noise detector works in the same way as the motion detector (we will not discuss it in any more detail): it basically records half-second-long sound pieces and compares their power.

11.4.3   Playing mp3 Alerts in MobSensor

Mobile phones support several multimedia types, and thus we should use this advantage in games as well. Below, we will show how MobSensor plays an mp3 when an alert is detected:

```
// variables in the class
private FileConnection mp3File;
private InputStream mp3FileInputStream;
private Player mp3Player;
private VolumeControl volumeControl;

public void playMP3Alert(){
  try {
    // open file connection
    mp3File = (FileConnection) Connector.open(
      "file:///E:/alert.mp3",Connector.READ);
    // open inputstream
    mp3FileInputStream = mp3File.openInputStream();
    // create player
    mp3Player =
      Manager.createPlayer(mp3FileInputStream,"audio/mp3");
    mp3Player.realize();
    // request volume control
    volumeControl=(VolumeControl)(
      mp3Player.getControl("VolumeControl"));
    volumeControl.setLevel(get_gaugeVolume().getValue());
  }
  catch(MediaException me){/* handle exception */}
  catch(IOException ex){/* handle exception */}
  try {
    if(mp3Player!=null){
      // prefetch
      mp3Player.prefetch();
      // start playing the mp3
      mp3Player.start();
    }
  }
  catch(MediaException me){/* handle exception */}
  catch(SecurityException se){/* handle exception */}
}
```

In the `playMP3Alert()` function, firstly a `FileConnection` is opened to the mp3 file, after which an `InputStream` is opened to the content. We can then create the player object (`mp3Player`) responsible for handling the multimedia content. Any player object has its own life cycle with the following states: `unrealized`, `realized`, `prefetched`, `started`, `closed`. We can see in the rest of the function how the player gets to the started state when playing of the mp3 will start.

We will not discuss MMAPI in this chapter in any more detail – a complete description can be found in reference [17], where the MMAPI and its classes are described in depth.

With this example we would just like to show how we can play any kind of mp3 file if the phone supports this multimedia content.

11.4.4 The User Interface of MobSensor

If we start the application main screen, we can see the most important information about the state of the application. We can reach the main functions from the menu, where we can start the motion and noise detector, view the settings, and reach the networking functions. Figure 11.10 illustrates the user interface of the application. After the 'boss' mode has been started from the menu, the main screen shows the network address of the boss and how many phones have already connected to the sensor network.

On the settings view we can set the sensitivity of the sensors and the difference values above which the detectors should alert. The last screenshot was made on an emulator and represents the motion detector. On the top of the screen we can see the difference number, which comes from the previously described comparison algorithm.

Creating UI for Java ME applications is relatively easy with the NetBeans visual mobile designer [18]. However, if we want to create custom UI, we have to implement our own canvas-based classes, as shown in relation to `GameCanvas` (Section 11.3.2).

MobSensor converts the mobile phone into a motion and noise detector. To use the application, we do not need to work on the small screen with limited controllers – instead, we just have to put the phone in an appropriate place and it will work automatically.

11.5 Summary

The goal of this chapter was to give an insight into MIDlet game development on Symbian OS. Since there are several publications on game design for mobile phones, we

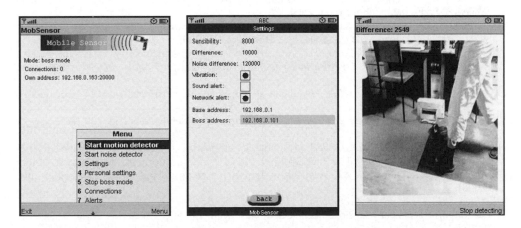

Figure 11.10 User Interface of MobSensor

have chosen the category of interactive games, where the application exploits the special capabilities of mobile phones, such as mobility, camera and microphone, networking technologies, etc.

In this chapter we have examined MIDlet capabilities on Symbian OS, and we have shown how multitasking works on it. Symbian OS treats Java applications as first-class citizens and does not pose any limitations on them, and therefore even complex MIDlets can run on Symbian OS-based devices. We have illustrated the processing power and memory usage of MIDlets with measurements. A comparison with native applications also confirms that complex Java ME applications have a role to play on smartphones.

In addition, we have discussed game development on mobile phones in general, and we have highlighted some important areas of APIs, such as the GameCanvas class and network-handling APIs. In order to demonstrate how we can use the methods introduced, we have outlined the MobSensor application, the core algorithms of which have been described.

We sincerely hope that this chapter will help the reader to take the initial step in implementing similar interactive applications.

References

[1] Stichbury, J., 'Games on Symbian OS', ISBN: 0470998040, John Wiley & Sons, Inc., Hoboken, NJ, 2008.

[2] 'Connected Limited Device Configuration'. Available at: http://java.sun.com/products/cldc [accessed 23 September 2008].

[3] 'Mobile Information Device Profile 2 Description'. Available at: http://developers.sun.com/mobility/midp/articles/midp2network [accessed 24 September 2008].

[4] 'Java Specification Request Overview'. Available at: http://www.jcp.org/en/jsr/overview [accessed 24 September 2008].

[5] de Jode, M., 'What Java™ Developers Need to Know about MIDP on Symbian OS', Symbian Developer Network, 2005.

[6] de Jode, M., 'Programming Java 2 Micro Edition on Symbian OS', ISBN: 978-0470092231, John Wiley & Sons, Inc., Hoboken, NJ, 2004.

[7] Stichbury, J., 'Symbian OS Explained: Effective C++ Programming for Smartphones', ISBN-13: 9780470021309, John Wiley & Sons, Inc., Hoboken, NJ, 2005.

[8] Ekler, P., Nurminen, J. K., and Kiss, A. J., 'Experiences of Implementing BitTorrent on Java ME Platform', CCNC'08, 1st IEEE International Peer-to-Peer for Handheld Devices Workshop, Las Vegas, NV, 2008.

[9] 'Java Specification Request 184'. Available at: http://jcp.org/en/jsr/detail?id=184 [accessed 24 June 2008].

[10] 'Java Specification Request 239'. Available at: http://jcp.org/en/jsr/detail?id=239 [accessed 24 June 2008].

[11] 'NetBeans Java ME Game Builder'. Available at: http://www.netbeans.org/kb/samples/mobile-game-builder.html [accessed 24 June 2008].

[12] 'Java Specification Request 82'. Available at: http://jcp.org/en/jsr/detail?id=82 [accessed 24 June 2008].

[13] 'Java ME Technology: Everything a Developer Needs for the Mobile Market'. Available at: http://java.sun.com/developer/technicalArticles/javame/mobilemarket/ [accessed 4 October 2008].

[14] Mason, S., 'Writing MIDP Games', Symbian Developer Network, 2008.

[15] 'Java Specification Request 135'. Available at: http://jcp.org/en/jsr/detail?id=135 [accessed 24 June 2008].

[16] 'Java Specification Request 234'. Available at: http://jcp.org/en/jsr/detail?id=234 [10 October 2008].

[17] Goyal, V., 'Pro Java ME MMAPI: Mobile Media API for Java Micro Edition', ISBN-10: 1590596390, Apress, Berkeley, CA, 2006.

[18] 'NetBeans Visual Mobile Designer'. Available at: http://www.netbeans.org/features/javame/index.html [accessed 10 October 2008].

Index

Mobile Peer to Peer (P2P)   Edited by Frank H. P. Fitzek and Hassan Charaf
© 2009 John Wiley & Sons, Ltd